# DON'T JUST DREAM OF GOLD . . . GO FOR IT!

How can songwriters like Diane Warren, Michael Bolton, Michael Kamen, and Jam and Lewis create smash hit after smash hit? How did Prince Be of PM Dawn and Chris Barbosa go from being club deejays to writing #1 songs? This knowledgeable insider's guide has all the answers and tells you what it takes for you to make it too. Easy hints and exercises get you started on a song. Specific guidelines give you the commercial edge on everything from lyrics to titles. Detailed discussions on demos, recording sessions, and making a master recording save you from costly mistakes. And clear business advice provides nuts-and-bolts instruction on selling songs, signing contracts—even on starting your own company. Whether you're a novice or a pro, you'll find everything a songwriter needs to know in

## THE COMPLETE HANDBOOK OF SONGWRITING

**Mark Liggett** began his career in the music industry in the 1970s as a songwriter. Before turning his efforts to production, he taught songwriting courses and started his own publishing company, the Record Breakers. Through the years his production efforts have earned him a Gold Single and a Gold Album in 1984 for Shannon's "Let the Music Play," a Gold Single in 1986 for "Boys Do Fall in Love" by Robin Gibb of the Bee Gees, and a Gold Album in 1992 for the New Kids on the Block's "No More Games" remix project. He has also worked with such artists as Billy Idol, The Spinners, Alfonso Ribiero (Fresh Prince of Beverly Hills), and George LaMond. Currently, Mark is co-owner of Ligosa Sound Studio and co-manages several groups on major labels.

**Cathy Liggett** is a free-lance writer. Mark and Cathy are married and live in Oh

# THE COMPLETE HANDBOOK OF SONGWRITING

## An Insider's Guide to Making It in the Music Industry

SECOND EDITION

BY

# MARK AND CATHY LIGGETT

A PLUME BOOK

PLUME
Published by the Penguin Group
Penguin Books USA Inc., 375 Hudson Street,
New York, New York 10014, U.S.A.
Penguin Books Ltd, 27 Wrights Lane, London W8 5TZ, England
Penguin Books Australia Ltd, Ringwood, Victoria, Australia
Penguin Books Canada Ltd, 10 Alcorn Avenue,
Toronto, Ontario, Canada M4V 3B2
Penguin Books (N.Z.) Ltd, 182–190 Wairau Road, Auckland 10, New Zealand

Penguin Books Ltd, Registered Offices: Harmondsworth, Middlesex, England

First published by Plume, an imprint of New American Library,
a division of Penguin Books USA Inc.

First Printing, August, 1993
10 9 8 7 6 5 4 3

 REGISTERED TRADEMARK—MARCA REGISTRADA

LIBRARY OF CONGRESS CATALOGING IN PUBLICATION DATA:
Liggett, Mark.
    The complete handbook of songwriting : an insider's guide to making it
in the music industry / by Mark and Cathy Liggett. — 2nd ed.
        p.   cm.
    Includes index.
    ISBN 0-452-27011-1
    1. Popular music—Writing and publishing.   I. Liggett, Cathy.
II. Title.
MT67.L43   1993
782.42'023'73—dc20                                          92-46335
                                                                CIP
                                                                 MN

Printed in the United States of America

PUBLISHER'S NOTE
This publication is designed to provide accurate and authoritative information
in regard to the subject matter covered. It is sold with the understanding that
the publisher is not engaged in rendering legal, accounting, or other professional
service. If legal advice or other expert assistance is required, the service of a
competent professional person should be sought.

*To Kelly and Michael*

# Contents

Special thanks to those individuals and organizations who have helped shape this book and/or our careers: Walt Aldridge, Dick Ashby, Chris Barbosa, Mark Blatt, Wes Boatman, Leon Brettler, Michael Brettler, Mara Bruckner, Ed Chisolm, Sergio Cossa, Ronnie Daniels, Jason Dauman, Maurice Gibb, Robin Gibb, Anne Godwin, Jerry Greenberg, Dave Jurman, Michael Kamen, Stephen Kipner, George LaMond, Jerry Lane, Rod Moskowitz, Jeff Pence, Evan Rogers, Debbie Rose, Charlie Roth, Matt Senatore, Terry Shaddick, Ashley Shepherd, Eliot Sloan, Billy Steinberg, Carl Sturkin, Curtis Urbina, Diane Warren, Janet Vogt, ASCAP, BMI, SESAC, and the Harry Fox Agency.

# Introduction

Conjure up an image of the songwriter, and either the vision of some reclusive type huddled over a guitar in a dingy, dimly lit room comes to mind, or the more grandiose image of a person swaying on a piano bench before a baby grand in the luxury of a spacious white-on-white living room.

But when you pan either of these dwellings, you're bound to find something else: an array of hats hanging from the bedpost or hatrack. There's much more to the reality of songwriting than the composers and lyricists of those two images. At least, there's much more to successful songwriters. Successful songwriters are quick-change artists, ready to jump at a moment's notice into the different roles of craftsman, disciplinarian, businessperson, team member, and realist. These are the roles they need to assume at one time or another to get them where they're going.

## The Songwriter as Craftsman

While it's true that some songwriters possess more inherent ability than others, when you scratch the surface of any writer, you'll soon discover a craftsman. Songwriting is something that can be learned, just like knitting or woodworking.

For over two decades, Billy Joel has been a prime example of a songwriter who has mastered his craft well. First off, the topics he chooses for his songs have mass appeal and run the gamut of emotions experienced by everyone, from "Piano Man" and "Just The Way You Are" to "Uptown Girl" and "We Didn't Start the Fire." Second, every line of his lyrics relates back to the topic. Third, his melodies set the mood and carry it. All of these elements are part of the craft—not the art—of songwriting.

And to become the renowned songwriter he is today, I'd venture to guess that Billy Joel has written at least a roomful of songs that you and I will never hear. Writing song after song is where the disciplinarian in a songwriter has to come into play.

Songwriting isn't some totally aesthetic, enigmatic process that just happens. It's a job. And the people who treat it as such are the ones who make it. Just like the executive who goes to his office each day, or the author who's at the PC every morning, you must set aside a certain amount of time each day to devote to your writing. Don't wait for "divine inspiration" to hit, because it can't be relied on. Divine inspiration is just an excuse to be a part-time songwriter. Sure, walking down a deserted street at 3:00 A.M. and watching the moon filter through the trees can be inspiring. But setting a routine and practicing your craft is what's really going to allow your talent to surface.

Above all, don't ever give up, just keep writing. Even the greats write some mediocre songs. If they didn't, their albums would contain ten hits instead of the usual two or three. Like Charlie Monk at April Blackwood Music Publishing used to tell me, "Great songwriters can write shabby songs, but a shabby songwriter will never write a great song."

## The Songwriter as Businessperson

By now you're convinced that songwriting is a job. And like any other job you'd do, it's one you want to be compensated for. Therefore, not only do you have to discipline yourself to do the work, but you also have to be business-minded about the work you do.

First and foremost, it's important to see that your song is a product, and like any other product, it needs to fit within a specific market and appeal to a target audience. The markets available to the popular songwriter include the various genres of music: pop, rock, country, rhythm and blues, dance, jazz, and gospel. In the outside business world this target-marketing strategy is called "product positioning." In the business world of music, it's commonly referred to as "cast directing." But whatever term you want to apply to it, the bottom line is this: if you can't figure out what market your song fits into, then one probably doesn't exist. Which means your tune won't have a good vehicle for exposure, and consequently probably won't earn any money. The business-minded tunesmith must channel his or her own creativity by viewing the song's commercial potential from the standpoint of the target audience.

Another aspect of being a businessperson reveals itself after you've written your song. Let's say you have a commercial, marketable song and you even have a taker for it, either a publisher, producer, artist, or record company executive. Terrific, right? Not so fast. First, they want you to make some changes on your tune. Or they ask that you give up part of your writing credit or all of your publishing rights. (This is discussed in more detail in Chapter 8, "Wheeling and Dealing.") Now what?

Whether the changes to be made are major or minor, or the amount of writing credit or publishing you're asked to relinquish is large or small, this can still prove to be a heart-wrenching situation for many songwriters. How far should you go to get a song signed? How much should you give up to get a deal under way? When should you compromise your artistic integrity?

Sometimes at the beginning, 50 percent of something is better than 100 percent of nothing, and songwriters just starting out are well advised not to pass up a deal, even a tough one. That's not meant to sound mercenary, just practical. Music is a business, and the politics of business often work against you in the beginning of your career, and for you when your career has been established. There may come a day when you'll be on top and have enough money in the bank that you won't have to forsake anything—including your artistic integrity. Since sound business practices are such a vital aspect of the songwriter's career, much of this book is devoted to increasing the writer's business aptitude.

## The Songwriter as Team Member

In the hierarchy of the music industry, the songwriter is the vital force whose songs give the publisher something to publish, the producer something to produce, the artist something to perform, and the record label a record to put out. But, paradoxically, the songwriter is often the lowest person on the music totem pole. This may be due to the sheer number of writers, but right or wrong, that's how things stack up. (If it makes you feel any better, what the songwriter loses in status, he or she makes up for when the money starts rolling in.)

However, regardless of who's higher up than whom, from the time that a song is created till the time that it's recorded, released, and established in the marketplace, everyone is dependent on one another, a part of the same team. It takes a sincere, combined effort for any song to get anywhere.

Actually, the people involved in this process are somewhat similar to defensive and offensive players on a team. The defensive players—the writer, producer, artist, musicians, background singers, engineers, mixing consultants—go in the studio and make the record. But merely putting a song on vinyl, so to speak, does not a hit make. So in come the offensive players—the publisher, record company, promotion people, distributors, club deejays—to make sure the record gets every possible chance to become a hit if it has the potential.

Of course, that doesn't mean that the writer, producer, or artist can't help with the promotion. Calls can be made to the radio stations to request the song. Stops can be made at the record stores to ask for the tune. Not only does that go on in New York or any other music town, but a network of families and friends around the country can do the same thing. Every last little bit helps to create a buzz on a new release. Radio stations aren't going to continue playing songs no one requests, for fear they'll lose their listeners and subsequently their sponsors. In the same way, record stores aren't bound to stock records that no one is asking for.

So, as hard as the songwriter pushes and prods to get

someone to record a song, once the song is recorded and released, the writer still has to press on and do whatever can be done to make the record available to the public. The only difference is, at that point you're not working alone. You're a part of a team.

## The Songwriter as Realist

As you read this book, you'll see that music is a subjective art form that you need to be objective about if you intend to claim success. And that's a job for a realist.

Tunesmiths must be able to pull themselves out of a creative mode and look at their work for its true merit and commercial value. Sure, you can ask your friends and even your mother for their opinions. But you know what? They're going to like everything you do. (Spouses, on the other hand, who are more concerned about keeping the electricity going or putting the next meal on the table, tend to be a little more honest!)

It's good to be able to recognize your strengths, but it's important to be aware of your weaknesses as well. If your melodies are so complicated that no one can get a grip on them, work to simplify them. If your lyrics seem trite, work to instill some freshness and life into them. We all tend to develop those things which come easiest to us, and slough off the more difficult tasks. Improving a weak point doesn't happen overnight, so be patient with yourself. However, if you've run the gamut and have really tried, yet still never see any improvement, by all means don't beat yourself up over it. You may be either a great lyricist or a great composer, and you can hook up with someone else who is one or the other. Each a master in one area, you can then proceed to make fantastic music together.

If, however, you just can't seem to muster any realistic

insight into your material, take your tunes to a few publishers. They'll let you know what you're lacking very quickly. People in the industry aren't paid to be nice to you, and their criticisms can be helpful, even if they're in the form of a rejection.

## Above All Else—Persistence

The objective of this book is to give you the ammunition you need to craft commercial songs and to get those songs heard, published, recorded, and making money for you. Yet without your inner fortitude to forge ahead, without your burning desire to make it, none of the tips you'll find in this book or in any other can do much to help you overcome the obstacles that songwriters face. That's because the underlying trait of those who succeed in this business versus those who don't is persistence.

How often do people watch "Wide World of Sports" or "Saturday Night Live" and say, "Yeah, I always wanted to be a champion skier," or "If only I could've been a famous comedian"? And that's as far as most people get— whimsically wishing they're something they're not instead of taking the initiative to work toward a goal.

By just persisting, you're automatically placing yourself in the top 10 percent of any field because most people sit on the sidelines and wish upon a star forever. Sure, it's tough. Sometimes you'll feel like you're caught in a catch-22 situation. You may find yourself lamenting, "No one will listen to my songs because they've never heard one before, but how will they ever hear one if they won't listen?" But you can get them to listen, if you're persistent enough. This book will show you how.

The cold truth is, no one is exempt from rejections. At some point in their careers, everyone has been rejected ten or a hundred times (whether they're willing to admit it or not), and nobody likes it. Yet if you've been objective about your material and really want to crash through to the top, you shouldn't let the rejections get you down. It's just a fact of life that there will always be people telling you, "No way." "Sorry." "Maybe next time." The answer is to wear the opposition down before they can wear you down. The great irony is, the same people who tell you that you'll never succeed are usually the first to pat you on the back once you do and say, "Kid, I always believed you had it in you."

And often you can actually build your inner strength by looking at rejections as learning experiences that translate into something positive to help you through your next attempt. Rejections don't always have to close doors, they can also open new ones.

For example, someone could hear your material and disregard the tunes themselves, but laud you for your production ideas, steering you in a direction you had never before considered. Or maybe as a singer/songwriter, your singing capabilities will take you further than your writing talent ever could have. Or maybe you'll have to sing for your supper for a while before you're given the opportunity to showcase your writing ability.

That's what happened in the case of the Bee Gees who, even though they couldn't read music, always seemed to have an endless capacity for composing award-winning songs. The Gibb brothers got their start in the Land Down Under as a singing trio in their early teens. Yet it was years before they were noticed. They finally landed a deal on Festival Records and, to further prove that success cometh not overnight, Festival put out thirteen records before the brothers plugged into the public's ear with "Spicks and Specks."

With that minor achievement in tow, along with

rough demos of "I Started a Joke," "Words," "Holiday," and "To Love Somebody," the Bee Gees felt confident enough to strike out for Nems Enterprises in England. There, the record company executives were awed by their myriad of talents, and the brothers were signed on the spot. The rest, as they say, is music history.

So who out there says you can't have a Top 10 record next year? Who says you can't walk up the aisle and collect a Grammy in five years? Make a commitment now to see just how far your star can rise. Because it can.

## "Take Two"

As you know, this is the second edition of *The Complete Handbook of Songwriting*, and we're really pleased that a subsequent edition came to fruition based on the merits of the first.

Overall, the book has been really fun, and it keeps resurfacing in the strangest ways. Recently, I was talking to a songwriter in Michigan trying to negotiate publishing on a song he'd written, and after a while the writer asked if he could have some time to think about things and promised to give me a call the next day. When he did call, he said he had stalled me because he wanted a chance to refer to a songwriting book he had—and when he reviewed the book once again he realized it had my name on it. We also appreciate the support we've gotten from the performing rights organizations and the teachers who have passed along the book's title in their songwriting courses and workshops.

However, with all the changes that took place in the music industry in the '80s, it was high time to bring the first edition into the new decade.

The revisions we've made in this edition reflect current changes in legal matters, copyright information, music formats, technology, and equipment, plus how all of these factors affect the songwriter, and discuss just what is expected of a writer in today's market.

In this edition, too, we've tried to pass along insights from major-league songwriters, publishers, jingle writers, and so on—people totally enveloped in the industry who have a passion for music—and a head for the business.

Anyway, I hope all of the information included in this updated edition will help you in your quest, and that someday when I'm driving in my car and slide a top-selling CD into its slot, the song I hear playing will be yours.

# 1

# Writing the Commercial Song

To start with the obvious, except for instrumental compositions, a commercial song is comprised of two elements: words and music. Some songwriters compose music and weave words around their notes; others write the words first and set them to music. Either way, what really makes a song come together is the marriage, or prosody, of the words and music. And in order to achieve that marriage or blending, a songwriter should first understand the components of music (melody, harmony, rhythm) and words (title, lyrics) and how these elements are best structured together. Additionally, there are other factors to consider, such as the length of a tune, the use of sex in songs, and radio formats, which will help the tunesmith gauge and add to the commercial potential of his or her song.

First, I'd like to give a brief overview of songwriting basics.

# The Music

## Structure

Anyone who receives songs from writers on a regular basis will probably tell you that an unstructured song is a dead giveaway of a novice songwriter.

Listen to the radio, and you'll notice that most songs do have a structure or pattern. There's repetition both melodically and lyrically and contrast between verses and choruses. All with good reason. A song isn't supposed to be an exercise in frustration for the listener. It's patterned to allow the listener to get a quick grasp on the song on the initial listening, to remember it easily and feel a part of it. Even so, it should also be structured interestingly enough so the listener will still enjoy the tune thirty or so listens down the road.

One of the most popular song structures is the AABA pattern, with the A sections being verses and the B section a chorus. In this pattern, the opening A verses repeat the same musical idea and are followed by the B chorus, which provides contrast with the verse and is usually the "hooky" part of the song. Finally, the A section, or the original musical idea, is repeated.

You'll note that some songs even include a C section, termed a "bridge" or "release," which brings in a totally different musical idea altogether. The bridge or release normally follows a chorus, but can also come between a verse and chorus if it seems the song is becoming too monotonous or the listener needs some sort of release. The bridge can be a simple chord change or a rhythmic change, but it should always be a melodic change to take the song and listener to a different plane.

The AABA pattern is predominant in country songs, ballads, and in any song where a story is being told and the lyrics are critical to the song. Its two-verse lead-in gives time for the writer to develop the story line and for the listener to absorb the message.

There are a number of variations on the AABA pattern, and some of these are:

ABAB    (verse, chorus, verse, chorus)
ABAC    (verse, chorus, verse, bridge)
ABABCB  (verse, chorus, verse, chorus, bridge, chorus)

Song forms don't seem to be nearly as rigid today as they were in the past. Still, you will find that the majority of commercial songs at least start with one of these song forms as their basic structure. However, if you have something else that comes to mind, a form that doesn't disrupt the flow but rather helps it or enhances the message or lyric content of your song, feel free to depart from any of these patterns. You can think of it like building a house. Basically, you lay down the foundation, but what you build on top of the foundation can be totally new and different—and hopefully, when you're all finished, it'll stand solidly.

Most often, each section of a song consists of eight bars, so in an AABA-patterned song you'd be looking at a common thirty-two-bar refrain. Even here, though, you shouldn't feel compelled to stick to eight-bar verses and choruses if more or fewer bars work better in what you're trying to accomplish.

## Melody

Commercial songs are made for singing, or at least for humming along to. So when you take guitar pick in hand or sit down to the keyboard to compose a song, you should consider:

**Simplicity.** Most commercial songs have simple melodies that are catchy, memorable, easy to sing, and easy to follow. If you're bent on writing involved melodies, be prepared to sell symphonic pieces instead of the kind of material commercial songs are made of.

**Range and Key.** Songs are generally written in a range and key that the average person can sing along to. My own criterion when I was writing songs was if I could hit all the notes, then the average studio singer probably could, too.

The most commercial keys for songs are the key of C with no sharps or flats, keys with one or two sharps such as G and D, or keys with one or two flats such as F and B. Most composers will also usually limit the range of their song to one octave plus a perfect fifth.

By writing a song in a range and key that only require average ability to sing along to, you're not only giving the man on the street something he can sink his amateur vocal cords into, you're also presenting your publisher with a song he can shop to numerous professional singers with varied abilities.

**Development.** Picture this: You're sitting in the cushy office of a publisher or record company executive. He puts your cassette demo into his tape recorder and cranks up the volume. After almost a minute, you begin to see his face scrunch up with puzzlement. After two minutes of listening to an intricate melody that's winding its way, he supposes, to nowhere, he looks at you as if you've just grown another head.

Take it from me, friend, those can be the two longest minutes of your life.

When a publisher, producer, artist, record company executive, or even your best friend hears your song, they expect you to get into it quickly so they can, too. Don't confuse them with a plethora of musical ideas or phrases. Stick to just a few (but not so few as to be boring), and repeat them throughout your song. That's the stuff memorable songs are made of.

Additionally, each part of your melody should build on the one before so the listener can understand where the song is leading to. Most often, the melodic lines in verses will be more linear than those in the hook or chorus. Even so, there has to be a melodic elevation or intensity that helps make the transition from one section to the next. When strung together, all sections should build to a climax.

**Classification.** Obviously, the melody and rhythm of your song should be geared to the genre of music you're creating, the mood you wish to set, and the target audience you plan to reach.

**Introduction.** I've saved discussion of the beginning of your song for last because creating the "killer" introduction is usually a task that falls in the lap of the producer. A songwriter needn't drive himself or herself to the edge trying to come up with a superlative introduction.

The introduction of a song is the instrumental section that sets up the mood and segues into the opening verse. The simplest way to develop an introduction is to select an interesting part of a melodic line that's able to lead into the verse and then modify it somewhat.

## Harmony

Harmony is achieved when chords are played against a melody in a way that complements the melody and enhances it.

Any schooled musician will be knowledgeable about chords and their variants—majors, minors, and dominant sevenths, to name a few; which chords make up standard jazz or R & B progressions; and which musical notes are harmonious with which chords—right off the top of their heads.

But what about the unschooled musician?

The fact is, there are any number of melodies that can be written over the same series of chords. Plus, you'll find that at any given time, there are certain chord progressions which are in vogue. So to improve your chord comprehension, you can try the following exercise.

Listen to any radio station's Top 40 countdown and select a song that's similar to a tune you could imagine yourself writing. Buy a copy of the song and give yourself plenty of time to figure out what chord progression underlies the melody. Then proceed to come up with your own melody over those chords. As your melody develops, you may find that you'll want to change some of the original chords so they won't clash with the new melody. After repeating this exercise a few times, you'll be pleasantly surprised at how your knowledge of chords will expand. As a side benefit, you'll probably have a grasp on commercial song structures.

### Rhythm

Rhythm is what gives a song its movement, tempo, beat, feel, mood, or groove. It's primarily established by the instruments making up the rhythm section of the song, that is, the guitar, bass, drums, and keyboard. So when you're making a demo, you'll want to be sure that these instruments are played in a manner that helps to establish the groove or tempo you have in mind.

Also, when you're establishing the rhythm of your

song, make sure you're aware of what market you're shooting for, and what type of radio station might play your record. After all, every record executive wants to feel that he or she knows what market your song will ultimately fit into, and the rhythm of your song is very much a part of how your song is perceived (and how secure he or she feels about any investment in your material!).

In many genres of music, record people don't always hear a song; they don't separate a song from an artist from a record. The record executive will most likely hear a finished piece of product, and many times that's in terms of a track, a unique rhythm, or something that's just different or on the cutting edge. Without establishing the proper rhythm for your song, you may end up camouflaging its potential, or may even date it. When you think about it, when an old song is redone into a contemporary hit, the songwriting hasn't changed—but the rhythm generally has. Many times that's all it takes to make material current.

The rhythmic pattern of a song can also be embellished by the way in which the lyrics are sung. And it's up to you, as the song's creator, to dictate which words should fall on which musical notes, and how the words should be phrased, stressed, or cut off. For example, by spelling out the word "P-A-S-S-I-O-N" instead of singing it, Carl Sturkin and Evan Rogers, founders of the Rhythm Syndicate, emphasized the rhythmic quality of their song to an even greater extent.

Remember, rhythm is the quality that determines how your song is perceived as a whole. It can either add nothing but nonchalance to a great song, or its novelty and catchiness can put a so-so song over the edge.

# The Words

In order to learn your songwriting craft well, you need to become a professional people-watcher. Witness how people react to their environment. Listen to their heartfelt stories. Eavesdrop on their conversations. Get a feel for what they feel. While songs do emanate from the depths of the songwriter's soul, they still need to project universal feelings—happenings that the masses can relate to. That's why love is such a popular theme for songs. Who has never been in love, wished they were, or hoped the pain of love lost would never trouble them again?

## Titles

When you see a title like "Hello" or "You and I" topping the charts, it's hard to believe that anyone would dare stress that an intriguing or catchy title is critical to your song. But it can be, especially when you're just starting out.

Your song's title is the first thing that a publisher, producer, artist, or A & R executive (see Chapter 4, "Shopping Your Demo") knows of it; it's your introduction to them. That means if your title piques their interest and raises their eyebrows, they're not only going to want to hear your song, but they're going to want to like it as well.

Titles are generally taken from the hooky part of a song, and may give a clue as to the song's lyrical content. A title can be one word ("Impulsive"), a repetition of words ("Ice, Ice, Baby"), or even an entire sentence ("I Guess That's Why They Call It the Blues"). They can be nonsensical ("Din Daa Daa") or something everyone can relate to ("How Am I Supposed to Live Without You").

Some titles are provocative ("Sexual Healing") or suggestive ("How Deep Is Your Love"). Others stem from clichés ("Better Stop and Smell the Roses") or contain messages ("The Times They Are A-Changin' "). You'll find that many titles display contrast ("Get Up to Get Down") or are a play on words ("Sleeping Single in a Double Bed").

Through the ages, girls' names have also been popular ("Maybelline," "Michelle," "Gloria," "Donna," "Joanna," "Oh, Sherrie," "Angelia"), and so have phrases that people use in their daily encounters when put together in the right package ("[I Want to] Kiss You All Over").

When you're working on your title, run your finger down a record chart and see which titles appeal to you and catch your eye. Listen to radio deejays and note the titles they seem to have fun with. Many times, you'll hear them incorporate a title into their spiel, like " 'It's Heaven' here at WCDE" or "We're playing your favorites 'All Night Long' at WKLM." A catchy title can be the catalyst that gets you through someone's door and gets your song heard, so make it as alluring as possible.

## Lyrics

Lyrics are the words that relay the theme of your song, and there are some general rules you should consider to do that properly.

**Structure Your Lyrics.** Lyrics need to be presented in a pattern just like music does. So, if you've written a song in the AABA pattern with eight bars per section, you'll want to write two verses, a chorus, and a final verse that are metered in the same way as your melody. Even if your music isn't ready at the start, help yourself out by writing lyrics in a pattern that can easily be molded into a song's musical structure.

**Select Words Carefully.** A song is just like a commercial. There's a limited time in which to tell your story or relay your message, so you can't afford to waste a word. Carefully select each word so that you can get across all that you set out to say.

Additionally, each line of your song should build on the previous one, and the words should climax in conjunction with the music. If your verses are well written, anyone should be able to come along and read them and have a general idea about what the theme of the chorus will be.

**Write to Your Song's Topic and Market.** Lyrics should be tailored to the type of music you're creating, the song topic you've chosen, and the market you're trying to reach. So, if you've composed a high-energy dance tune, your lyrics should be just as energetic and aggressive. And in the same way, if your subject is the lament for a lost love, the words should exude sentiment and plaintiveness.

The words you choose should also reflect the language of the market you're aiming for. A rock band doesn't reach the ears of teenagers with lyrics akin to "Strangers in the Night," nor would an R & B singer and a pop artist use the same lingo to describe a beer-drinking extravaganza with the guys. Use the colloquialisms of the people you're trying to appeal to. If you're not all that familiar with the market, study it more or seek help in writing the lyrics. Whatever you do, don't abuse the language. I've heard rhythm and blues lyrics written by some white folks who carried the street jargon so far in an attempt to sound hip that it sounded ludicrous.

**Be Conversational.** Today's lyrics are more conversational than ever, rather than waxing poetic. In fact, I'll never forget my anguish over that realization when I wrote my very first song. My opening lines read, "With the break of dawn came the morning sun. And with the morning sun came the memory of last night and what we'd done."

When I showed the lyrics to an executive at a record company, he was visibly turned off just after reading those two lines. As he explained to me, people don't talk like that. The public wants to hear things expressed the way they would say them. A songwriter is trying to win the listeners' hearts, not a blue ribbon in a poetry contest.

**Choose Singable Words.** Even for the best professional singer out there, some words are just more difficult to sing than others. So after your lyrics are down on paper, test them out by singing them out loud.

You'll find that vowel sounds are easily sung and can be sustained for long notes or endings. Also, shy away from too many sequential "s" or sibilant sounds, which can be disturbing on tape.

**Repeat! Repeat! Repeat!** Capitalize on the cleverness of your lyrical hook by repeating some of its words or the entire series of words throughout the chorus. As with repetitious musical ideas, this will greatly enhance your song's memorability.

**Use Rhymes That Flow.** Some of today's songwriters shudder at the growing use of soft or false rhymes such as "pour" and "sword." On the other hand, many contemporary writers feel that forcing pure rhymes like "meet" and "feet" is too constricting and can dilute their message.

So, without a documented right or wrong way, the

songwriter is left to his or her own rhyming devices. But the mechanism you utilize should not distract from the tone of your song or its story. Your rhymes need to go easy on the listener's ears as well as the listener's sense of reality.

**Go Heavy on the Paint.** Since you have a limited time in which to tell your story, the more visual words you use, the quicker the listener can see the picture you're trying to paint or feel the emotion you wish to convey.

In my opinion, country writers are the most skilled users of visual imagery. Their picturesque words set the stage of a song on the first listening, and yet by the time the song is heard a dozen times, their careful choice of each word allows the listener to add another prop to the setting.

Nowadays, visual imagery is even taken one step further, since videos are being used to entertain the public and merchandise records. So as you're writing your lyrics, think about how they might translate into a video art form. By starting out with a look at the bigger picture, quite often you wind up painting a better one.

# The Hook

The hook is the catchy part of a song. It's the repetitious part that's implanted in your mind after hearing a song just once, it's the words that everyone remembers, it's the melodic line you just can't get out of your head.

No matter whom you play your song for, everyone's ears are conditioned to listen for your song's hook. And since everyone is on the edge of their seat waiting to hear it, it's best not to keep them waiting too long. There's no way to define the exact entry point for your hook, but as a general rule it's a good idea to introduce the hook early in your song.

Typically, a song is structured with the hook as its chorus, and many song titles are lifted from the hook. But the hooks themselves are not so typical. Some hooks are based primarily on a melodic line, as in "Someday," sung by Mariah Carey. Contrasting lyrics might be more pertinent to the hook, as in Anne Godwin's "Gotta Get Up if You're Feelin' Down." Hooks can also be one-liners like "(Everything I Do) I Do It for You" or a rhythmic pattern such as "M-M-M-My Sharona."

Whatever type of hook you utilize in your song, remember that its purpose is to reel in the listener. The hook is what will sell your song to the music executive, and it will ultimately sell your record to the public.

## Putting Words and Music Together

When a man and woman take their vows, it doesn't much matter who asked whom. What matters is that they get along. Likewise, when you set out to write a song, what you're striving for, just like those two people, is compatibility.

The following guidelines will help you maintain the compatibility between the words and music that comprise your songs:

* Structure your words and music in the same pattern.
* Create a similar mood, both melodically and lyrically.
* Blend your music and words by allowing each syllable or word to fall on a musical note or notes, and by adhering to the same meter and rhythmic pattern.

- Target both your music and lyrics for a specific artist or a particular genre of music.
- Write words that are easy to sing and melodies that are easy to sing along to.

By following these simple steps, you'll have the foundation for a workable union of words and music.

## The Search for Ideas

You can choose to write a story song like "Coward of the County," a message song like "Another Day in Paradise," a concept song like "Things That Make You Go H'mmmm . . . ," or even a novelty song such as Weird Al Yankovic's "Eat It." But where do ideas come from? How do you get started?

Concepts for songs can be found in everything around you and in everything you experience or witness other people experiencing. Most people become so accustomed to the numerous advertisements, TV shows, magazines, news briefs, billboards, newspapers, and conversations that bombard their senses on a daily basis that they practically tune them out. But it's from exactly those types of media that ideas evolve.

Songs can be written about current events or the latest fad. Ideas can be gleaned from articles you read or just from a phrase that pops out of a sentence. You can write of your own emotional triumphs and agonies or those of a friend. You can observe the strangers around you and eavesdrop on their conversations in elevators, restaurants, bars, or even the health spa. Look at the world around you, listen to what's on people's minds, but be sure to jot your ideas down quickly because they too easily slip away.

Sometimes, too, the best ideas are purely accidental,

although it takes a true songwriter's instinct to pick up on them. Smokey Robinson, a Motown Miracle, is proof of that. When he and Al Cleveland were doing some writing together years ago, it was a slip of Al's tongue that led them to write "I Second That Emotion." Evidently, they had taken a break from their writing to do some Christmas shopping, and while Al was talking to a saleslady, he inadvertently said, "I'll second that emotion," when what he really meant to say was, "I'll second that motion." Everyone laughed, but Smokey picked up on the slip and, his mind already in gear, they went back home and wrote the blockbuster hit that afternoon.

Since a song is the communication of a feeling, experience, or observation that a vast majority of people can relate to, everything in the world is a subject for writing about. What's right under your nose is always the hardest thing to see. But the songwriter who can zero in on the obvious and relay it in a unique way is the writer who has a lock on the songwriting craft.

## The Question of Musical Training

If you took the number of successful songwriters and divided them according to those who had years of formal training and those who were unschooled, I'd wager that it would be a fairly even division.

Formal musical training can be extremely helpful and could put you a step ahead not only in terms of what you know, but in the self-confidence that that knowledge brings you. The actual process of writing may become less of a strain, too, when you have a true grasp of music's rules and boundaries and are able to handle chordal progressions or arrangements with relative ease.

Nevertheless, natural musical ability, combined with a

love of music and a fervor to work relentlessly, has been the key to success for many writers with little or no musical background.

Trained or untrained, it's a rare occasion when a writer hits it big on the first song. But Chris Barbosa is one of those exceptions.

Now a producer-songwriter, Chris used to work part-time as a deejay spinning records for parties and at clubs. During that time he saved up money to purchase a drum machine and a Roland Bass Line, thinking that he could use these to incorporate sounds into the records he was spinning. Being a gadget freak to begin with, Chris got hooked on these electronics and it wasn't too long before he was talking his grandmother into helping him out with a synthesizer purchase.

The day the synthesizer arrived Chris immediately hooked it up and started familiarizing himself with it. After a few hours, he brought all of his machines together, began syncing up some of his previously programmed drum and bass line patterns, and then added melodic lines over these parts with the synthesizer. That night, the track for "Let the Music Play" was created. It was Chris's first songwriting attempt and when put together with lyrics by Ed Chisolm, the tune went on to become a gold record.

When Chris wrote "Let the Music Play" he knew nothing about music except what he had picked up from his deejay experience—what songs got the crowd on the floor and what kept them there. Since that time Chris has taken some music lessons and says it's helped speed up his writing. But he admits that if the rules begin bogging him down or cramping fresh ideas, or even make the song too complicated, he dumps them and proceeds on gut instinct.

So, songwriters don't always need a degree of some sort to prove their writing ability. With so many instructional outlets at their disposal, they can train themselves if they have a mind to do so. Writers can always learn by listening to the radio, playing album after album, tuning in to cable music stations—MTV, VH-1, and so on—going to concerts, visiting nightclubs, and hanging out in the studio. And if they feel that some kind of structured training would be beneficial, outside of conservatories the songwriter can pick up some night classes or sign up for songwriting workshops.

I would just caution that no matter what the degree of your musical training, you should handle it with care and not let it chain you down. Sometimes trained studio musicians will break out in a cold sweat and beg not to play a melodic line that breaks all the rules. Yet once they do play it, they'll often admit that the line does work within the context of the song.

The fact is, the majority of the population isn't musically trained. They evaluate a song based on what their ears tell them—either a song sounds good to them or it doesn't, either they like it or they don't. And since it's the public's ears you're trying to appeal to, the songwriter has to learn how to hear things the way they do.

## Length of Songs

Within any given hour of airtime, a radio station's program director needs to be sure the station is playing enough records to keep its audience attentive, and still have time left over to run commercials. That's why the length of most commercial songs doesn't exceed four minutes.

However, some R & B dance and urban stations may play longer-running records or even twelve-inch mixes, which can run anywhere from four to over six minutes in length. In the event a dance record crosses over into another radio format, such as pop radio, a shorter version is made available to those stations.

The length of a song is also a consideration when it comes to video shows or channels like MTV, since it's unlikely those shows would devote any more time than the standard four minutes to a song. Unless, of course, it's a real showstopper and as highly acclaimed as Michael Jackson's fifteen-minute "Thriller" video.

## Crossovers

A crossover is a song that gets airplay in more than one music market, such as when a country song makes its way onto the pop stations, or a rock song is played on an R & B station.

Currently, the industry is experiencing a shifting period in which a lot of musical genres are blending together, so crossovers have become extremely prevalent. However, the beginner songwriter who aims at writing a crossover hit is usually biting off more than he or she can chew. Writers should concentrate their efforts on creating songs that are either suited for a particular artist or that fall within a specific genre of music so that a specific audience and firm foundation can be gained.

Believe me, if you write an R & B song that pop radio listeners want to hear, they'll hear it, because crossovers occur when the material is right and when the time is right for the material. When Chris Barbosa and I produced "Let the Music Play," our aim was to produce a twelve-inch R & B dance record. Ironically, when the production was finished the record had a strong pop hook. Consequently, the record jumped from the dance charts to the R & B charts and then went pop. Of course, its success in the pop arena was helped substantially because a major record label had bought the song from the independent label that had originally distributed the twelve-inch version. But that shows that when a song displays crossover potential, someone will usually step in and take it as far as it can go.

Ballads seem to cross over more often than any other type of song. Contrarily, they're also the hardest type of song to break. Teenagers hear the up-tempo tunes for the first time in clubs or at the local roller-skating rink, and then wander home and call their favorite radio station to request it. But where do you break a ballad? Nowhere, except on the radio. And the program director usually has to spy the name of a well-established artist on the record label before he'll give the record a spin. But remember, with the ballad's mass appeal and long-lasting quality, if you should write one that crosses over, you'll be in the black for quite a long time.

## Radio Formats

If you don't have a specific target audience for your song, and a radio format or a means for your song to be heard, chances are no record company will be willing to release your record. Remember, songs that fall in the cracks usually tend to stay there. So when you're writing, you must ask yourself: Is there a radio format in existence that my song will plug directly into?

As a songwriter today you have more choices than ever, since radio stations have become even more segmented. Through the years, new radio formats have come into being, such as AOR (album-oriented rock), MOR (middle-of-the-road), AC (adult contemporary), DOR (dance-oriented rock), urban (dance-oriented and/or rhythm and blues and possibly rap), and, last but not least, New Age. Yet these new formats are basically offshoots of the major music markets: pop, R & B, country, rock, and jazz.

You'll note, too, that in recognition of these various formats, publications such as *Billboard* have even more record charts and track sales on more types of music than ever before.

The bottom line is, in order to give your songs the chance to be heard, be sure to build them on solid ground, and remember there's no ground more solid than a song directed to a specific radio format.

## Sampled Music and Music Loops

In the early days of rap music—mostly back in the early eighties—when the genre was still little known except to passersby on urban street corners, rappers would simply rap over records. But when the popularity of the music grew, rappers got off the street corners and into the studio. Only at that point, with all the electronic and digital equipment at their disposal, they could do more than just rap over a song. They could piece together snippets and beats of songs, or loop music—basically they could do whatever their little creative hearts desired.

In the beginning, no one really thought much about whether or not these "snippets" and "loops" constituted a copyright infringement because there wasn't really enough money involved for publishers to chase people down. But at the point when rap really exploded and became a mainstay of popular music, around 1990, all of that changed. The money got bigger and so did the reality that sampling and loops did sometimes infringe on copyrights. Therefore, the process of clearing samples came into existence.

For many publishers, the use of samples has breathed new life into old catalogs, and though it's a pretty standard part of the creative process in a lot of rap and dance music, it now goes outside those realms into rock and pop. And who knows? Country could well be next.

The fact of the matter is, if you, the songwriter, write your songs with samples or loops in mind or demo them that way, at the point that you sell your song and before it's commercially distributed, your samples may need to be cleared. That decision is usually based on the length of the sounds or music you sampled and how it's used in your song. Though the law is still very unsettled where sampling is concerned, there is the possibility that you could be accused of copyright infringement if you don't go about things the right way.

In one legal case to date, a judge swiftly ended a dispute with the words "Thou shall not steal" and ordered all of the defendant's product to be taken off record store shelves before the weekend came to an end. Yet it will take more outcomes of more cases in the future before the legal boundaries of sampling are better defined.

Wendy Spielman, president of The Sample Doctor, Inc., a company that specializes in aiding writers in clearing procedures, suggests that when you're in the studio, as the initial stage of the clearing process, you need to make up a sample clearance sheet. This sheet should be set up to include:

- the title of your song
- the title of the song being sampled
- the writer and publisher information, which can be taken from the actual label on the record or from the label copy on tapes and CDs
- a description of what you took from the song—horns, bass, whatever
- the timing of the amount that you took, how many

times you looped the part, and where in your new
song you placed it

Wendy's company has a list of clients that includes
such names as Chubb Rock and Prince, and she's the first
to admit that the clearing process can be a time-consuming, frustrating, and expensive experience. She also ad-
vises writers who will be seeking permission to use
samples from other records to be careful about the use of
profanity in their own songs. Many times, copyright owners and/or artists don't want to be associated with foul
language or crude sentiments and will deny permission for
use because of this.

## Sex in Songs

Sex sells. In books, movies, ads, magazines, and songs.
It brings people's fantasies into focus and form, and wakes
them from the everydayness of things. Plus, it gives kids
something to talk about and giggle at.

Although in today's society it appears that where sex
is concerned it's open season and everything's fair game,
it's still wise not to overshoot the boundaries of good—or
semigood at the very least—taste. So when you're using
sex in your songs, make it suggestive or disguised rather
than blatant and intrusive. Not only because it's sexier for
the listener to use his or her imagination, but also because
anything too crass just isn't going to make it on to many
radio stations across Middle America. The majority of
radio stations aren't going to risk losing listeners and advertising dollars for your one overheated song—no matter
who you are.

So use sound judgment when you use sex in songs.
Titillating titles that alert the primordial senses like "Love

Is Only Inches Away" are great because they do draw the listeners in, but don't turn them off by enumerating the graphic details. Cleverness, subtlety, and even cuteness work. They worked for Peter Frampton in "I'm in You," for Lennon and McCartney in "Come Together," and for the Bellamy Brothers, who sang, "If I told you you had a beautiful body, would you hold it against me?"

## The Writer's Signature

A writer's signature is his or her unique style, the identifiable characteristics of a particular writer. When you hear an Elton John, Carly Simon, or Black Crows song, don't you usually know the song has to be theirs?

Every songwriter strives for a style that separates him or her from every other writer and makes his or her material easily identifiable. And rightly so.

But along with all the pluses of developing your own style, there can also be some minuses if you take it to extremes. Like when someone starts writing songs that sound so much alike that the public becomes bored with his or her style and record sales start dropping.

Lionel Richie did a great job of keeping his fans enthralled when, after his hits "Truly," "Still," and "Endless Love," he then displayed the versatility of his talent and delighted his fans with "All Night Long."

As a writer, you want to show all facets of your talent and learn how to be identifiable, but it's important not to be too predictable.

## Collaborators

Throughout the ages, numerous teams have spawned unforgettable works—Gilbert and Sullivan, Lennon and McCartney, Leiber and Stoller, Bacharach and David; the formidable list goes on and on. But even with that sort of company in mind, some writers are just too hell-bent on their own egos to look at their work objectively and admit that they could use the help of a collaborator.

Collaboration doesn't lessen a songwriter's worth. Nor is it supposed to be an opportunity for two people to outshine one another. The idea behind collaboration is for two people to combine their talents and efforts and work together for a common goal: a great song. Two heads coming up with something superior is always better than doing something mediocre on your own.

So, if your forte is really the music and, as much as you've tried, your lyrics still seem to be holding your songs back from breeding interest—or the other way around—do your songs a favor and face that reality. Recognize your strength and take pride in it, but acknowledge your shortcomings. Find yourself a collaborator.

A collaborator can bring in fresh ideas when yours have gone stale, or can be the nudge you need to get you over the finish line when you've gotten just so far on a song and can't seem to complete it. Quite often, collaboration becomes a give-and-take situation with both people contributing in both areas, so that the lyricist might come up with a better melodic line in the verse, and the composer might hit on some stronger words for the hook. Collaboration gives a songwriter the chance to improve on a weak area by observing someone else's strong suit.

With the changes in musical technology, too, and the current emphasis on production, the songwriter who isn't capable of getting a competitive demo off the ground might want to consider collaboration with a tech person—someone who can use a synthesizer, drum machine, sequencer, and so on and get the writer's ideas down on tape.

There are many people who are covert songwriters, so no matter where you live, if you look hard enough, you should be able to find a collaborator. You can check with the bands in your area, talk with high school and college instructors, and check out any other musical outlet in your vicinity, such as churches, choirs, music stores, music clubs, and songwriting workshops. Through one of these, you're bound to find someone who's interested in writing the same type of music as you. You can even run ads in your local suburban and college newspapers.

On a broader scale, a performing rights organization, a publisher, or the SGA (Songwriters Guild of America; see Appendix D) can also be instrumental in helping you track down a suitable collaborator.

When you do find a collaborator, at the onset be sure there's a meeting of the minds in regard to how the writing credit will be divided. You might think you have 80 percent of a song completed and have asked someone to come up with only the 20 percent of the ideas needed to bring the song home. But your collaborator might feel that he or she has contributed 50 percent to the song as a whole. So clear up the gray areas by figuring out at the start who is going to get what percentage, and then get it down on paper in black and white.

Also, if you are collaborating with a tech person, you should keep in mind that, technically, a song consists of melody and lyrics and legally that's what the writer's share of the money is intended for. So when you're negotiating the songwriter splits, if you did write the melody and the lyrics (the song), don't give away the house.

If you run into a situation where you've written a melody and decide to hand over the song to two or more lyricists, always be candid about it. Let these people know that you've given the tune to several lyricists and that you're going to pick the best from the lot, and that all unused lyrics will be returned to their creators.

It's true that you might go through a few partners before you find the person who clicks, the person who has a compatible talent and personality and shares your goals, tastes, and working habits. But if you look long and hard enough, you will find the person who's right for you.

## Writing and Rewriting

Some days you're bound to feel like a sheer genius working at your craft. And then other days, the Writer's Block Monster will loom over you and you'll sit paralyzed with a blank mind.

Rest assured that the monster visits everyone from time to time, and you can't let him make a complete zombie out of you. If an idea isn't working, go on to the next one. And if that idea doesn't work, maybe it's time to take a day off and go fishing. Quite often, all it takes is a fresh, aired-out mind to put your creative flow back in motion again. Sometimes, too, when you feel yourself stagnating, you might need another set of eyes to help you see what you can't. So ask someone to review your work for you, someone whose opinion you value and who will give you their honest reaction.

Also, never be afraid to revise your songs or start them over completely. After all, great songs are not written— they're rewritten. No one writes a song, or anything else for that matter, perfectly on the first go-around. Good material has always been revised and fine-tuned by the time you hear it.

# Close-up of a #1 Song: "(Everything I Do) I Do It for You"

Undoubtedly you've heard the work of Michael Kamen—you just may not know you have. Kamen is the classical music talent that rock bands call on when they want to embellish their tracks with orchestration à la Queen Reiche's "Empire" LP and Pink Floyd's "The Wall." Kamen's name and melodies are also at the heart of many memorable film scores like *Lethal Weapon 3* and *Robin Hood: Prince of Thieves*. In fact, Kamen's "(Everything I Do) I Do It for You" (co-written by Bryan Adams and Robert John "Mutt" Lange) was the theme song for *Robin Hood* and also the biggest song of 1991, resting in the number one position of the Top 40 for seven weeks.

Kamen admits that it's very tempting after a success—and with the luxury of hindsight—to try to say why a song attained hit status. "But the truth is," says Kamen, "you can never say unequivocally why a song is a hit. At best, you can only come up with some possible causes."

In the case of "(Everything I Do) I Do It for You," the circumstances surrounding the song were charged with positives. First off, it gained wide exposure from a hit motion picture, which, in turn, gave it instant recognition on radio. It was performed by pop/rock superstar Bryan Adams, and the legendary Robert John "Mutt" Lange was the producer.

However, many songs have made the leap from film to radio and have even been created with the same sort of megastar setup, yet few manage to achieve that degree of success. For instance, as Kamen himself points out, *Lethal Weapon 3* had the awesome collaborative team of Kamen, Eric Clapton, David Sanborn, and Sting, but just didn't go the distance the *Robin Hood* ballad did.

So what made "Everything I Do" so magical? How did

this very special song come to be? Well, believe it or not, the pure melody of the song—its chords and structure— was actually conceived by Kamen some twenty years ago. At that time he couldn't adapt it for any of the projects he was working on, so he tucked it in the back of his mind, hoping that someday he'd have the opportunity to use it. As he reviewed the *Robin Hood* film, the melody came back to him, and ironically, the song ballad that had lived inside of him for many years seemed to be a perfect match for one of the most well-known story ballads of all time.

Actually, "Everything I Do" wasn't just an incredible match for the movie, but in purest songwriting terms it has what every songwriter is working toward—the perfect marriage of words and music. And it's a marriage that seems effortless and uncontrived in every way—as if it was "just meant to be." This ease is even more appreciable when you realize that musically the song is much more sophisticated than most other successful popular songs. It's not written in a traditional AABA pattern, but rather has an ABCABCDBA$_2$C pattern. To explain that a bit, there's an A-section verse, a B-section change, a C-section chorus, and after this sequence is repeated twice, it's followed by a bridge, the B-section, an altered A-section, and then the outchorus.

However, most people would never guess at the intricacies of the song, which is what's so outstanding about it. It's like a tapestry of musical sections all woven together, yet seems to flow seamlessly from section to section. There aren't any great distinctions or distractions between the sections; the song simply unfolds beautifully and, again, effortlessly.

The easy nature of the music gives the song its totally genuine and sincere quality. And that's exactly the tone the song should have because "Everything I do, I do it for you" was the heartfelt disclosure Robin Hood made to his love, Maid Marion. His promise to her was the genesis of the lyric. It's the ultimate commitment, a love that goes beyond here and now and a love that's worth dying for. Fittingly, the lyrics aren't clever or terribly poetic, but what they are (as you can read) is written directly to this statement and in the same voice. The words are real and honest with a straight-from-the-heart appeal that goes deeper than any imagistic or flowery words ever could.

"(Everything I Do) I Do It for You"

Look into my eyes—you will see
What you mean to me
Search your heart—search your soul
And when you find me there you'll search no more
Don't tell me it's not worth tryin' for
You can't tell me it's not worth dyin' for
Ya know it's true
Everything I do—I do it for you

Look into our hearts—you will find
There's nothin' there to hide
Take me as I am—take my life
I would give it all, I would sacrifice
Don't tell me it's not worth fightin' for
I can't help it there's nothin' I want more
Ya know it's true
Everything I do—I do it for you

There's no love—like your love
And no other could give more love
There's nowhere—unless you're there
All the time—all the way

Oh, you can't tell me it's not worth tryin' for
I can't help it there's nothing I want more
I would fight for you—I'd lie for you
Walk the wire for you—yeah, I'd die for you

Ya know it's true
Everything I do—I do it for you

Looking back, there are other factors that might have contributed to the success of "Everything I Do." The song dealt with an emotion that everyone could relate to. There was nothing like it on the airwaves at the time. But, again, all of this is only conjecture and could apply to the success or failure of any song.

The point is, a songwriter always needs to strive to write the best song possible just as Michael Kamen did. Every day I hear songwriters say if Nirvana or Michael Bolton would record their song, it would be a smash. But let's face it, you really can't use that as your measuring stick—because any song recorded by an artist of that stature is bound to have some chart success.

So whether you're writing a ballad, rock or novelty song—or whatever—remember objectivity. Work hard, use your skills, and remember you must create a song that works so well even an unknown artist would have success with it. Make that your goal. Because no one ever knows which songs will make it. In the wise and very experienced words of Michael Kamen: "Songwriting is like preparing a meal. You shake all the same ingredients into a pot— sometimes it's just right, other times it misses the mark and you're not exactly sure why. Ultimately, I find I'm most successful when I don't set out to write a "hit." Rather, I let success sneak up on me while I'm going about the business of working hard and writing songs."

Walt Aldridge, "No Getting over Me," "Holding Her and Loving You," "I Am a Simple Man":
    Many times new writers have a song or two and tend to clutch onto those when they really need to get on with the business of writing more songs. I don't mean

writing too quickly or too much and not taking the time to develop your ideas. But writers should submit the song or two they have, and in the meantime, continue writing more songs. It takes years to develop a sense of when to write more or write less, when to turn the burners up or down—even seasoned writers have a difficult time with that. But for the new writer it's best to just keep writing. It helps you find out what you do well and your hit may be the song you haven't written yet. After all, the more seeds you plant, the more likely you are to grow a watermelon.

Diane Warren, "When I'm Back on My Feet Again," "When I See You Smile," "If I Could Turn Back Time":

Don't give up, if you believe in your heart that you're meant to be a songwriter, don't give up. I knocked on doors, I followed people down the street in my car, I ran after people trying to give them tapes. Of course, this is a business where you'll be seeing the same people for a long time; you don't want to really turn anybody off. You just got to work at it, you got to keep your grasp together, you got to write great songs, you got to go out and convince the world that they are great.

Billy Steinberg, "Like a Virgin," "So Emotional," "True Colors":

My advice would be to believe in yourself. I worked my Dad's farm with him "just in case" music didn't work out for me. But at the same time I never quit writing or playing with my band. Our break came one day when the girlfriend of one of our band members who happened to know Linda Ronstadt got a tape of one of our songs to her. And that was the start. Also, I've always loved words, and my partner Tom Kelley and I do things a little differently because I write the lyrics and then we work on the music. Most other writers do it just the other way around. But for us the music really has to make the lyric shine—and when it does— when it gives life to the lyric, then we know it's right.

Carl Sturkin/Evan Rogers, "P-A-S-S-I-O-N," "Soldier of Love," "Street of Dreams":
    Our pearls of wisdom for a new writer would be—

1. Don't bore us—hit us with the chorus.
2. Dare to be stupid.
3. Remember, there's not as much luck involved in this business as people like to think.

# Making a Demo

## What's a Demo?

Yes, I admit it. I started my career as a teenage dabbling songwriter. Throughout college, when meager funds left me without anything to do, I'd hole up alone in my room and write songs. Or I'd stalk the halls of the dorm strumming out new tunes when tennis injuries kept me behind while the team traveled to tournaments without me. And more times than I care to recall, you could find me wailing to the moon on weekends when the girls attending our suitcase college packed it up and headed home to Mom. Songwriting was a cheap companion. It was my cure-all.

At that time I had no idea what a demo was. But then in the winter of my senior year I began to take my songwriting hobby a little more seriously. It had been an exceptionally austere, accident-prone, and celibate season, and I realized that I had actually accumulated a fair amount of tunes. So, I decided to find out just what, if anything, could be done with my efforts. I had visions of walking in to see a publisher who would instantly beg to hear all of my songs, declare me songwriter of the year, and grant me fame and fortune.

However, nothing like that happened. At Christmas break, I took myself to Muscle Shoals, Alabama, the prestigious recording center. I walked into a place called Fame Recording. When I asked the receptionist how I could go about getting my songs heard, she simply said, "You need to make a demo." As visions of Rolls Royces and Grammy Awards retreated from my head, I inquired, "What's a demo?" She told me what it was—a recording of someone singing your song accompanied by instruments. It's a shortened name for demonstration recording, and it's called that because it demonstrates the potential your song may or may not have in the commercial market.

What that receptionist failed to mention, though, is what a revelation even the roughest recording of your own song can be. Recording your song on tape and hearing it played back is like standing back to take in a wall you've freshly painted. You can suddenly discern the places in the tune which require touching up, glossing over—or even the spots where you've missed the boat completely.

After you've written your song, you should record a rough tape of it on your home system. After listening to this reference tape several times, you'll be better able to determine what instrumentation should be used on your demo, what sort of vocalist would sound best on the song, and even whether the original arrangement couldn't, indeed, stand some rearranging. This tape will also serve as a reference recording which will aid you in tightening up the song's musical direction and your production ideas before the studio clock begins ticking away your dollars.

Before you actually record the demo, though, stop and ask yourself: Do I plan to shop my demo to a music publisher, a producer, an artist, or a record company

executive? (More on these people later.) Do I ju
pitch my talents as a songwriter, or additionally
lish myself as a singer/songwriter?

As you'll soon read, the answers to these qu
play an important role in the development and acce
of your demo. This is where the first major decisio
cerning your demo comes in. So, take the time to d
where you're going before you head there.

## Gearing Your Demo to the Music Publisher

When catering your demo to a music publisher, your
main objective should be to show the potential of your
song. Music publishers are in the business of owning and
placing songs.

Music publishers require broad-based demos that afford them the flexibility of shopping songs to ten or even
a hundred artists before a buyer comes to the surface. By
stylizing your song too specifically, you're decreasing the
number of artists the publisher can peddle the tape to, and
lessening the chances of the song being recorded. In other
words, while the demo should still be a good representation of your song and a decent production, try to avoid
locking in the song too tightly, unless you are, indeed,
trying to place your song with a specific artist or act.

When choosing a vocalist for your demo, remember
too that he or she should be good—but not too good. The
music publisher doesn't want a vocal performance that
would cause a prospective artist to reject the song due to
sheer intimidation, and someone who sounds like Mariah
Carey's baby sister could do just that.

By allowing your demo a sort of "open-endedness,"

'isher's ability to place
.terested in signing your
e extra money to make an
. a demo that is cast more

*[folded corner text, partially visible]*
st want to
to estab-
estions
ptance
con-
ecide

## Demo to the Producer

either in the market for songs for a
or for songs in general, or they're looking
to produce. So, depending on your goals,
can be most helpful.

presenting your material to a producer, you
emain aware of the fine line between making a
mo and overproducing one. Don't do what some
riters do, and look at it as an opportunity to slack
on the production. That's just a poor excuse for a poor
mo. While it's true that producers are regaled as having
the "best ears" in the business, they're human, too, and
can't always "hear through" an unprofessional demo.
Your demo needs to display the song's direction and establish the song's groove.

However, producers have this other funny human
trait called an ego. That's why you should also refrain
from overproducing a demo you present to them. Like
you, a producer has a creative flair when it comes to
developing a song. By creating an extremely elaborate
demo, you are likely to diminish his input and overall
excitement about your song. Let the producer feel like he
can add the finishing touches that can make your song a
hit.

# Gearing Your Demo to the Artist

You wouldn't go to a butcher shop to have your shoes repaired, so why would you send Amy Grant a demo entitled "Get Up, I Feel Like Being Your Sex Machine"? Instead of familiarizing themselves with a market and its artists—where these artists have been and where they're growing to—some songwriters indiscriminately mail out the same demos to every performer from Anka to Zappa.

Ninety-nine percent of the time, if you haven't done your homework in this area, it shows with a lack of results. But . . . well, there is that one percent, as in the case of the hit "Bette Davis Eyes." Donna Weiss and Jackie DeShannon collaborated on that song eight years prior to anything ever happening with it. After it had sat for some time generating dust particles instead of interest, Donna played the song for her friend Kim Carnes, a rising country star. Kim had just gained widespread recognition for her duet with Kenny Rogers, "Don't Fall in Love with a Dreamer." Now working on a solo project, Kim had the clout to put the tune on her LP *Mistaken Identity*. Only rather than cutting the song in the country style that was on the demo, she cut it in a rock 'n' roll groove that proved very successful.

It is possible that your song may veer onto a path of music you never dreamed possible, but the chances are slim. Doing preparatory work before sending out demos to artists is much easier and surer than fighting the unbeatable laws of probability.

# Gearing Your Demo to the Record Company Executive

Most of the time, when a songwriter presents a demo to an A & R—artist and repertoire—executive at a record company, it's because the song is suited for an artist signed to that particular label.

However, if you're a singer/songwriter trying to get a deal you'll also be dealing with A & R people, since they're in the business of seeking out and signing up new talent, but in that instance, a master recording rather than a demo would be your best presentation vehicle. (See Chapter 11, "Mastering the Master.")

A master recording is a final recorded version of a song that is ready to be made into a record. Obviously, it offers a superior sound and can better display the professionalism of your band or solo performance. And a professional, quality sound is a key element in obtaining a deal with a record label.

Within an arena of fierce competition, the A & R executives are blasted daily with recordings bearing all the latest recording techniques from some of the best people out there. Consequently, the master recording is what the A & R ears know and hear best. So if you're pursuing a singer/songwriter career, give yourself a fair shot by matching the sophisticated recordings of your rivals.

Remember, though, that although record company executives are interested in songs, their primary focus is on the development of artists. Either they're searching for an artist to compete closely with an artist on another label, or they're looking for a totally original artist who stands apart from the mainstream of musical talents instead of merely silhouetting the others before him.

# The Importance of Making a Competitive Demo in Today's Market

The record industry is a risky business at best. And though everyone is *supposed* to have golden ears, and everyone is *supposed* to know a hit song when they hear one, that's just not reality. NO ONE *really* knows. So the more you can do to make your product less risky, the better your chances will be to get your product to the public.

In short, you need to make the best demo you possibly can—a demo that eliminates doubts and guesswork and shows your song for all that it is. That doesn't necessarily mean that every demo you do has to have the polish and finish of, let's say, a Wilson Phillips production—unless, of course, you're trying to sell a song to Wilson Phillips or are competing in that arena. But the point is, you should make a demo that outshines or is at least comparable to the other demos within the specific genre of music you're writing for.

Additionally, the Tin Pan Alley days are truly a thing of the past. No one is strolling into music industry offices strumming a guitar and auditioning their songs live. Music is more sophisticated than ever, and musical equipment is, too. And that means, as you'll read in the section on midi equipment, that more than ever before a larger segment of the population now has the tools (and doesn't necessarily have to have the schooling) to create songs and produce demos. Obviously, it doesn't take a marketing major to figure out that when supply far outweighs demand, competition is heightened.

So a lot is expected of today's songwriter in terms of making a solid demo, and it can be a bit frightening. But on the bright side, today's songwriter also has access to sampling techniques and equipment that can turn out some decent product in a relatively inexpensive way. By taking a drum groove out of a record and looping it, taking a guitar part out of another record and sampling that, adding a keyboard pad, and so on, you could sample enough parts to create the track for your song, and the only thing you'd have to do is get a microphone and do a vocal.

The bottom line is this: When you think you have a finished demo that's ready to be shopped, picture yourself as the person sitting on the other side of the desk. After listening to this demo, would you be eager to open up your checkbook? In the long haul, taking the time to ask yourself this question and giving an honest reply can surely help you do your best to meet the competition head-on.

# Demo Styles

Once you have an idea of what you want to show with your demo, you must decide what style of demo to make. Different types of demos are suggested for different styles of music. These can be divided into two categories: the ballad demo and the up-tempo song demo.

## The Ballad Demo

Because of the ballad's characteristic slowness and the importance of the lyric, finding the right singer for your demo is your first must. The singer must be able to clearly enunciate the words and to create a mood with his or her expressive singing. Vocal execution is critical to the success of the ballad demo.

The production of this type of demo can be fairly simple. Most often, a piano or guitar will be sufficient accompaniment for the singer. However, if you should desire more instrumentation, a rhythm section should do the job (keyboard, bass, guitar—electric or acoustic—and drums). Because the vocalist is so crucial to the execution of your demo, the rhythm section isn't always necessary to show the potential of your ballad. However, if you should choose to incorporate more instrumentation into your demo, be aware that it should reinforce your song's mood and lyrical content.

(By the way, a typed lyric sheet should always accompany a demoed ballad. In this way, the listener can get the full impact of the song's story on the first listening.)

## The Up-Tempo Song Demo

Besides the actual melody and lyrics intrinsic to your song, the up-tempo demo needs to convey drive and energy. This drive and energy are established from the groove that you give your demo, and the groove is derived primarily from the rhythm section—keyboard, guitar, bass, and drums.

In today's music, rhythm sections are very often derived from old records that are looped in a one-, two-, or four-bar pattern or samples of little snippets of beats from an old record that are strung together to create a new groove.

Depending on the genre that you're dealing with, the "track" that you create can sometimes be more important than the actual song (melody and lyrics). To me, a good example is C&C Music Factory's "Gonna Make You Sweat." The actual track or groove was an undeniable dance hit as it was (and went on to be a pop hit as well), but the producers, Clivilles and Cole, added a rap and some vocal embellishments that were just the icing on the cake.

# Demo Costs

When I was working for a music publishing company years ago, I remember a songwriter who made his way into the office to give a live performance of his tune. This was truly a rarity, and proved to be somewhat devastating for the writer.

After the writer had strummed and sung out his creation, he went on to rave about his song—its impact, its potential. But the man behind the desk stopped him flatly and said, "You believe in this song? Then you put your money into it. Go make a demo."

In the nature of things songwriters have to be the first to put their money where their songs are—to jump on their own bandwagons. Your belief in your song is reflected in the efforts you make to represent it. However, many writers might be abundant in the creativity department but are usually tapped dry money-wise, and walk a financial tightrope while trying to get their careers off the ground.

Therefore, the following information is designed to break down demo costs and help you minimize them so you can make as good a demo as your dollars can afford.

## Studio Costs

If you're making a demo at home on a multitrack cassette deck—whether analog or digital format, or any other format for that matter—the only costs involved will be the microphones and the tape.

But if you plan to go the studio route, a 4-track studio will run approximately $10 to $30 an hour and an 8-track configuration will run anywhere from $15 to $50 an hour. Either can turn out a solid demo.

The hourly studio rate is known as the "card" or "book" rate, and though it may be printed up in the studio's brochure, it is rarely etched in stone. Studio managers may be persuaded to lower the rate if you're a new customer, if you intend to pay cash up front, or if they could just use the business. So never be reluctant to barter. More favorable rates may also be negotiated if you're willing to record during off-peak hours, such as weekends or through the night. Yet another way to cut costs is by block-booking the time. If you intend to spend more than ten hours or so in the studio, you're guaranteeing the studio the use of a quantity of hours, which, in turn, should decrease the hourly rate.

When booking a studio, you also need to confirm any additional charges. Generally, an engineer is included in the hourly fee, but ask before you book. You may also need to outlay money on equipment and instrument rentals, so figure out what you'll require in advance. Most studios are equipped with standard instruments such as drums, acoustic piano, and amplifiers, all usually available free of charge. Outboard equipment such as reverbs, compressors, limiters, equalizers, synthesizers, phasers, noise gates, and echo effects can cost extra. Again, be sure you've asked ahead of time about all of these items to prevent a traumatic shock when presented with the bill.

## Tape Costs

All studios are set up for a particular type and size of reel-to-reel tape, so ask the studio manager what tapes they require and their costs. If you purchase the tape at the studio, it will be tacked onto your final bill and will probably run you much more than if you purchase it outside the studio prior to your session. Tapes can be purchased from a wholesale distributor, or a local stereo center can provide you with considerable savings, too.

Ampex and Scotch are the most commonly used reel-to-reel tapes and come highly recommended. With regard to cassette tapes, which you'll be buying in order to make copies of your demo, name brands such as Ampex, TDK, and Maxell are recommended. Metal and chromium oxide tapes share first place in terms of high quality. From there, ferrochromium is the next best, with normal bias being the lowest-quality tape. If you've decided to use a digital format in recording your demo, I would still recommend a DAT by Scotch or Ampex.

You've heard the adage "Time is money"? Well, when buying cassettes this is especially the case. Copying one song onto a ninety-minute cassette is certainly money down the drain. Twenty minutes (ten minutes per side) is all you need. Why pay for more?

## Musician and Vocalist Costs

Sometimes you'll be able to play and sing on your own demos, but if you're not equipped to be a one-man band, you'll need to hire outside musicians and vocalists.

Where do you find them? Well, you could spend money running ads in the classified section of your local newspaper, but it's unlikely that you'll really need to. There are a variety of sources to investigate which won't cost you anything except maybe some footwork, some time, and a little ingenuity. First, look for their "For Hire" ads in the classifieds. Then, search out your local high schools, colleges, conservatories, music stores, music instructors, nightclubs, bars, church choirs, friends, and friends of friends.

Literally hundreds of musicians and vocalists are dying to get into the studio. And no matter how long your session runs, most musicians will work on a flat-fee basis.

Don't be at all surprised if you ask a guitarist from the local university to do a session for $15 and a six-pack of beer, and he jumps at the chance. Studio experience is priceless, and most musicians know it.

Union musicians and vocalists aren't to be shied away from either. It's very common for them to work for much less than union scale if and when there's a lull in their schedules. However, if the demo is sold to a label, then they'll have to be paid in accordance with union terms. Likewise, if nonunion musicians and vocalists perform on a subsequent master recording, they're obligated to become union members. The two unions established for musicians and vocalists are the American Federation of Musicians (AFM), which represents musicians, arrangers, contractors, and copyists, and the American Federation of Television and Radio Artists (AFTRA), which represents singers, actors, announcers, narrators, and sound-effects artists.

Another way to reduce musician fees is to locate a synthesizer player in your area. That way, one person can do the work of several musicians.

Whomever you hire for your demo, make sure everyone is well rehearsed before entering the studio. Nothing burns up studio time and your dollars more quickly than a vocalist who doesn't know the melody or a guitarist who just can't get that one lick quite right.

## Choosing a Studio

Price plays an indisputable role when deciding on a studio, or anything else for that matter. Yet there are other criteria to be considered before finalizing your studio choice.

First off, there's the number of tracks to consider.

Four- and 8-track configurations are quite suitable for a good-quality demo; a 24-track studio is most often used for master recordings. (While the 4- and 24-track studios should be able to produce comparable sounds, the 24-track is more advantageous when making a master because the additional tracks provide more control over the recording right up to the final mixing stage. For example, a 24-track studio can have 24 instruments, each on its own separate track. This separation can prove invaluable when adjusting the final levels or when deciding to drop an instrument in or out of a certain section of a song. The 16-track studio can also be used for master recordings, but rarely is since it runs close in cost to a 24-track studio without being as well facilitated. As a result, 16-track studios are becoming increasingly obsolete.)

But remember, with a 4-track studio, you can only have four instruments on separate tracks. Therefore, if you need to use eight instruments, you'll have to double things up. When mixing, this won't allow you to lower the guitar level while keeping the piano at the same volume if those instruments are recorded on the same track. Also, if you later realize that the piano doesn't work with the guitar in the verse, there's no way of dropping one instrument out without dropping out the other.

Another consideration in choosing a studio is the acoustics of the room. This is extremely important because different rooms are conducive to different types of music. For instance, when recording rock 'n' roll songs you'll want a live sound. So go in and snap your fingers, and if there's an echoing effect, you'll know the room is "live."

However, the room isn't the only thing that determines the "live" quality. The setup of the instruments does, too. For a live sound the instruments aren't plugged directly into the mixing board; rather, they're recorded over amplifying equipment. In this way, the ambiance of the room will be picked up and the additional noise, even the flow of the air, will give the tape a dirtier, rougher quality. When you plug instruments directly into the board, the recording is unaffected by any surrounding noises and the result is a cleaner sound on tape.

Since every studio does have a different sound, always ask to listen to a tape that was recorded at the studio you're thinking about booking. And check out the rooms yourself.

Studio engineers make a difference, too. But you may not know much about the engineer and how well you can work together until after you've been at the studio a time or two. Still, the engineer is like your technical right arm. You should be able to tell him what effects you want on the demo, and he should be able to deliver.

The engineer spends most of his time turning the knobs on the mixing board, fine-tuning or EQing (equalizing) every frequency through the board. Basically, this means he adjusts the levels of the bass and treble and the softness and loudness of each instrument or vocal part separately, which in turn creates an overall sound.

You can do the same sort of thing on your own stereo, and probably have before. By maximizing the treble, the music comes across as high and tinny. When cranking up the bass, the effect is boomy, and makes your heart feel as though it's jumping through your chest.

Similarly, boards in different studios also produce different sounds. Some boards will produce punchy sounds, others weaker or thinner sounds.

Gradually, by keeping your ears open, you'll learn about the various studio equipment and more about what the engineer is up to, all of which will aid you in gaining more control over the outcome of your demo.

## Technological Changes Through Midi

Though music is an ongoing, constant part of our lives, the music industry, like most other industries, is in a state of continuous flux. And part of the reason for the changes is the development of new instruments and equipment available to people involved at every level of the business—musicians, producers, engineers, artists, songwriters. Overall, midi is one such technological advancement that has broadened music and the opportunities available to those involved in it.

Midi is an acronym for musical instrument digital interface. It's a language like any other—German, Spanish, French—but a language that allows one instrument to communicate with other instruments.

Basically, with midi you have one master keyboard (the controller) which tells the other keyboards (the slaves) what to play. Though this sounds very simplistic, don't be fooled. Midi has been unbelievable in finally actualizing the dreams of music people. Years ago, if you had a vision of a sound in your head, something that was made up of two or three composite sounds, it was just too laborious with analog synthesizers to even try to get it on tape. To layer sounds you'd have to go through the process of recording one patch on one track, another on another track, another on another track, and on and on. But with midi, you can do it all at once by just lining up two or three sound modules or synthesizers and letting them talk to each other through this musical language. The different sounds are cued to come in at different places in your recording and the result is this gorgeous, grandiose sound. You can hear the ting of a bell, the swell of the gong, the string melody—all of the sounds you can hear in your head, you can finally get to tape.

## How Midi Evolved

This may not be the world's most historically comprehensive account on the evolution of midi, but it is an eyewitness account of how I saw midi taking shape in studios over the years.

Midi began appearing on the music scene in the early eighties, but while it was coming into its own there were other things out there also attempting to relay messages in musical formats. For example, the sequencers at that time used DCB (digital control buss) or CV to gate (where the CV—"control voltage"—turned a note on and the gate turned the note off). In fact, I remember the first time I ever saw a sequencer. It was in early 1983 at Unique Recording in New York. We were doing a session, and somebody said, "Hey, so-and-so is bringing in a sequencer tonight." And my immediate response to that was, "What's a sequencer?"

At the time I was working with Robby Kilgore, who was technically one of the top guys in the country, and when that little box appeared in the studio that night (it was an Oberheim DSX, by the way), his eyes were as big as half dollars, he was so excited. However, I was still asking, "What's a sequencer?"

Later, I came to realize that a sequencer is like a miniature computer. You feed it instructions or data and through midi (or at that time, some other language), it passes that information on to your synthesizer or sound module, telling it what to play. To me, it's almost like a player piano. You've got the roll of paper with the little niches cut out of it, and the machine that mechanically turns the roll round and round so that the piano keys play a particular song. Well, the sequencer is like that mechanical roller and sends information to the sound module so that like the piano, it can play what it's told to.

But, anyway, back to my story. That night at Unique we were all so enamored with the sequencer we played with it for hours, totally forgetting that we were burning up studio time and money. And after several hours of trying, we still couldn't get that little machine to correctly spit out the entire eight bars of music that we had played.

Why weren't those early sequencers successful? Well, everyone knew they wanted to have machines talk to musical instruments, but they were still scrambling to come up with something that could become a standard in the studio. When those first rounds of sequencers tried to communicate with synthesizers, it was like you trying to communicate with someone who speaks Russian when you only know ten words of the language.

At the same time that the sequencer people were going back to the drawing board, the DX7 had become a super-popular synthesizer. Before the DX7, synthesizers and sound modules were mainly analog, and although the DX7 may not have been the first digital synthesizer, it was quickly accepted as the best because it had midi and, believe it or not, it actually worked on a consistent basis!

So what began from all of this was a sort of leapfrog situation. Advances in one piece of gear spawned advances in other pieces of gear, so that when synthesizers began improving, the sequencers had to get better—which they did.

Sequencers began using midi and could easily talk to the new digital synthesizers. However, to program the sequencers was no easy feat. Though new and improved, they often needed to be programmed in "step time," meaning everything had to be articulated musically into the sequencer, and it required a trained musician to perform that task.

But what about all of the people who were musically creative, but not musically trained? The manufacturers were really missing the boat by not having a sequencing unit they could use, too. So they developed one, and it was a sequencer that employed "real time." With this type of sequencer, through midi and a keyboard you could tell the keyboard to tell the sequencer what you were playing, and you could slow things down so that even a nonmusician could virtually sequence parts at a slower speed—one note at a time if he or she wanted to.

Again, technologically everything continued to leap forward and new developments in synthesizers followed the advancements in the sequencers. Synthesizers became even more refined, more user-friendly, much smaller and more manageable. No longer did you need an entire room to house your large array of keyboards. Instead, with the development of sound modules, you were looking at a piece of gear that was about nineteen inches in width and one to three rack spaces high, so the corner of a bedroom provided ample space to house a pretty impressive arsenal of sounds.

So, as a result of all of the advancements in midi over the years, we have equipment that is very forgiving and can be used by people at all levels of musical expertise, gear that is more compact and manageable in size, plus, it's equipment that is more affordable in price—and that's how we get to . . .

## Midi Equipment for Making Demos at Home

Parallel to the development of sound modules was the development of workstations. Workstations look like a regular synthesizer, but incorporate a keyboard controller, sound banks and usually a synthesizer, and a sequencer all within itself. The M1 was one of the first workstations to make this "all internal" idea popular, and what made it even better was that with the M1 you no longer needed a drum machine because it had very usable internal drum samples.

Over the years, the workstation concept has improved with the addition of more voices. In other words, most had eight voices, meaning you could only utilize eight notes at a given point in time. That meant that after laying down the kickdrum, high hat, snare, and toms, you would only have four notes left to play bass, key pads, and so on if they were playing at that same moment. Therefore, workstations were further developed to incorporate more voices and more outputs, which ultimately resulted in more versatility and control in all aspects of the creative process.

So, if you decide to purchase midi equipment to make demos at home, you can go about it in two ways:

1. *Modular Style.* By purchasing your equipment modularly or in separate components, it may cost you a bit more, but you may ultimately have more control over your results. It's also a way that you and a couple of your friends could go in together and buy some gear, splitting the expenses and the equipment.
2. *Workstation Style.* Remember that the workstation houses a controller, sequencer, and synthesizer all in one. They offer compactness along with their streamlined approach, but remember, what you hear is what you get. So make sure you like what the workstation has to offer before you take one home.

Whether you're using modular equipment or a workstation, you'll also need to have some means to record your vocals or live instrumentation. Your recorder can either be in an analog or digital format. My suggestion in each category would be the TASCAM 8-track cassette portastudio, which is an analog portastudio with a built-in mixer; for a digital studio the Alessis A-DAT is also very impressive. The A-DAT is also 8-track, but doesn't offer a built-in mixing console.

And now, the information you've been waiting for—how much will all of this cost? Well, for everything you need to make demos at home, here are some approximate prices (keep in mind, too, you can look for used equipment):

Modular Route
| | |
|---|---|
| Sound Module | $1,000 |
| Computer | 1,000 |
| Software | 400 |
| Controller | 500 |
| Amplifier | 500* |
| Small Speakers | 250* |
| Microphone, misc. gear | 500 |
| Total (Approx.) | $4,150 |

Workstation Route
| | |
|---|---|
| Workstation | $2,500 |

(The workstation can range from $1000 to $5000, depending on whether it's new or used and its level of sophistication.)

| | |
|---|---|
| Amplifier | 500* |
| Small Speakers | 250* |
| Microphone, misc. gear | 500 |
| Total (Approx.) | $3,750 |

*Instead of purchasing an amplifier and a set of small speakers individually, you may want to purchase self-powered speakers which have their own amplifier and are more portable. These could run you anywhere from $200 to $500, so you'd be saving money, too.)

Don't forget that added to these totals will be the cost of an analog or digital recorder. The analog portastudio will run you approximately $2,000, and the digital recorder will probably be a little over $3,000. Additionally, as I mentioned before, the lower-priced digital recorders don't normally have built-in mixers, so you can add on another $1,000 or so for a mixer if you go this route.

With this amount of equipment, and depending on your level of expertise, you should be able to accomplish a lot and turn out a very good-quality demo at home. But that doesn't necessarily mean you'll never, ever have to set foot in a studio. After all, if you're working on something that needs to compete directly with Phil Collins or Steve Winwood or someone of that caliber, you have to remember that they're not recording on an 8-track at their houses.

However, if you do need to compete at a high level but need to keep costs low, you can do your homework at home and complete your project at a bigger studio. In other words, the gear we've talked about here is all portable, so that if you have all of your parts running live or virtually and they're sequenced, you could bring your sequencer and synthesizer into the studio and run it live off the time code on your tape machine (this is assuming your tape machine has the vocals on it). That way, you can mix it in a studio where you have outboard equipment at your disposal along with the benefit of a large recording console and an experienced engineer. Overall, in terms of low cost and high quality, this sort of arrangement offers the best of both of those worlds.

# DATs

DATs are digital audiotapes, meaning they employ a digital recording format as opposed to cassette and reel-to-reels, which are analog formats. They are about two-thirds the size of a regular cassette and were designed as a convenient way to store source material and as a good referencing medium for people in recording studios and professionals involved with productions.

With DATs, producers finally have something they can take home that is very representative of what their recording actually sounded like in the studio. Before, with cassettes, there was always a loss in sound quality and variances between cassette machines, so you could never be sure how close your cassette was to your two-track mixed-down master tape.

Basically, DATs have taken the place of 15-ips and 7½-ips reel-to-reel tapes because they can offer a genuine representation of a recording without the bulkiness and inconvenience of a reel-to-reel. In the past, the busy A & R executive had to take a little bit of time to play a reel-to-reel. The tapes were usually stored tails out, and he'd have to lace the tape onto the machine and rewind it before he could even listen to one song. But now, he can slip a DAT into a DAT machine, push a button, and it's rolling. There's the same convenience of a cassette, yet it's a much higher-quality listen.

In the future, manufacturers plan to have cassette machines that will have a digital head as well as an analog head. Right off the bat, Sony developed a DATman conceived in the same vein as the Sony Walkman. It actually fits in your hand and has stereo microphones so you can go out in the field and record.

Which brings us to another advantage DATs offer— their copying capability. In an analog format, whether you're dealing with cassettes or reel-to-reels, the noise floor gets louder as you make one copy to the next. That's because there is noise associated with analog recording. That doesn't mean that a good analog machine isn't as good if not better than any digital machine. But what it does mean is that a fifteenth-generation copy of the original source material on a DAT will sound very, very close to the original. Contrarily, if you did fifteen generations on a reel-to-reel, even if it was 30-ips half-inch (the best analog format), you would definitely notice significant sound degradation and the noise floor becoming louder. The same would be true of a cassette, only the degradation would be even more drastic. You couldn't even stand listening to a 15th-generation cassette.

One thing that you will lack with a DAT is editing capabilities, unless, of course, you have the special equipment (sound tools) required to edit digitally.

# CDs

Record product has evolved from 78s, to LPs and 45s, to 8-track tapes and cassettes, to CDs. CDs, as you know, are compact disks. They are the commercial version of DATs and are a means for companies to release product in a digital format. But where DATs are usually 44.1 or 48 kilohertz—which is the sampling rate—CDs are always at 44.1 (the higher the number, the higher the sound quality or sampling rate).

One of the great things about CDs is that they wear well and have consistent sound quality throughout. By contrast, vinyl records get scratched and broken, and since the outer tracks of the record have the best sound quality, as you get closer to the inside of the record you'll detect more harmonic distortion.

# Acetate Dubs

As you know, demos are presented on cassette tapes and DATs whenever possible. For the music industry executive, cassettes are an answer to the fast-paced nature of the business, since they can be conveniently listened to in the office, in the car, on a jet, or anywhere else, for that matter. (And for you, that means more chances of having your song heard.)

Before cassettes arrived on the scene, though, acetate dubs and reel-to-reels were the popular mediums for a songwriter to display his or her talents.

Even though an acetate dub is in the shape of a record, it isn't a record. As is obvious from its name, the dub is cut on acetate, not vinyl, and can only be played a limited number of times (somewhere between five and fifteen playings) before the acetate becomes worn and starts to sound muddy and scratched like a 78-rpm record that was dug out of someone's attic.

Rather than being used for demos, nowadays the acetate dub is more commonly used as a stepping-stone when mastering a 12″ record.

## Lead Sheets

A lead sheet displays the musical notation of a song's melody along with the chord symbols and words, and is usually handwritten, as opposed to sheet music, which is printed up.

Lead sheets were first born out of necessity, since they were the songwriter's only medium for representing his or her tunes. Writers would have their songs written out on lead sheets and take them to a publisher, who would turn the sheets over to an in-house piano player who, in essence, auditioned the songwriters' tunes.

For the most part, however, lead sheets are no longer in vogue. Due to the technological advances in the industry, combined with the fact that a lot of today's music publishing personnel can't read music, they've become increasingly extinct. Nowadays demo tapes serve the same purpose as lead sheets once did in the past.

It would be unfair to say that if you use lead sheets, it follows that your songs are dated. But, be it right or wrong, that's my immediate conclusion when someone sends me a cassette demo and includes a lead sheet in the package instead of the lyric sheet that should be there (see Chapter 4, "Shopping Your Demo"). Though I really try to keep an open mind as I slot the cassette into the player, once the music starts playing, damned if my preconception doesn't come true, because nine out of ten times the song is clearly out of touch with contemporary music and sounds like a tune that's been sitting in someone's underwear drawer for a decade or more.

You may send lead sheets when you register your works with the U.S. Copyright Office, but even then it's not necessary—the Copyright Office, like other music-related enterprises, accepts a demo cassette.

If a circumstance does arise when you need a lead sheet of your song (maybe someone has to work on the song's arrangement or it's being used as liturgical music or whatever), you can easily find people to make one up. Almost any music teacher, music major, arranger, musician, or anyone who's knowledgeable about music should be able to do a lead sheet for you either by hand or on computer. Or you can always look in the Yellow Pages under "Music Copyists." Depending on your relationship with the person who is going to transcribe your song and the degree of his or her professionalism, the lead sheet will probably run you anywhere from $20 to $50.

## How to Present Your Demo

Chapter 4, "Shopping Your Demo," is devoted entirely to just that. It will tell you how to make the best physical presentation of the demo itself, how it should be packaged, and give tips on how to get it to the people you need to reach. However, right now I'd like to give two tips. One is that your cassette demo should be accompanied by a typed lyric sheet (especially necessary with a demoed ballad!), and in the event you're selling yourself as a singer/songwriter, a concise biography as well.

Second, you may have a hundred tunes in your songwriting collection, but would even you, their creator, want to listen to all of them at one sitting? Even fifty of them? Or fifteen? Probably not. You'd most likely skip over to your very favorites. Well, the person you're presenting the material to feels exactly the same way. So, never submit more than three songs at one time. Three songs are ample for determining if you have what it takes, and any more than that will only oversaturate and burn out your listener.

## Showcasing Your Tunes

I'm sure you've seen it happen on the late movie. You know, the one where the record company executive wanders into a club, hears a songstress, signs her up, and she's deemed an overnight smash. The next day she's a multimillionaire and he is, too, because they got married at a sunrise service and they continue to live happily ever after in piles of money and gold records. Sure! But the movie is right about one thing: one unsolicited showcase leading to an overnight sensation usually only occurs on the big screen.

Showcases are live performances targeted to an audience of record company executives, producers, and publishers. They are normally arranged after a demo has been received and is well liked.

Sometimes a band or performer gains enough of a

reputation that the music moguls will seek them out on their own. There was a group in our tristate area, the Afghan Wigs, who after developing a sort of following across the country had A & R execs and publishers eagerly coming to catch their show in a little burg in Kentucky. But not all discoveries are made that way. Many times you have to set the stage, and you have to make the push to get the right people to come hear you.

So, if you wish to showcase your material and/or band, submit a demo with a brief biography and an invitation to see and hear the act. With a little luck, your demo will serve as a strong enough enticement to bring in the audience you want.

## Demo Firms

Trade publications such as *Billboard* provide listings of demo firms, that is, companies which specialize in making demos.

Many demo firms are top-notch, reputable companies. However, since you'll probably be dealing with a demo firm via the mail or phone, it's in your best interest to check out their track record before submitting your song. Ask for a tape of a demo they've done which falls into the same genre of music as your song. Also request a list of their demos which have been placed with publishers or record labels. For extra protection, consult with the Better Business Bureau, SGA, or any friends you have in the industry.

Going through a demo firm may prove to be less expensive for you, but it will never be as educational, because the studio experience is one which will pay for itself song and song again. So, if you can stretch your dollars, make the demo yourself. By learning the business from the board on up, you'll gain a better grasp of the industry as a whole. Your creativity will expand with the discovery of new gadgets and sounds, and you'll be more in control of your future as a songwriter.

## Remember . . .

Always keep a copy of your demo on file. This should preferably be a reel-to-reel tape stored tails out or a DAT.

Also, keep a cassette copy of your demo with you at all times—in your briefcase, your purse, or the glove compartment of your car—so that you can be prepared for anything, either circumstances you've planned for or opportunities that seem to fall out of the sky. As anyone in business will tell you, success is when preparation meets opportunity. In other words, always have a cassette copy of your demo handy.

# 3

# All About Copyrighting

Okay, so you've written some songs, made a demo, and you're ready to go. But it's usually a good idea to protect yourself before you start showing or showcasing your music. Copyrighting protects your work from unauthorized copying, proves ownership of your work, and assures you that you will reap the monetary rewards of your labor.

Over the years, the U.S. copyright laws have undergone many revisions. The current law is the Copyright Act of 1976, which went into effect on January 1, 1978. In order to take advantage of the law, it's important for every songwriter to understand how it works.

## What's Subject to Copyright?

Basically, copyright protection extends to books, magazines, pantomimes, choreographic works, paintings, murals, motion pictures, advertising materials, fabric designs, musical works, and sound recordings. But we'll only concern ourselves with the art forms pertinent to the songwriter—musical works and sound recordings.

The most familiar type of musical work is a song wherein both lyrics and music make up the work. A sound recording is the performance of a song on tape. Sheet music and phonocords are the forms musical works and sound recordings are published in, respectively.

A musical work and a sound recording are considered to be two independent and separate works. That is, each time someone records a song like "Stand by Me," a new and separate sound recording is created. Yet the song itself remains a musical work in its own right.

## What Can't Be Copyrighted?

Ideas for one, no matter how novel. Because, just think, if ideas could be copyrighted, there'd only be one song about unrequited love (instead of one zillion), or one praising sunshine or the unabashed thrill of piloting a fast car—and that would certainly limit the possible topics for songs.

In the same way, often-used phrases like "I can't get you out of my head" and titles of songs can't be copyrighted, since they lack sufficient literary content. You're free to write a song entitled "Every Breath You Take," and Sting couldn't take the life's breath out of you. However, if you attempt to market your song in a way that confuses the public about its authorship, you'll be opening a Pandora's box of legal problems.

# When Does a Musical Work or Sound Recording Qualify for Copyright Protection?

The U.S. Code, Title 17, Section 102(a), states that in order to qualify for copyright protection, a work must be original to the author and fixed in a tangible medium of expression.

But let's back up a moment and figure out what that's really saying.

First of all, "original to the author" means created by the author independently of any other work. Again, that doesn't necessarily mean a work that's entirely novel. After all, there's nothing new under the sun, and the repetition of that cliché further proves it.

"Fixed in a tangible medium of expression" means that the work is put down on paper, tape, canvas, or in a form that can be perceived or communicated for more than a transitory period. So, if you're lazing around on the patio, strumming your guitar and singing a song of yours to a friend, that doesn't fix the song in a tangible medium of expression. However, if your tape recorder is pushed to "record" or if the song is being transcribed as it's sung, that changes matters, because the moment your work is fixed is the moment it's created and, therefore, can be registered for copyright protection.

# What Rights Does Copyrighting Provide?

Under the new Copyright Act (U.S. Code, Title 17, Section 106), the owner of a copyright is provided with five exclusive rights:

1. The right to reproduce the copyrighted work in either copies or phonocords.
2. The right to prepare derivative works based on the copyrighted work.
3. The right to distribute copies or phonocords of the copyrighted work to the public.
4. The right to perform the copyrighted work publicly.
5. The right to display the copyrighted work publicly.

## Are There Any Limitations on Those Rights?

Funny you should ask.

While the new Copyright Act is straightforward in enumerating the exclusive rights of copyright owners, it also outlines the limitations which affect those rights. For all types of works, the Copyright Act allows for "not-for-profit" and "fair-use" exemptions.

The not-for-profit exemption means that a copyrighted work can be used in noncommercial circumstances such as for educational, religious, charitable, and governmental functions.

The fair-use exemption, however, is not quite as cut and dried. This exemption applies to copyrighted works used for the purposes of news reporting, teaching, criticism, comment, or research. The use must be limited and can't hamper a work's commercial market or value. And that's where the problems come in—in determining just what is permissible use and what's over the limit.

Let's say a contemporary poetry teacher photocopies the lyrics of a Don Henley song for his class to review. That may be considered fair use. But if in order to avoid buying sheet music, the teacher makes multiple copies of many lyrics, the courts might rule that to be unfair use.

Another example where fair use becomes questionable is in record reviews. A music critic would hardly want to review a song like Don Henley's "End of the Innocence" without quoting some of the lyrics. Yet if the critic reprinted a considerable amount of the lyrics or the sheet music in its entirety, this would infringe on the salability of Henley's musical work. People wanting to perform the song could merely purchase the publication the song was quoted in and would no longer need to buy the album or sheet music. And there's nothing fair about that. That's why critics generally get the go-ahead from the copyright owner to reprint the song and then will add a copyright notice and the words "used by permission" to the material.

For recorded musical works, rights are further limited by a special provision that says the rights to reproduce the work and publicly distribute published phonocords are not reserved exclusively to the copyright owner.

Therefore, once the copyright owner gives the initial permission to have phonocords of the work distributed to the public, any other person may obtain a license (known as a compulsory license) to make and distribute phonocords of that musical work also—but only to the public for the public's private use. Of course, that person must notify the copyright owner and pay the royalties due the owner for each phonocord manufactured and distributed. (The mechanical royalty rate and royalties will be discussed in detail in Chapter 9, "How Your Songs Earn Money.")

Those who intend to use phonocords for commercial purposes—broadcasters, discos, jukebox operators, background-music companies—must also obtain a license directly from the copyright owner. But in these cases, the copyright owner is not forced to license the work or to be confined to the designated statutory royalty rate.

The compulsory license does allow for a revamp of the musical work's original arrangement, but only to the point that it may conform to the style of music the licencee is looking for (i.e., a Beatles song subdued to fit Muzak standards). The song cannot be rearranged to the extent that its basic melody or intrinsic characteristics are changed, and it cannot be put in medleys or sampled without permission.

The copyright owner of a sound recording also faces restrictions because the right to publicly perform the sound recording is not deemed exclusive to him. In fact, that right may be enjoyed by anyone who obtains the phonocords. When you hear a song on the radio, both the song and the sound recording have been publicly performed. But since the right to license the public performance is exclusive to the copyright owner of the song and not to the copyright owner of the sound recording (remember, they're viewed as two individual works), the radio station must get permission from the copyright owner of the musical work, and the owner receives performance royalties when the song is aired. (Performance royalties are also explained in depth in Chapter 9.) The copyright owner of the sound recording doesn't receive royalties and his consent is not required. Congress is considering amending the Copyright Act to change this, but as of now, that's how it stands.

## Who Can Be a Copyright Owner?

Only the creator of a work or his or her agent can file an application for copyright registration. Yet the rules change somewhat when there is more than one person involved, as in the case of a collective work, a joint work, or works made for hire.

## What's a Collective Work?

It's a culmination of several independently copyrighted works.

Say, for instance, you have a piano songbook featuring songs by James Taylor, Carole King, Elton John, and others. Each of those works already has an individual copyright. But a copyright must also be obtained for the folio by the author or the person responsible for putting the songbook together. This can only be applied for after the author has been granted permission from each creator to reprint their particular songs. However, that permission doesn't allow the author to reprint or distribute the songs in any other manner, such as individually or for use in a subsequent songbook.

## What's a Joint Work?

It's two songwriters joining together to write music and lyrics. Each party is considered a co-owner of the songs. Paul McCartney and John Lennon are co-owners of the joint work "Help!" (Unless, of course, ownership has been transferred to a publisher, which I'll be discussing shortly.)

## What Are Works Made for Hire?

Works made for hire are divided into two categories:

1. *Works created for an employer within the realm of a writer's employment.* Here, the employer or the person responsible for hiring the songwriter becomes

the owner of the song unless both the employee and the employer sign an express written agreement stating otherwise.

2. *Specially ordered or commissioned works used as a contribution to a collective work like a movie, television series, and so on.* In the absence of a signed, express agreement to the contrary, the copyright ownership stays with the writer who was commissioned to create the work.

## How to Obtain a Copyright

First off, you need to understand the difference between a copyright notice and registering a copyright claim.

To supply your work with a copyright notice is simple—you just place a notice on your work. The U.S. Copyright Office doesn't issue copyrights on creation; it registers copyright claims.

When you place a copyright notice on your work, it's a signal to the rest of the world that you are the creator of that particular work. Registering a copyright claim does the same thing, but unlike the copyright notice, it additionally gives you the authority to sue in the case of infringement. It also authorizes the court to presume that you are, indeed, the copyright owner, putting the alleged infringer in the defensive position of proving otherwise.

## What Does a Copyright Notice Look Like?

1. *Symbol.* On musical works, the copyright symbol may be expressed with the word "Copyright," the

symbol © (the letter c in a circle), or the abbreviation "Copr." The © is recommended, since it meets international copyright requirements.

On copyright notices of sound recordings, the symbol ℗ (the letter P in a circle) is used as the international symbol of protection adopted by the Phonograms Convention.

2. *Year.* Technically this is the first year of publication of the work. However, if the work is unpublished, display the year of its creation. On a copyright notice for a demo, put the year you're shopping the demo.

3. *Owner.* This is the present owner of the copyright. Many times you'll also see "all rights reserved" added, which gives additional international copyright protection in countries under the Pan-American Convention.

So, the copyright notice for your songs will look like:

© 1993 Al Key
All rights reserved

This notice will appear on the first page of all sheet music or whenever the song or lyrics are found on an album jacket or used in a record review.

The copyright notice protecting the sound recording on record albums, tapes, CDs, and other phonocords will be written as:

℗ 1993 Breakaway Records
All rights reserved

Although it's common practice to post this notice on both the bottom rear of an album jacket and on the record label as well, the law only requires one place or the other.

# Is It Really Necessary to Put a Copyright Notice on an Unpublished Song or Demo?

Let's put it this way. It certainly can't hurt, and I would recommend it without a doubt. The notice will help show that you claim the rights to the work and will help to avoid problems in the event that the work is published. If you're submitting a demo on a cassette, you may want to write or type the notice directly on the cassette, rather than on the cassette case. However, remember that your notice should include the year that you're shopping the demo—not necessarily the year that you wrote your song. Publishers—or anyone, for that matter—don't want to think that they're listening to something that's been sitting in someone's drawer for years.

# Must a Copyright Notice Be Placed on Published Works?

Since the United States became a member of the Berne International Copyright Treaty in 1989, it is no longer necessary to place a notice on published works. Even so, the U.S. Copyright Office will tell you that it is still strongly encouraged.

# How Do I File a Registration for Copyright?

Published and unpublished works are registered by filing application forms with the U.S. Copyright Office.

Most often, the forms you'll need to file are the Form PA for songs and the Form SR for sound recordings.

To order these registration forms, you may either write to the U.S. Copyright Office, Library of Congress, Washington, D.C. 20559, or call the Forms Hotline at (202) 707-9100 and leave a recorded request.

Information specialists at the U.S. Copyright Office are prepared to answer any and all questions regarding the methods of securing a copyright and registration and may be reached by calling (202) 479-0700, Monday through Friday, from 8:30 A.M. to 5:00 P.M. But they're not there to offer legal advice, so if that's what you're looking for, you'll have to consult an attorney.

Since the U.S. Copyright Office processes over a half million pieces of mail each year, don't be alarmed if a certificate of copyright isn't delivered to you immediately. It may take a few months or so to receive it. Rest assured, though, that all incoming mail is stamped with a date, and that becomes the date your registration is effective. If you're concerned about whether or not the Copyright Office will receive your material, you can always send it via registered or certified mail and request a return receipt. Remember, too, that the Copyright Office doesn't check one work against another; they merely register the works.

## How Do I Submit Form PA?

For either published or unpublished works, Form PA is the application form that's required. Accompanying the form should be two copies of any published work or one copy of any unpublished work. These copies can be in the form of cassettes, phonograph records, or lead sheets. Also enclose a check or money order payable to the Register of Copyrights for $20 to satisfy the registration fee.

When registering more than one work at a given time, the $20 fee still applies. However, on Form PA you'll need to identify the collection of songs under an umbrella title like "Collective Works of Stephanie Wright, Series I." If this collection is being submitted on a cassette, it's also wise to identify yourself on tape, indicate the number of your songs on the tape, and give the number and title of each song as an introduction to its recording.

## How Do I Submit Form SR?

Form SR is required for registering a copyright of a sound recording. You go about it the same way you would when registering a published song. That is, you need to submit two copies of the sound recording along with Form SR and enclose a $20 registration fee. This is the set fee no matter how many songs are included on the recording.

The album jacket or any printed material published with the sound recording should be sent with the phonocord. In a situation where the copyright owner has the rights to both the musical work and the sound recording embodied in the phonocord, Form SR can register copyrights for both works simultaneously.

## What's a "Poor Man's Copyright"?

Some songwriters make use of the "poor man's copyright" to avoid the $20 registration fee, particularly when they've composed a substantial number of songs which have never been commercially released.

This is how the poor man's copyright works: A songwriter mails himself a copy of his own song via certified mail. Upon receipt of the package, the songwriter doesn't open it. Rather, he puts the package away in a safe place. In the event an infringement action is filed and a court case ensues, the songwriter could then submit the package as evidence.

The poor man's copyright isn't a sure bet, though. For one, the court will need to be totally convinced that the songwriter's testimony is valid and that the package hasn't been tampered with or opened while in the writer's possession. Also, those who use the poor man's way out aren't provided with the benefits granted to registration applicants.

For all the hassle, impending uncertainty, and cost of postage, I'm hardly sure it's worth it.

# How Long Does Copyright Protection Last?

Under the former copyright law, U.S.A. protection began at the date of publication and lasted for twenty-eight years, at which time the copyright could be renewed for an additional twenty-eight years.

With the new Copyright Act, protection begins upon creation—or when the work is fixed—and extends, in most cases, for the life of the author plus fifty years after the author's death. For example, if a song was created in 1979 and its author died in the year 2000, the termination of the U.S.A. copyright would come about in 2050. This applies to all works created on or after January 1, 1978, and to works created on or before January 1, 1978, but registered as unpublished as of that date.

There are variations on this theme, of course. For joint

works created on or after January 1, 1978 (when the work was not made for hire), the termination is based on the life of the last surviving author plus fifty years after that author's death. For anonymous authors, pseudonymous works (those created under an assumed name), or when the work was made for hire, the copyright lasts for seventy-five years from the year of the first publication or one hundred years from the year of creation, whichever expires first. There's one stipulation, though. If the identity of the author of an anonymous or pseudonymous work is revealed before the expiration, the termination terms will change to become the life of the author plus fifty years.

Once copyright protection expires, the work goes into the public domain, giving everyone free use of it without any obligation to the former copyright owner.

In case you're wondering what happens to copyright owners who registered works prior to January 1, 1978, they've been taken care of, too. For those enjoying their first twenty-eight-year term, the Copyright Act does require a renewal at the end of that term, but will then automatically extend the duration for forty-seven years to allow them a seventy-five-year term.

Copyright owners in the midst of their second twenty-eight-year term—that is, their renewal period under the old law—are granted an extension to provide them with a seventy-five-year duration.

## Can Ownership of the Copyright Be Transferred?

Yes. It's done all the time.

Since copyright is a property right, ownership can be transferred in whole or in part by either contract, lease, license, or gift.

The most common type of transfer is from songwriter to publisher. Once the songwriter has signed a publishing agreement for one of his or her songs, the ownership of the song and the copyright transfers to the publisher. Sometimes the publisher winds up publishing the song, other times the song will never be heard of again. Nonetheless, the publisher is under no obligation to give the song back to the writer, unless there's a reversion clause in their agreement or unless the publisher wishes to return the song voluntarily.

In order for any transfer to be effective, there must be a written agreement signed by all parties involved. It's a good idea to then have this agreement recorded with the U.S. Copyright Office. To prevent any legal complications, the agreement should specifically spell out that the right to sue for infringement violations of the copyright is transferred with the copyright itself.

## Can Transfers of Copyrights Be Terminated?

The new act has set up the "thirty-five-year rule," which allows for two separate time periods for termination of a transfer.

Transfers not including the right of publication may be terminated at any time during the five-year period that begins thirty-five years from the date of the execution of the transfer. For example, if a transfer takes place in 1995, the transfer termination could be executed between the years 2030 and 2035.

If the transfer does include the right to publish the work, the transfer may be terminated during the five-year period that begins either thirty-five years from the date of the first publication, or forty years from the date of the execution of the transfer, whichever comes first. So, if you transferred your publishing rights to a song in 1994, and the song is published in 1995, the termination of the transfer can occur between the years 2030 and 2035. However, if the same song is not published until 2005, then you or your heirs may terminate the transfer between the years 2034 and 2039, or between the fortieth and forty-fifth year after the date of the transfer in 1994.

## What Constitutes an Infringement?

Earlier in this chapter, the five rights exclusive to the copyright owner were mentioned. An infringement occurs when any of those five rights is violated or additionally when unauthorized copies of phonocords are imported. At that time, the copyright owner has the authority to bring suit.

There are certainly blatant examples of infringement, such as when someone photocopies and sells sheet music of your song, or creates a new arrangement of your song without your consent. Even if that someone is your best buddy, it's still an infringement of your musical work. Likewise, an infringement of a sound recording takes place when someone tapes the sound recording and makes and sells phonocords from that tape.

Often, though, copyright infringement comes about subconsciously rather than consciously. Either way, to constitute a violation, the amount from the copyrighted work must be substantial and there must be a way the infringer had access to the work. Such was the case when George Harrison was brought to trial for infringement. It was determined that his 1970 release "My Sweet Lord" incorporated the same musical phrases as the Chiffon song

"He's So Fine." Not only that, the phrases were set up in a highly similar pattern. Since the Chiffon song had made the charts internationally in 1962, it was presumed Harrison had access to it. And because the repetition of the same phrases was so extensive, Harrison was found guilty.

In music, standard chord progressions, stock phrases, and the imitation of successful contemporary sounds will always exist. Because of that, as clear-cut as the new act has strived to make matters, there will always be fine lines and questions. Drawing the line between what's a little and what's a little too much is not always so easily done.

## What Should I Do if a Work of Mine Is Infringed Upon?

First, contact an attorney. Then be sure that your work has a registered copyright. Otherwise, no legal action can be taken.

If you have neglected for whatever reason to register a published work, the Copyright Act does provide a three-month grace period in which to do so. However, no provisions of that sort are allowed for unpublished works. So to be on the safe side, register unpublished songs immediately, and register published songs as quickly as possible, or at least within the three-month grace period.

## How Can I Avoid Infringing on Someone Else's Work?

You hear songs blaring from your radio, music spilling over you in a store or over the phone, and even strangers whistling tunes in elevators. So whether you realize it or not, you're apt to be influenced by someone else's work.

And let's face it, in any era, certain popular sounds reign, and everyone borrows from each other to some degree in order to incorporate those sounds into their own record, thereby adding to its commercial value.

But remember, as discussed in Chapter 1, "Writing the Commercial Song," if you should use samples and loops from other songs throughout your song, depending on the length and usage of those snippets, you may need to have the samples cleared before your song is commercially distributed in order to avoid copyright infringement.

If you don't intend to spend the money to go through copyright clearance procedures and want to hedge against infringing on another person's work, my advice would simply be this: Don't ever start your songwriting process with someone else's song and think that you can mold it into your own, because the foundation of the song may be so solid that your attempts to change it won't really be successful. Always start with your own song and then integrate any riffs or sounds you've picked up into your own work. That way the song can't stray too far, and it will always reflect your unique style.

# 4

# Shopping Your Demo

Back in the days when men were men and songs were songs, writers would meander their way through Tin Pan Alley with guitars strapped to their backs, hoping to secure a live audition with any publisher who was willing to listen.

But times have certainly changed, and these days the songwriter's chances of getting a live audition are slim. Today, the songwriter's material is represented in the form of a demo, and there are certain measures I recommend the writer take in order to have the best possible chance of having his or her demo heard and well received.

## Presenting Your Demo in Person

A firsthand presentation is always optimum, for two reasons: One, people always have a harder time saying "no" to someone's face, versus a voice on the other end of a phone or in a letter. And two, presentations allow the writer to start developing relationships with people in the business.

For the songwriter living outside the major music centers, the one-to-one presentation can be an expensive endeavor. Even so, saving up the money to spend a week in New York, Los Angeles, Nashville, or any other city which seems to hold promise for you could make a notable difference in your career.

Of course, you'll want to schedule appointments beforehand, and you'll want to meet with the people who can do you some good. So if you're contacting a publisher, you should ask for an appointment with the professional manager. And if you're contacting a record label, your appointment should be made with the A & R executive who is in charge of the type of music you're selling.

Regardless of whom you present your material to, be sure you're prepared. It could be that your music may not make much of an impression if you're just starting out, but *you* should, because the impression you create will keep the doors open for you as your career develops.

When you're mailing out demos, you'll be sending cassettes, but when you get the opportunity to present your songs in person, cover all the bases. That means, you'll want to carry along a cassette demo, a lyric sheet, and if possible—though it's not mandatory—a DAT copy of your song. That's because many music industry executives have DAT machines in their offices nowadays. If you have a DAT copy of your song, hand that over first, assuming that the person you're presenting to would rather listen to that. Of course, if you're asked for a cassette of your demo, you'll have that on hand, too.

As for the lyric sheet, if you're presenting to a publisher, artist, or manager, give him or her the lyric sheet right off. However, it's been my experience that producers and A & R executives generally prefer to get an overall feel for the music and then, if they like what they hear, they'll usually ask to see a lyric sheet.

# Submitting Your Demo by Mail

Prior to mailing your demo, contact each company ahead of time to make certain they'll accept unsolicited material. Some companies do not, in which case you'll be wasting your time and postage. If the company will accept your material, explain what type of songs you're submitting (dance, pop, or whatever) and ask whose attention your package should be directed to. This is especially necessary when you're submitting a demo to a large company where there are numerous executives assigned to various genres of music.

Your package should include:

1. *Your demo on cassette.* For everyone's benefit, a copyright notice should appear directly on the cassette. (Remember, your notice should state the year you're shopping your song, not necessarily the year in which you wrote your song.)

2. *A brief cover letter.* Write a couple of short paragraphs describing your songs and thanking the recipient for his or her time and consideration. If you've had any commercial success, be sure to mention this to your recipient, too. But keep it brief. This isn't the time to rave ad nauseam about yourself.

3. *A lyric sheet.* A copyright notice should be included on this, too.

4. *A concise biography.* The biography should be included if you've already had some commercial success as a songwriter or if you're pitching yourself as a singer/songwriter. It should be extremely brief, only a paragraph or two, outlining any valid experience you have had. In the case of a singer/song-

writer, if you've sung background vocals on a recording or belong to a band, by all means let the
listener in on it.
5. *A self-addressed stamped envelope.* You'll want every
chance to have your demo returned to you with a
response.

Since you won't be there in person to present your
material, let the package tell something about your image
to distinguish you from the masses. Companies are bar-
raged with demo packages week in and week out, so if
your dollars permit, try using an imaginative logo, color-
ful mailing stickers, or printed stationery. All of these
things will help to get your package noticed and remem-
bered, as long as your package retains a polished professional look. Don't get too bizarre unless that's truly the
impression you're trying to convey. As insane as the
music industry is, no one really wants to deal with a
madman unless they're absolutely forced to or are convinced there's money to be made.

## Tip-Top Tapes

Since you'll either be mailing your demos on cassettes
or leaving cassettes behind for a record executive to listen
to at his or her convenience, there are certain guidelines
you'll want to follow in preparing the cassette itself:

**Limit the Number of Songs.** Three songs is the maxi-
mum number to record on your demo tape. In all
honesty, I prefer two. If someone doesn't care for your
first two songs, they'll be predisposed not to like the third
one anyway, or they may not even bother to listen to it at
all. If two (or even one) of your tunes are well-liked, you'll
always be asked for more.

**Don't Give Too Much of a Leader.** A leader only needs to be two to three seconds long. Some people tend to overcompensate with thirty seconds or so of un-recorded tape, and that can be lethal. A person receiving your demo in the mail may not wait that long for your song to come on or may get interrupted by a phone call and never return to it. In the same way, when you're presenting in person, a lengthy leader can make for a most uncomfortable situation as the two of you stare into silent space for what seems an eternity. Double-check the tape, though, to make certain you haven't lost the intro of your tune by recording over the white or blue unrecordable portion of the cassette tape.

**Record on Quality Tapes.** When you're submitting a lot of demos by mail, the dollars can mount up. But you can still purchase good-quality normal bias cassettes at decent rates by buying them in bulk at a local wholesaler. If you don't know a wholesaler, check with a studio in your area and find out who their supplier is. Specify that you're interested in twenty-minute cassettes, though (ten minutes on each side), since that will be more than ade-quate recording time for your two to three songs.

**Obtain the Best-Sounding Copy.** Most often, a studio engineer will be making your cassette copies, and he'll usually take the time to turn some knobs to achieve a good reproduction. However, listen to your copy before you leave the studio, and if you're not pleased with it, request another run-through.

**Don't Circulate Old Cassettes.** Circulating a scratched-up, mangy-looking cassette makes a recipient think your tunes have been previously sent around and many a person turned them down. Even if your songs are dynamite, one look at that dog-eared cassette is going to bias your listener's opinion.

**Label Your Cassettes Properly.** First off, print the song's title and the name of the group or artist performing it. Next write down the name of a person to contact and list a phone number or numbers. Include a copyright notice directly on your cassette also.

As explained in the preceding chapter, the notice should include the copyright symbol ©, the word "Copyright," or the abbreviation "Copr.," the year, and the name of the creator. Remember, even if your song was written ten years ago, no one needs to know it. The year on the copyright notice of a demo is the year you're shopping the tape.

The final label should look like this:

> "Fair Game" sung by Vital Signs
> Contact: John Doe 555-1234
> © 1993 Jane Doe

### Listen to Your Cassette Copies

Recheck your copies to make sure everything's there that's supposed to be, and nothing's there that isn't supposed to be. And, as silly as it sounds, make certain the tape is rewound. Expecting an overworked music executive to take the time to rewind your tape may only get it thrown into the trash can.

**NEVER Send Out Your Last Cassette, Because You Probably Won't Get It Back.**

**Always Keep a Cassette of Your Tunes Handy at All Times.** You never know who you might bump into.

## Follow Up and Build Relationships

Prior to mailing out your demos, it's a good idea to keep a record of the companies or people the tapes were sent to, the date they were mailed, the date you should make your initial follow-up call—approximately ten days after the mailing—and the date of your second follow-up call. It's also helpful to make a note of the name of the receptionist or secretary to whom you speak, so you can add a personal touch to your calls. (Incidentally, this record is also valuable when shopping your demos in person.)

Follow-up calls are a lot of work, and can make for some pretty hefty long-distance phone bills. But they're a means of showing interest in your own career, and they keep your name at the top of everyone's mind while establishing over-the-phone relationships at the same time.

Politeness and a little conniving are one of the best ways to start out your initial follow-up call. Let ten days pass by after you've mailed your package, and make your conversation similar to the following:

SONGWRITER: My name's Samantha Stinson, and I mailed a demo to your company approximately ten days ago. I realize it's still too early for any feedback, but a few of my demos didn't reach their destination, and I'm just calling to see if it got to you.

SECRETARY: What's your name again?

SONGWRITER: Samantha Stinson. I sent the demo in an orange envelope. (The secretary spies the orange envelope at the bottom of a pile, pulls it out, looks at the return address, then places it, most probably, on the top of the pile.)

SECRETARY: Yes, it's here.

SONGWRITER: Great. Do you have any idea when someone will get a chance to listen to it?

SECRETARY: Kelly usually listens to tapes (a variety of
possible answers here) (a) on Fridays; (b) the third
week of the month; (c) within a week after they
arrive.

SONGWRITER: Okay, great. Thanks so much . . . uh,
what was your name again?

SECRETARY: Chris.

SONGWRITER: Thanks, Chris. You've really been a big
help to me.

With that type of follow-up call, you've established
several things: (a) the secretary is now familiar with your
name after hearing it twice and looking at it once in print;
(b) most likely, your envelope was pulled from the bottom
of a pile and placed on top; (c) you now know when
someone will be listening to your demo and that means
you know when to place your second follow-up call; (d)
you've also found out the secretary's name, so you can
now start developing a relationship with him or her.

Allow the amount of time to pass that the secretary
indicated before placing your second follow-up call. If
your package is still sitting in the pile at that time, let a few
more days pass before calling back again. If, on the next
call, someone still hasn't listened to your demo, you can
appeal to the secretary. Explain that you really need to get
your project wrapped up in the next week or so (don't give
an unrealistic deadline like the next day), and if there's
anything the secretary can do to get your song to the
person it needs to go to, you surely would appreciate it.
You can also say other people are interested in your
demo, whether it happens to be true or not, but don't
exaggerate the situation by stating that everyone is dying

to get their hands on your song. That's a line that everyone's heard a million times, and believe me, it won't work. Find a workable balance in your conversations. Don't come off too pompous; yet don't appear desperate. Be businesslike, but it's good to show a little personality, without getting too personal. In short, be human so others can relate to you.

From the outside, the music industry may appear to be huge and overwhelming. But once you're on the inside, you'll find that it's much smaller than you had imagined, and an extremely mobile business, with many of the same people rotating from one company to another. Therefore, you can't afford to alienate anyone or disregard any opportunity to form contacts.

If you get to the point where you're dealing exclusively with one person at a company, do your utmost to try to develop relationships with some of the other people there. That way, when the time comes that your contact moves on, you'll have two contacts at two companies instead of just one.

Also, even when you think you're speaking with the lowest-ranking person in the company, always be pleasant and polite. Quite often, a receptionist, secretary, or assistant has more pull than you realize and can make the difference as to whether or not your demo gets heard. In fact, at many small firms where there's just a handful of employees, the boss often rounds up everyone to listen to demos. Plus, who knows? The secretary you get to know could end up sitting in the boss's seat one day.

## Be Accessible

When someone wants to respond to your material, they're not likely to hire a modern-day Sherlock Holmes to track you down, so make sure you're easy to reach.

Include a self-addressed stamped envelope in your demo package. Have a phone machine so anyone can leave messages while you're out. Even if you're the transient type, have a stable mailing address and phone number even if it's your parents'. After all, a person is only going to try to get in touch with you a couple of times, and if you're too irresponsible to give them a means or place to contact you, it's doubtful that they'll keep trying.

## Something Up Your Sleeve

While it's true that you have to be easy to reach, you'll find that business people on the other side of the fence are most difficult to peg down. That's mostly because so many people are always tugging at their coattails.

In my years of peddling tapes around Manhattan, I discovered some tricks that helped me speak to the people I needed to reach, and I hope these will work for you too.

As a general rule, the business hours of most record business administrators are sporadic. Some might come to work at 9:00 and leave at 5:00, but more often than not, the executives usually arrive at 10:00 to 11:00 A.M. and are in the office until 6:00, 7:00, or 8:00 P.M. Also, the boss might work twelve hours one day and just pop into the office for a quick check the next.

However, secretaries still tend to put in a typical nine-to-five day with an hour off for lunch. So, I found that I was most successful in speaking to the boss when the secretary wasn't there (either during lunch or after he or she had gone home for the day), because at those times the boss was manning the phones. In fact, since it's always the secretary's job to insulate the boss by screening calls, I also discovered the boss was usually easier on me than the secretary had been.

Another little trick you can pull out of your hat is this:

Find out from the secretary what time the boss usually arrives in the morning (here, you might use a pseudonym to avoid being a pest). If the secretary says 11:00 A.M., just give the boss enough time to get a cup of coffee and begin reviewing the day's schedule. Then place your call at 11:15. Since the boss hasn't been swamped with calls yet, he or she is more likely to speak to you. Also, since the boss hasn't yet had a chance to slot in every quarter-hour of the day, you might get lucky and find they're free to see you on the same day.

If you're located in a music city, you can also let your legs do some walking. Find out which clubs certain producers and A & R persons frequent or which pubs the administrators trail off to after work. Search out the people who are solely interested in the type of music or act you've put together, and cater to them. It may take some time to complete this type of research. But once you've been around long enough, you'll be able to note the trends and get some helpful scoops through the grapevine.

# Know Who's Who and Who's Doing What

People inside the music business could never keep up with all of the industry happenings and names if they didn't read the trade publications. And when you're on the outside wanting in, you should be especially aware of these publications and how they can help you.

By perusing a publication like *Billboard*, you can easily determine the popular songs and trends, the names of groups and artists who are debuting and on the rise, and what everyone's all-time favorite artists are up to.

From the charts alone, a songwriter can glean an abundance of information—no matter which classification of music you're interested in. You can scan the Pop, Black Singles, Country Singles, Adult Contemporary, Dance/Disco, and even Rock Album charts to find the names of producers, record labels, and publishers. In short, all the names of people and companies you need to reach are right there.

In Appendix C you'll find a list of trade publications, tip sheets, and other music-related publications and newsletters which can keep you current with the industry. It's important to read up on these and remain aware of who can help you—and then, of course, to take the initiative to seek those people out.

## The Competitive Edge

Most often, you'll be submitting your material to companies in the major music cities of New York, Los Angeles, and Nashville, or you'll be setting up appointments and traveling to these places. Still, there are some steps you can take on the home front in the interim.

If, on your own, you've gone so far as to have made a master of your song, you might take a dub to a local radio station and ask if they would consider playing it. (However, most stations, particularly those in larger cities, will be reluctant to play a record that isn't in the stores and consequently unavailable to the public.)

Another alternative is to contact a record distributor near you or a "one-stop" in your area. A one-stop is a wholesale store that carries record products from various distributors. It's here that record store owners and jukebox operators may come to purchase the tapes, CDs and 12″ records they wish to stock. Someone at either of these outlets may be able to refer you and your record to a prospective buyer.

What's more, you can also act as a talent scout in your

own right, right in your own hometown. Search out the bands or solo acts in the local clubs, bars, and studios and see if any are worthy of performing your songs. Also, keep your ears open for a group or performer who's looking for material. By combining your individual talents, you might light the fuse that will launch your careers simultaneously.

## Act in a Credible Manner

Many times songwriters will try to pawn off one of their songs as something that it's not. For example, a writer will bring in a country tune, and when you reply that the song's really special, but you just can't do anything with it since you have no country music contacts, the next thing you know they're on their hands and knees, begging you to get an R & B artist to cut the same song.

That may sound ludicrous to you, but it does happen—more times than I've cared to experience. It's the kind of discrepant and melodramatic performance that makes a writer appear ignorant and oh so desperate.

Even in the worst of times, maintain your dignity, and thereby your credibility. If you really believe you can change your song so easily from one genre to another, don't ask someone to imagine it, go make a new demo and let him hear it. Songwriters who do otherwise waste everyone's time, make themselves look totally ridiculous, and risk losing the contacts they've worked so hard to make.

## To Give Up or Not to Give Up?

That is the question. And a question only you can answer. I'm not speaking of discarding your songwriting career altogether, I'm merely talking about when to give up on shopping a particular song.

Sometimes, no matter what you do with a song, it just isn't destined to find its niche. In fact, some songwriters will tell you that they arrived at their smash tune by taking the best elements of four of their songs and melding them into one.

It's true that you can't trust all the ears of the people in the industry all of the time. But if you go to fifty people or so and no one shows interest in your tune, it may be time to reconsider your song's potential.

On the other hand, I couldn't tell anyone to give up on any song they wrote if they truly believed in it. So often, peddling a song can be a numbers game, just like selling insurance or encyclopedias. Sometimes you just have to hit enough people before the law of averages takes over and you land a favorable response.

I played the numbers game a lot. Many years ago, I peddled a dance song called "Sure Shot." I owned the publishing on the song and, after listening to the radio, really believed the song was competitive and deserved to be heard. So I went to everyone I could to shop it, and that meant a list of thirty-six people. Thirty-five of those people turned me down, but the thirty-sixth person signed the record. The outcome? Well, the record didn't storm out of the stores, but club deejays liked it, and it became the number-three dance record in the nation.

Your chances of getting your song published or recorded depend on how open the market is for your type of product at that particular time. Sometimes it also depends on how much money will be needed to successfully promote the song. So if you get to feeling frustrated about your work, remember that it might not be that your song is unworthy, you might just be a victim of circumstances.

And if you really reach an all-time low, take a minute

to recall the now-greats who were once in the same position as you. For years, Bruce Springsteen played in beer joints all over the Northeast before his talent was recognized. Nirvana was traveling the Pacific Coast in a station wagon and sleeping in cow pastures for a long while before the majors acknowledged them. Then there are Willie Nelson and Elvis Costello (who got noticed while singing and playing guitar on the steps of a convention center in London where CBS executives were meeting)—one day all of their hard work finally paid off.

Some people call it "paying your dues." Others say, "your time has come." Still others call it "luck." Whatever it's called, don't let "it" get you down. There are many overnight successes out there that were many years in the making. So keep plugging away—you could be one of them.

# 5

# The Music Publisher

**What's your criteria for signing
one songwriter over another?**

Michael Brettler, Shapiro, Bernstein & Co., Inc.:
   "In choosing one writer over another, I'd say the
first thing I look for is quality. Also, someone who's
prolific. Someone I can get along with—I wouldn't want
to be in a position where I hate hearing that Songwriter
A is on the phone. And someone who's aggressive and
will make their own additional connections."

Mara Bruckner, Emerald Forest Entertainment:
   "Several factors go into a decision to sign a writer.
The most important, in my opinion, is the ability of the
writer to write songs that are unique and special as
opposed to generic and formulated. They must have
interesting lyrics and melodies, yet fit into a general
framework which makes them accessible. At the same
time, they must be somewhat commercial (for lack of a
better term), meaning that they can be covered by many
different artists and that they sound like hits.

"The current climate for songwriters is very collab-oration-oriented, and so I'd like to feel comfortable in being able to set writers up to cowrite with artists and know they could be flexible in any given situation.

"It also doesn't hurt if the writer has production skills and could conceivably take on various projects in a writer/producer capacity. Strong connections and a track record are also a plus."

Evan Lamberg, EMI Publishing, Inc.:

"For me, there are two sides of it. There's the music side, where the writer has to have a special talent for either writing songs with great hit melody content or writing superior lyrics. And then, because music is a business, the writer needs to have their head on straight. They need to act professionally—show up at meetings on time and handle themselves properly. I work with writers on a very personal level and spend a lot of time with them. I need someone I can work with as a team, pull our resources and energy together and get great results."

## The Role of the Music Publisher

The music publisher will in all likelihood be your prime target when you are ready to peddle your demo.

Out of the circle of people you could shop your songs to—publishers, producers, artists, managers, and record company executives—the publisher is usually the most accessible to the songwriter. That's because, unlike the other music industry people just mentioned, the pub-lisher's primary job is to place songs; therefore, it follows that he's most interested in finding them. He is also more adept at hearing the potential of a songwriter's work through a demo, whereas record company executives, for instance, are more attuned to the hit potential of a master recording. The publisher's ongoing efforts and plentiful contacts afford the songwriter a multitude of possibilities for getting songs recorded, and it's usually the publisher who is most willing to spend time—and even money—to develop the songwriter's talent.

Music publishers can be as small as one-man operations or as big as large corporations. Some publish virtually any type of songs, others specialize in one genre of music. Sometimes you'll discover a publishing firm that has been run by the same family for generations. Other times, you'll hear of artists and producers who form a publishing company once they've acquired the publishing on a song they plan to record. And in this instance, they'll usually hire someone to handle the publishing administration.

But whatever the size of a publishing company, the duties of the music publisher are to serve as:

A *salesperson*. While you're at home churning out songs, your music publisher is studying the trade magazines and tip sheets, phoning his numerous contacts, and shopping your song to anyone who might be instrumental in getting your tune recorded, whether it be a manager, artist, producer, or A & R executive.

Once the publisher does get your song recorded and released, he'll often work along with the record label to promote the song in any way he can.

*The copyright administrator.* In order to protect your song's copyright, the publisher files the required registration forms and song copies with the U.S. Copyright Office. Additionally, the publisher further protects the writer's work from illegal exploitation. He does this by taking legal action in circumstances where records and/or tapes of a song are being reproduced and sold without authorization (pirating), or when there occurs the unauthorized recording and selling of a performance of a song (bootlegging).

A *revenue generator*. While the songwriter is the person who brings a song to life, the publisher is the person who turns that creation into a money-making entity.

After securing a deal for a song, the publisher further exploits the song's copyright and thereby creates additional revenue for both himself and the writer by:

◆ Attempting to get cover versions (recordings by people other than the original artist) of a song. Using the record as his demo, the publisher will shop a song to as many artists as possible in an effort to get those artists to recut the song.

◆ Trying to secure printed editions of a song. When a song has achieved a relatively high degree of success, the publisher will work to have printed editions of the song made available to the public through retail outlets. Printed editions include the printing of the song for sheet music, songbooks, folios, and stage and marching band arrangements.

◆ Subpublishing the writer's song overseas. For a publisher to acquire a subpublishing deal, a song usually has to have charted in the United States, or the subpublisher has to feel that the song will have appeal in his territory. In Chapter 9, "How Your Songs Earn Money," some of the standard practices involving subpublishing deals are outlined.

A *revenue collector and distributor*. The songwriter receives performance royalties directly from the performing rights organizations he or she is affiliated with. However, the writer receives mechanical, synchronization, and printed editions royalties from the publisher. (Each of these money-making sources is discussed at length in Chapter 9.)

In other words, the music publisher can be the song-writer's most helpful business partner. But just as impor-tant, the publisher can also be the songwriter's best friend by acting as a creative advisor, guiding the songwriter in the studio, and introducing the songwriter to potential collaborators.

## The Big and Small of It

Before signing your songs away, you should investi-gate both large and small music publishers to decide where the potential of your songs will be realized and where you'll feel most at ease.

It would be unfair and unwise to completely stereo-type and pit large music publishers against the smaller ones. But it's helpful for you to have an overview of the benefits and drawbacks of both so you can keep these in mind during your initial encounters.

First off, the large music publisher will probably have an equally large reputation. An association with him can clearly give you ready-made credibility. Along with the larger publisher's prestige comes sizeable resources, which can also prove to be rewarding where the writer is con-cerned.

For instance, the large publisher's vast catalog of songs ensures a steady flow of income, so it's more likely he can afford to advance you money on the songs you sign to him. What's more, the larger publishing firm obviously maintains a larger staff, with each member having his or her own set of contacts. That can all add up to massive exposure and promotional efforts for your song before and after it's been cut.

However, because of his size, you might find it more difficult to pique the interest of the large publisher. Not only that, once you have his interest, it might be more difficult to keep it. Here, the publisher's professional manager sometimes views the songwriter as a "producer of product" rather than an individual. Additionally, there are more deadlines to be met, and the writer is pressured to produce while knowing he or she is only one writer in a sea of others who are also submitting material and vying for attention. So you might discover that the larger publisher lacks the intimacy that a smaller firm will display— "might" meaning that you should keep an open mind while retaining this thought.

However, if you're a writer who really thrives on personal attention or is looking for guidance, the smaller publishing firm may be what you're looking for.

In contrast to the larger publisher, the smaller one operates on less capital and doesn't have money to throw around. In some respects, that can be beneficial for the writer because it guarantees the writer much greater longevity and peace of mind in knowing his or her material won't be so quickly passed over for a newer project. It's also safe to assume the smaller publisher will work extremely hard to push and promote the material he's already staked money in, since every dollar is a little harder to come by.

However, because of the small publisher's financial limitations, he may not be able to supply you with an advance or even cover your entire demo costs. Even more, he may not be eager to sign a song that's represented by a poor-quality demo, since he doesn't have the funds to experiment in hopes that a new demo can bring out the song's underlying potential.

Common sense may lead you to conclude that smaller publishers should be ruled out simply because they're likely to have fewer contacts than the large publishers. But this isn't necessarily true. The smaller firm's connections can be just as far-reaching and notable as their larger competitors'.

Whatever music publisher you decide to go with, investigate its credentials beforehand by checking with any of the performing rights organizations, SGA, or even the Better Business Bureau. In addition, make certain you consult with a music attorney prior to signing any contracts.

## How to Find a Good Publisher

There are several ways to go about searching for a good publisher.

**Check Out Label Copy.** Visit the record store and look for the albums, tapes, and CDs of an artist you feel your songs would suit. On the jacket, you'll generally find the name of a publishing company, and can call Directory Assistance for their phone number.

**Scan the Record Charts.** As mentioned previously, names of publishers can be located by scanning the record charts in publications like *Billboard*.

**Look in Your Own Backyard.** Mingle with the people in your town who are in the music business, whether they own a recording studio or a major music store. Since these people have chosen to make music their life, it's probable they've also attempted to publish a song at one time or another. So put on your supersleuth cap and give them a try. They may have a lead on nearby publishers, or they may have an acquaintance in Nashville or New York who will know of someone. And since you're a hometown girl or boy, it's likely they'll be eager to help you.

**Contact a Performing Rights Organization.** In Chapter 9, I'll be discussing these organizations at length, but for now just know that eventually every writer needs to be affiliated with either ASCAP, BMI, or SESAC. These organizations are set up to service songwriters, and they're another source of information.

## Publishing/Production Companies

Unlike in the past, the trend in today's music industry is to become self-contained. What this means is that artists or producers will often bypass the publisher and develop their own stable of writers from whom they may draw material. Under these circumstances everyone (excluding the publisher) benefits. First, the artists and producers benefit by being able to share in the publishing revenues, thereby increasing their incomes. And, second, the job of finding material becomes less arduous for them. For the writer, this type of "family" atmosphere lends a sense of security in knowing he or she will always have a home for his or her material. Plus, there's a better chance that the writer will be able to hang on to a piece of the publishing, thereby increasing his or her income also.

Since publishers in general haven't been entirely successful in breaking through this clique of writer-artist-producer, many have had nowhere to place the material in their catalogs. As a result, many publishers have adopted the attitude of "If I can't beat them, I may as well join them," and have established publishing/production companies as a way to survive this competition.

By running a production company simultaneously with a publishing firm, the publisher establishes another means of income. Whether the publisher doubles as a producer or hires an outside producer, he is able to create master recordings of songs in his catalog, which he can then peddle to a record label.

As with anything else, dealing with a publishing/production company has its good and bad points for the writer, and you need to assess the situation.

Publisher/producers sometimes only look for songs when they're in need of material for a particular project. They tend to use the songs on that recording and then move on to the next project. Of course, that's immediate gratification for the writer, who can witness the publishing and recording of his or her song within a short time period. But what if the song has all the makings of a standard? What if the publisher/producer's album project stiffs and no one ever hears of your tune and it's lost forever? What if, with all good intentions, the publisher/producer has spread himself too thin and just doesn't have the time to solicit cover versions of your song? Of course, if you've written a faddish dance tune that probably doesn't promise prolonged longevity, this could be an ideal setup for you. But do take the time to look at all sides of the matter.

Besides the instant gratification, working with a publisher/producer can be advantageous for the writer for two other reasons. First, quite often it gives the writer the chance to work more directly with the artist. The writer then can develop a personal relationship with the artist that with luck will outlast that particular project. Second, in his day-to-day activities the successful publisher/producer is often approached by labels that represent outside artists. Naturally, if these artists are in need of material, the publisher/producer can point these prospective takers in the direction of his writers.

## The Professional Manager

When you make an appointment with a publishing company, the person on staff whom you'll want to meet with is the professional manager. He's the person responsible for screening all new material.

Because of his musical background and his position within the company, the professional manager can become a very important individual in the eyes of the songwriter. On the creative end, he will offer editorial criticism and structural evaluation, and will oversee the production of demos in the studio. In business aspects, the professional manager serves as the liaison between the business people at the publishing company and the writer, whose priorities sometimes differ. The professional manager is also responsible for the execution of budget allotments and contractual negotiations.

Throughout this book, I've stated numerous times that you'll seldom get to audition your songs live for anyone in the industry. Well, the professional manager is one of those rare cases where you may get that opportunity.

Once you've proven yourself to the professional manager by bringing him consistently good material, it's likely that all he'll require from you is a rough representation of your latest song or song idea.

If the professional manager feels that your song has potential, you'll be able to make a "working" demo in the publisher's small recording facilities. The "working" demo will give a more accurate idea of just how recordable and commercial the song really is, and both of you can then decide if the song is far enough along or worthy of being demoed professionally. Many writers find this type of working relationship immensely beneficial, as it frees them from demo costs while allowing them to gain simple studio experience at the same time.

The music industry is in constant motion and high job turnover is common. So you may have your song signed by one professional manager only to learn several months later that he's moving on to another company. As a result, you may find yourself in a position where his successor doesn't have the time or the inclination to look into his predecessor's last project (meaning yours!). If this should happen, your only course of action is to try to rejuvenate interest in your tune with the new professional manager. And if all else fails, try to swallow your disappointment and begin anew with your new professional manager. However, don't lose sight of the former professional manager. You never know when or where you may hook up with him again.

## Staff Writers

Years ago, publishers employed staff writers as a matter of course. These staff writers wrote exclusively for their employers and normally drew a salary which was usually an advance against any future monies the writers' songs would earn.

Today, there are fewer companies willing to employ staff writers. Even so, there are still many writers who would be willing to relinquish their independence and be bound exclusively for the financial security the position affords.

Since things are so different today, the staff writing positions that are available aren't always set up as they were in the past.

For example, a small publishing firm with minimal operating capital might put a writer on staff if he or she is willing to pull double duty as a professional manager, or perhaps work in another area of the company performing clerical duties or whatever. While this situation might not be optimal, it could still prove to be a valuable experience for a songwriter who's new on the scene, and at least provide a way to get his or her foot in the door.

Publishers might also be more inclined to hire someone who isn't just a writer but is also a producer/arranger—someone who has the ability to demo not only his or her own material but also other product that the publisher already has.

Many times when publishers do hire staff writers, the writers are expected to produce a certain quota of songs within a specified time frame. For their work, these writers will receive a weekly salary—and I'm purposefully being conservative on this—that normally lies between $200-$400 for new writers and $400-$1,000 for a writer who has had some commercial success or a singer/songwriter who has a deal on a label or has generated excitement from labels. These salary advances are recoupable against any royalties the writers' songs might earn when recorded and released.

Generally, a staff writing position is contracted for three to five years, although within that period the contract usually comes up for renewal several times. To give you a typical example of how this might work, the staff writer may be presented with a contract stating an employment term of a "one-year initial period plus two one-year option periods." This means that at the end of each year the staff writer's contract comes up for renewal. So given this example, after the initial period of one year, the publisher can continue the renewal process for two more years, thereby binding the writer exclusively for a total of three years.

You should note that in most contracts of this nature, it's usually only the publisher who has the option to disengage from the contract at the time that it's up for renewal. The staff writer doesn't have that option, and is bound, so long as the publisher wishes to continue the relationship, for the duration of time specified in the contract whether it be three, five, or whatever number of years.

Since a contract of this nature could tie up the writer

for a period of time, he or she will want to give careful consideration to all terms stated in the contract before signing it. Chapter 7, "Songwriter Contracts," deals with recommended contract terms and specifically outlines items the writer will want to look for in an exclusive songwriter agreement.

## Standards

There's really no set criterion that's used to classify a standard. Basically, the standard is a classic, a song that has been popular over many years, has mass appeal, and is recorded time and time again in various genres of music including orchestrated versions, Muzak, and so on.

Creating a tune that's destined to be a standard is the dream of every songwriter. Likewise, finding tunes that have the potential to become standards is the goal of every publisher.

Why? Because a standard is sought out and used by artists, advertisers, producers, musicians, and film producers. And it's through the ongoing use by both professionals and amateurs alike that the standard can provide an annuity for the publisher's and songwriter's children and grandchildren.

Over the years, standards have originated from a variety of sources, including Broadway shows, radio, television theme songs, and movies. All music categories enjoy their standards. There's rock 'n' roll's "Johnny B. Goode," the jazz standard "In the Mood," R & B's time-transcender "Respect," and country's "Ring of Fire." Contemporary songs that make the standard grade are "Yesterday," "Hotel California," and "Fire and Rain."

# Song Sharks

Be aware that song sharks are not music publishers. In fact, they're exactly what they sound like—individuals or companies that deal unethically with songwriters and nibble and nibble at the songwriter's financial resources until they've succeeded in getting every last red cent.

Up front, every songwriter should know that:

- A legitimate music publisher will never charge you a fee to publish a song.
- A legitimate collaborator doesn't charge you for writing lyrics or composing a melody (whichever part you've asked for help on). Instead, the collaborator receives an agreed-upon percentage of the writer's share of the copyright.
- Legitimate record companies don't ask a writer for money to pay for the costs involved in making a record or pressing it up (or for anything else, for that matter).
- No one on earth can "guarantee" you a hit record.

The song shark's measures to get at the songwriter's funds are deceptive and fraudulent. Sadly enough, many a frustrated, uneducated, or naive writer is taken in by the bait of song sharks who splash magazine pages with ads claiming, "Big Money in Songwriting," or "We need YOUR Lyrics and Poems for Our Hit Melodies," or "We Guarantee YOU a Hit."

Of course, the song shark will never ask for money in an advertisement—they're slicker than that. But after you respond to the ad and submit material, they'll hail its potential and then ask you to send money in order for the company to begin initiating the steps required to make your tune a smash. Once the songwriter has made his or her initial investment, the song shark has the writer hooked because, logically, the writer isn't going to back down after turning over a precious sum of money, right?

Know that song sharks use various techniques to suck the blood out of songwriters. They ask for money to "publish" the writer's tune, which only means that the songwriter will receive a nice-looking printed copy of his or her song that no one else will ever see.

Of course, if the writer is looking for a collaborator, the song sharks are there to offer commercial lyrics and melodies for a fee. Only one has to wonder, if the lyrics and melodies are so "commercial," why don't they ever get on the radio? The answer is simple, really. The song sharks only store a few melodies and a few sets of lyrics, which they indiscriminately link to everyone's material. And that makes their job a lot simpler when it comes to their next step: asking you for the money to make a demo. If you've requested one of their melodies to accompany your lyrics, all they have to do is record a vocal overdub of your lyrics onto one of their prerecorded standard melody tracks. This assembly-line technique allows them to pocket a heap of the money they've received from the writer.

For just another "small" fee, the song shark will also record the song, press up copies, and submit them to radio stations. The thing you have to understand is that radio stations receive hundreds of new records every week. And not only do most of those never receive airplay, but a great number of them aren't even listened to by the station's programmer. This is especially true if they are records which haven't been sent by an established recording firm. So even though the song shark might submit a record to a radio station, they really don't promote the record, nor do they have the clout to do so. As a result, the record never gets heard and consequently never sells, and the writer never sees a return on his or her investment.

Yet another ploy to be aware of is the song shark who claims your song will be broadcast on the radio. To live up to that claim, the song shark will simply buy inexpensive airtime (with your money) on a low-wattage station, which won't do you any good either.

Bear in mind that in an effort to reduce the number of song sharks and to dissuade songwriters from becoming entangled with them, the performing rights organizations have made it a point not to grant affiliation to any publisher who solicits or accepts payment from writers wishing to have their songs published. Likewise, writers are not eligible for membership on the basis of work which they paid to have published or recorded.

If you should come across an ad promoting a "music publisher," be sure you know whom you're dealing with before you dive in—or you could get in way over your head. Check out the legitimacy of the individual or company with either the Better Business Bureau, SGA, or your performing rights organization.

# 6

# Record Producers, A & R Executives, Arrangers, and Artists

## Record Producers

### The Role of the Record Producer

When the music industry was in its embryonic stage, record producers were mostly found on staff at record companies. These staff producers were paid a commendable salary and were given royalties on the records they produced for either signed artists or new talent which they were encouraged to seek out. In fact, in those days, many staff producers also acted in an A & R capacity.

As the record industry evolved and finally plummeted to its slump in the late seventies, few labels could afford to keep staff producers on the payroll. So, out of necessity, these jobless staff producers could only continue doing what they knew best—producing. Consequently, the role of the independent producer was created.

Today, some labels still employ staff producers, but their numbers are considerably lower than in previous years. That's why, in this day and age, the spotlight generally beams brightest on the independent producer.

Not only do independents front their own money to make a master recording in hopes of being able to sell that master to a record company, but there are other independents who go the route of trying to secure a production agreement with a record company, although that's much easier said than done. This production agreement guarantees that the independent will produce one or more of the label's artists and/or will be allocated a budget to acquire and produce new talent for the label. With this type of arrangement, the independent can maintain a somewhat steady work flow and yet is still not exclusive to the label, making him free to make other production deals with various labels and artists.

Because of the producer's myriad responsibilities, his word has clout. The producer is the person who puts all the elements of a project together, supervises them, and is held accountable for the end product.

What happens is this: Initially the producer finds a song and matches it up with an artist. His choice of songs will guide the artist in a creative direction, and by producing that tune in a particular way, he hopes to bring success for the artist in the predesignated market. The producer's creative guidance is essential even to the extent that he'll book time in a particular studio that has a reputation for getting a particular sound for the type of music he's producing. What's more, the producer selects musicians with that same goal in mind.

Generally, it's also the producer who peddles and sells a master recording and makes certain all contracts reflect the best interest of the production team, including the production agreement, the artist's contract, and finally the master purchasing agreement.

Additionally, the producer is normally responsible for the project's budget and handles payments to musicians and studios. If the project exceeds the allotted budget, it is again the producer's neck that's on the line.

Producers come from everywhere. Some are former songwriters, arrangers, or musicians with musical training; others can't read a measure of music. So don't be duly impressed or unimpressed by a producer's musical background. What's more important is that the producer has a good ear for determining a song's potential and can hear the ways to make that song a marketable commodity. It's the producer who decides what parts of a production get mixed and which ones get nixed, so whether or not the producer comes up with all of the ideas for a song's arrangement or can even play those parts makes no difference. It's when you slip in the CD and listen to the end product that you'll hear the producer's capabilities speak for themselves.

While everything the producer does inside the studio is critical, just as important is his ability to deal with things going on outside the studio. To do that, a producer must have a keen business sense and a wide number of industry contacts. Even more, he specifically needs to develop relationships with record company executives, know what type of masters to shop to whom, be a pro at dealing with people, and be able to cope with the politics involved in bringing a deal to fruition.

Many times, artists and record labels rely solely on the producer and let his choice of songs go unquestioned and his time in the studio unscrutinized. There are even producers who hire other people to do the production work for them and will oversee the project by making regular visits to the studio to see that the project remains on course. However, when the project is brought home in the end, this producer still wins praise, and rightfully so, since he had the smarts to hire the right combination of people to accomplish what he wanted.

Yet there are situations where a label will want to maintain close supervision over a production. In that circumstance, though, it's usually because the producer is a newcomer to the business and doesn't have a long-standing track record.

## The Songwriter and the Producer

Since the producer is the hub of most wheels and the person with the most say-so, it's important that, as a songwriter, you develop a good relationship with the producer.

The names of producers are easy to find by reviewing record charts and the label copy on albums, tapes, and CDs. You may have to go through a record company or publisher before you find out the exact address and phone number of the producer you're searching out, but it can be done, and it's definitely something you should take the time to do.

However, before embarking on your producer hunt, take time out for an objectivity session with yourself to make sure the material you're submitting to a producer is suitable to what he's done before. If you're a singer/songwriter, be certain you're aiming your talents at a producer whose expertise lies in the same genre of music as your own.

Unlike the A & R director (see the next section), the producer doesn't require a master recording. But by the same token, your demo should be a decent representation of your song and display its direction. For a producer, the demo should be like a treasure map leading the way to the buried treasure, which is, of course, a hit song.

Most often, the songwriter who is willing to wheel and deal is the one who will pique the producer's interest. So don't be flabbergasted if a producer tells you he doesn't even want to hear your demo unless a portion of the publishing is available. It could be that he works semi-exclusively with a publisher, but even if he doesn't, he knows that a chunk of the publishing will whet the appetites of the record labels he shops the master of your song to.

It would be safe to say that most independent producers are trying to build their own corps of people—writers, artists, musicians, and even publishers—so they can rely on the same group of talents and keep the success generating from one project to another. Still other producers grow to have their own publishing firms, management companies, and sometimes even their own record labels. So when a producer is looking for a writer with promise, he's also looking for a writer with a sense of loyalty.

Once you do develop a relationship with a producer and he brings you up the ladder, show some allegiance and gratitude. After all, he's probably the person who took a chance on you by putting up the money to make a master of your song. And he's the one who put his credibility on the line when shopping your song to a label. Sure, you may surpass him one day. But try not to forget where you got your start.

# A & R Executives

## The Role of the A & R Executive

The A & R (artist and repertoire) executive is employed by a record company. His job is to act as the liaison between the label and its artists, pursue and sign new talent, audition and purchase master tapes, and sometimes even produce an artist affiliated with the label.

Like the producer, the background of the A & R executive is varied. At one time, this executive may have been a producer, songwriter, artist, musician, or manager, or may have come up the ranks through a publishing company. But whatever his past experience, you can bet the A & R director is heavily into music.

If you're shopping a master recording yourself, you'll

soon learn that record companies have different arrangements with their A & R staffs. Some A & R executives are allotted a budget each year with which to develop new acts or purchase master recordings. Others are designated a certain number of acts and masters they may sign. At some labels, too, the A & R executive is given full rein and is the sole decisionmaker on the purchase of masters. But in many cases, labels require their A & R executives to convene and play masters for each other, and a thumbs-up or thumbs-down signal is elicited from their round-table decision. So don't be too quick to write off an A & R director as wishy-washy if he's incredibly taken by your product on Monday and yet turns you down on Wednesday. He usually doesn't have the final say-so in the matter.

The A & R executive also spends many days traveling, doing paperwork, and acting as a troubleshooter and peacemaker. When a producer isn't happy about a clause in his contract, he calls the A & R executive, who, in turn, consults with the label's legal department. If an artist is having problems in the studio, it's usually the A & R director's job to clear the air.

Additionally, the A & R executive is heavily involved in the conceptual direction of a project, making sure the artist's image doesn't stray from the targeted market. He does that by overseeing the album artwork, photo sessions, liner notes, and credits, and by helping to decide on songs and which single off an album will be released first and what any of the follow-up singles may be.

## The Songwriter and the A & R Executive

Whether you're a songwriter or a singer/songwriter, you may be able to find a home for your talents with the A & R executive. That's because he's always working at both ends, looking for material for signed artists and pursuing new artists for the label to sign.

Quite often in today's economy, even A & R directors at the major labels are taking a "safer" approach when going about the business of signing new talent. Though the A & R executive may hear a great master recording a singer/songwriter has submitted to him and may even believe in it, he might wait for an independent label to break the record so he can get a free look-see before stepping in and making a commitment.

In the present market, too, you may also find more A & R executives who are willing to listen to demos than you did eight or ten years ago. It seems that labels are getting back into truly developing acts and not going for a trendy, one-shot deal. After all, it takes a lot of money to get a record heard by the public, and labels want to know they're going to recoup that money time and again. So they're back out in the clubs and bars looking for real, honest-to-goodness talent—people they can build on and bank on.

As you've probably already figured out, the A & R executive is an especially busy person and perhaps the most difficult administrator in the business to pin down. If, in attempting to make an appointment with an A & R director, you're asked instead to drop off your tape, don't be disheartened. But do use the follow-up tactics outlined in Chapter 4, "Shopping Your Demo." It's important that your name keeps popping up in their offices and that you do your utmost (short of becoming an annoying pest) to develop relationships with these people.

Once you have developed a relationship with an A & R executive, follow his career. There's a tremendous rate of turnover in this position, mostly because it's a "damned if you do and damned if you don't" proposition. If an A & R director is designated to sign up so many acts or purchase so many masters a year, but doesn't find enough worthy of the label, he may be out the door. Conversely, if the A & R director does sign up enough acts or buy enough masters, but they don't produce any revenue, again he may be asked to clean out his desk. Then there's always the A & R executive with a super track record who still loses his job when a new president takes over the company and brings along his own tribe of executives.

But even with the high rate of turnover in this position, you'll find that it's generally the same group of executives who are circulating from one record company to another. By keeping tabs on your A & R contacts, somewhere along the line they may be able to help you.

# The Arranger

### The Role of the Arranger

You can think of an arranger as someone who creates all the pieces of a recording's musical puzzle and fits those pieces together in a way that provides an overall pleasing effect.

In other words, before a song is adapted into a commercial recording, an arrangement is needed. Musical parts for various instruments and vocals have to be created in order for the song to make the jump from its simple demo form to a full commercial recording form. It's the job of the arranger, who most often gears his arrangement in accordance with the producer's wishes, to create those musical parts and write each of them out for the musicians and vocalists involved in the recording.

Arrangers may be hired to create full arrangements as just described, or may be asked only to arrange specific parts of the production, such as vocals, strings, horns, or the rhythm track.

Fees for arrangers can vary considerably. You might find a college music major who's willing to do the job for

$50 just because he's eager and hungry. Yet an arranger who's red-hot may not even talk to you unless you're willing to shell out $1,000. Normally, though, an arranger's fee will range between $450 and $1500, depending on the type and extent of the arrangement requested and the arranger's reputation.

Many arrangers are also contractors and will hire the musicians needed to play the parts they've charted out. For that added responsibility, though, they'll normally want a few extra bucks, since by contacting the musicians, handling their payments, and taking care of any paperwork involved with union musicians, they're actually absorbing some of the producer's headaches.

Today you can't really say that it's common or uncommon to have an arranger involved in a master recording. The decision to hire an arranger really lies with the producer and depends on his own personal preference and the confidence he has in his own arrangement ability. Many producers have always worked with arrangers and always will. Others depend on "head" arrangements, meaning they usually go into the studio with a song's bass line and drum pattern intact and then build the record from there off the top of their heads.

## The Songwriter and the Arranger

When a songwriter proposes to go into the studio to make a master recording of a song, he or she may feel that the expertise of an arranger is needed. Then, too, the songwriter now turned neophyte producer may also want to hire the arranger as a sort of studio security blanket.

If called upon, most arrangers will tell you they can do most any kind of arrangement fairly well. But, for your money, you want to find the arranger who is the best at the particular type of arrangement you're looking for. So get specific. If you want a string arrangement, find out if an arranger is better at aggressive string parts, symphonic ballad-type strings, or classic George Martin Beatles-style string parts.

More than that, you want an arranger who is skilled in arranging the same type of music that you're working on. So before making your selection, check out the arranger's demo reel and ask a lot of questions. It goes without saying that you can hire the most renowned arranger in town, but if he isn't adept at arranging the type of music you're producing, it isn't going to do you much good.

Once you've decided on an arranger, be as specific as you can about the arrangement you want. That's especially important if you haven't worked together before because you really won't know if he hears parts the same way you do. So give the arranger a starting place and much direction. Actually, the easiest way to do this is to hand the arranger a record containing parts you want him to create. Even go so far as to give the arranger the notes you want played if you have them in mind.

After the arranger has the arrangement worked out, get together with him outside the studio to make sure it's exactly as you wish. Otherwise, you may be in for a costly lesson. If you haven't listened to the arrangement beforehand and once the musicians play it in the studio you find you don't like it, you'll still have to pay the players before sending them home and will have to pay for the studio time you used as well. Even more costly, you'll also have to have the arrangement revamped and bring the musicians back to play and be paid again.

Probably the best way to find an arranger is by word of mouth. On a local level, you can check out people who are involved with jingle production in your area, or search out music conservatories, colleges, high schools, local bands, music stores, and music teachers. Any of these people may be able to create arrangements for you or can possibly turn you on to the people who can. If you're shooting for a specific arranger, you'll generally find his or her name on the back of an album cover. If the arranger isn't listed there, put in a call to the record label, and they'll be able to point you in the right direction.

## The Artist

When I was in college, a lady named Karla Bonoff wrote some popular tunes for singer Linda Ronstadt. As it turned out, a few months after Linda released those songs, Karla was given a record deal of her own and decided to release some of those same songs on her album. The funny thing was, I remember that many of my friends, having no clue as to the material's origin, were shocked that this Karla Somebody would dare attempt to rip off Ms. Ronstadt.

Because an artist is the vehicle for getting a writer's songs known, the general public is seldom aware of the songwriter behind the scenes or even as much as considers the possibility of his or her existence. How often have you heard someone refer to a tune as "Oh, you know, the song by So-and-so," whether So-and-so had anything to do with writing the song or not?

While the songwriter as an individual does, for the most part, take a backseat when it comes to public recognition, the songwriter's material is extremely instrumental in heightening the recognition the artist receives.

An artist chooses material based on certain criteria— what market the material will place him or her in, what kind of image will be established, and what part the material will play in the artist's evolution. Like other professionals, artists have a conception of how they would like to see their careers evolve—where they're starting out from and where they wish to go—whether it's from light rock to heavy metal or from country to pop. Many are seeking to grow in a way that will allow them to capture the largest market possible.

For example, you'll see someone like Sheena Easton, who started out singing adult contemporary pop with her hit "Morning Train," where she gained a very mainstream following. A few years later, her audience was broadened even more with some country followers when she sang the "We've Got Tonight" duet with Kenny Rogers. Finally she caught more fans in the funkier pop genre when performing songs written and produced by Prince.

So although no songwriter is fortuitous enough to possess a crystal ball, he or she still has to try to predict what direction an artist will grow toward and cast songs accordingly. It's probable that a new artist is trying to plant roots in a base market before investigating new turf, and when that's the case, your song can surely resemble a first cousin of the artist's initial hit. But as an artist develops and becomes established, don't try to pawn off songs akin to those on his or her first album; rather, consider the artist's maturation. Needless to say, when you're casting material in a circumstance like this, realism counts, because even with Gloria Estefan's wide acceptance, for example, it's doubtful she'd jump at the same sort of tune Bonnie Raitt would.

While the artist is always conscious of his or her personal development, he or she must also keep pace with changes in music as a whole in order to remain contemporary in their particular league. So you, as a songwriter looking to place your song with an artist, must also stretch your outlook to that same degree.

It could happen that you'll write a tune that's suitable for more than one artist, yet the song won't click in until that one-and-only artist comes along to make the tune a smash. "New York, New York" didn't succeed with several artists before Frank Sinatra cut the tune and made a huge splash with it.

Remember, it takes the combination of special key ingredients to make a song successful: the proper marriage between song and artist, the arrangement, production, and timing.

## The Unknown Artist vs. the Established Artist

As an artist grows in status, his or her input becomes more valued, and in the chain of getting your song recorded, it's the established artist who will have the final say-so. Suffice it to say that no one is going to tell an artist of Madonna's caliber which outside songs she must accept.

However, if your song is headed for the fairly new or unknown artist, its reception is going to be pitted against the opinion of either the producer, record company, or manager—or all of the above. The reason is, when a new artist is granted a record deal, the label will generally try to link this unknown element with a known one—the known element usually being the producer. That's because if the producer has a track record that merits attention, radio stations will be apt to give the record more of a chance. So in that case, the known element, or producer, will probably be making the decision on which songs are the most commercial and which will get the artist headed in the right direction.

In either situation, you may have to use your publishing as an inducement in getting your song recorded, no matter how great it might be. The known artist is likely to use his or her reputation as leverage and tell it to you exactly like it is: you need his or her name more than he or she needs your song. With the unknown artist, you may have more leverage, since it's your song that's launching his or her career. But even if the unknown artist lets you off the hook, don't be surprised if the label, producer, or manager tries to finagle some publishing out of you (see Chapter 7, "Songwriter Contracts").

Besides being flexible where publishing is concerned, a songwriter should also be open-minded about the interpretation of his or her song. You have to realize that artists and producers are creative people, too, and may make adaptations to your song. The artist's unique style might tend to change the characteristics of your song somewhat, or the producer may make changes due to the song's length, arrangement, or to solidify the direction he's chosen for the artist.

In fact, songwriting contracts commonly state that changes may be made by the publisher if he feels they are necessary to make a song more commercial. So you may not have the final word anyway.

No matter what hassles ensue, the fact remains that the songwriter and the artist need each other. In the beginning, it's usually a song that sells an artist, and in time it's usually an artist who sells a song.

## The Money Myth

A great many songwriters have the misconception that an artist's revenue is actually cutting into the writer's own. Unless you and the artist have arranged to share in the publishing and/or writing credit, nothing could be further from the truth.

Artists generate income from royalties made off record sales and from payments for their performances in clubs, in concert, and on TV. The songwriter's money stems from mechanical royalties from record sales, performance royalties each time the song receives airplay, and, theoretically, each time the song is performed live or taped for TV.

If you stop and think about it, a songwriter can actually become more financially secure than the artist. Artists usually only get one chance to make their money, and their careers can be a roller coaster ride of ups and downs with a few peaks followed by a downhill slide. On the other hand, a songwriter and a song are never really dead. The song can continue to circulate, be recorded by any number of artists, and with luck can become a standard. That means a songwriter can enjoy a substantial income for years into the future and can even pass the copyright along to his or her heirs. Besides that, because of the songwriter's anonymity where the public is concerned, no one is the wiser when a songwriter is crafting songs from a rocking chair at age eighty-three, whereas few artists can still round up the fans to fill a concert hall at that age.

## How to Locate Artists

It's unlikely that you'll get to speak directly to an artist, but you can get to their contacts or managers in the same ways that you track down producers and publishers: Scan the charts. Review the label copy that accompanies albums, cassettes, and CDs. Then start making phone calls.

You'll probably have to go through the publisher, label, or producer to get to the artist's contact or manager. But since many artists aren't always so keen on taking outside material, working from the outside in could be your best bet anyway. The publisher, producer, or record label may be able to persuade the artist and manager in a positive direction regarding your material, or if that doesn't work, they may be able to channel it elsewhere.

## The Role of the Artist's Manager

Some artists wish to be left alone to create, and prefer to turn over the business end of their careers to someone else. Others have quick business minds, but the demands of their whirlwind schedules don't leave any time for business. In either case, it's the manager who fills the artist's needs.

At the outset, the manager tries to take an artist's raw talent and mold it into something marketable. He takes the artist under his wing and is instrumental in linking him or her with a producer, in getting a demo made, and in acting as the artist's representative when shopping the demo to record industry administrators.

If a manager is fortunate enough to get his artist a deal, he'll work in conjunction with the A & R executive to create and embellish the artist's image and direction. With the label's publicist, he'll book interviews and promotional tours. And with a booking agent, he'll set dates for live performances. Overall, the manager oversees the artist's career by organizing each day while keeping a long-term goal in mind.

The artist's manager is always on hand to build the artist's confidence a step at a time. One way he does this is by setting up gigs in small clubs and then letting the artist progress to larger ones. Once the manager decides the artist has enough experience under his or her belt, he begins to book dates for bigger audiences and finally major concerts and tours.

Additionally, the manager acts as a strategist by helping to determine how the artist will be promoted, what material is right for the artist's image, and how the artist will evolve and change with the times.

It's standard for a manager to receive a 15 to 25 percent cut of everything the artist makes, depending of course on the artist's stature. There are some huge artists who require the aid of several people to handle their affairs. This may involve a business manager to schedule business appointments and studio sessions, another hired primarily to set up live performances, and still another assistant to maintain their personal affairs. In those cases, the percentage of the cut will greatly vary, or these individuals may even be placed on a yearly salary.

Since the manager is receiving a percentage of the artist's income, and in most cases overseeing the artist's entire career, he's another person who has some input into the acceptance or rejection of outside songs. And since many managers set up publishing companies, he might be another person trying to nibble at your publishing as well. But publishing, or lack thereof, may not be an issue if the material is hot enough, because the manager will still receive a percentage of the artist's income off of record sales.

## Choosing a Manager

As a singer/songwriter, when should you hook up with a manager, and what type of manager should it be? Unfortunately, there's no straightforward answer to that question. It's something you have to do when the time and person are right for you.

Some singer/songwriters who are just starting out feel comforted with a manager on their side to set them up with a producer, help them get a demo or master made, and represent them to record companies.

Other singer/songwriters wait to hire the services of a manager until they've had a hit on their own. The thinking here is that until that time, their money is their own, and they may be able to negotiate for a lower percentage of the manager's cut with their career and a hit record in tow. Besides that, they feel that being tied to a manager too early in the game will lessen their chances of hooking up with a better-known manager who has the contacts to take their career as far as it can go.

As with publishing companies, there are pros and cons surrounding both the large management firm and the individual manager. The well-known management firm is going to be established, respected, and have a plethora of contacts. Plus, if the firm is already handling a major act, it's conceivable they can use that as leverage to get you started. For instance, if someone desired to book Guns n' Roses for a concert, their management firm could grant that request upon one condition—that they book you as the opening act—thereby parlaying their lesser-known act on the strength of their biggie.

Still, you might know a person who's truly interested in your career and you as a person, perhaps even someone in your family. This person may not have far-reaching contacts at first, but in the plus column you can assuredly list their qualities as honest, hardworking, and sincere. Depending on the type of person you are, this person could make you feel more at ease with your struggling by providing boosts when you need them. In fact, just knowing someone is honest can bring about peace of mind, since generally monies are allocated to managers who, in turn, pay the artists what's due them.

If you wish to enlist the services of a personal manager, you can find their names in *Billboard's International Talent and Touring Directory*, which you can probably find in your local library. Additionally, you can review the label copy on albums, tapes, and CDs of artists whose work and acts resemble your own. If you don't see the management firm listed there, call the record label and they'll be able to help you out. Since this manager is already handling an act similar to yours, he may be open to taking you on, too. But even if that's not a possibility, he may be able to pass your songs along to the artist anyway.

# 7

# Songwriter Contracts

I've never been too fond of people who say, "Do as I say, not as I do." But in the instance where the songwriter becomes linked with a music publisher by signing a contract, I must admit that's the advice that comes to mind.

When a string of people helped me get my first appointment with a music publisher (namely, my former tennis coach lived next door to a former classmate of Charlie Monk, who ran April Blackwood Music Publishing in Nashville), I was eager, willing, and ignorant.

After I dropped the former classmate's name over the phone, Mr. Monk said he'd be willing to see me, but that I should call back later in the week. When I did call back, his time was tied up again, and he said it'd be best to wait and see when we could get together in the early part of the coming week.

So when Monday rolled around, instead of waiting around, I drove to Nashville. Once inside the April Blackwood doors, I explained to the receptionist that I'd spoken to Mr. Monk, and he said we could meet early on in the week, and might this be the day? I asked.

As things turned out, it wasn't the day that I met Charlie, but I was turned over to a lady named Judy Harris. Judy happened to like my material, although she wasn't too eager to sign it since it was in a semi-rock genre and seemingly out of place in Nashville. But when I returned a month later with new material, I was offered a contract with April Blackwood, which I signed Johnny-Hancock-on-the-Spot.

The point is, I really don't think I reacted any differently than many other new songwriters do when offered their first publishing contract. I was so excited about what this prospect could mean, and so ecstatic that I'd finally found someone who liked my songs, that I hastily jumped at the chance.

You can believe I didn't sit back easily in my chair and calmly say, "Well, Judy, I'll have to have my attorney look this over." (What attorney? I didn't have an attorney!) Nor did I say, "I'm disturbed about clause three on the first page," or, "What about changing this to read . . ." The fact of the matter was, I didn't know enough to ask about or for anything. I wasn't aware that I could ask for an advance as a reimbursement for my demo costs. I didn't know to ask for a time reversion clause. Consequently, when April Blackwood didn't have any luck in getting my songs recorded, the songs never reverted back to me, and I never saw any of the money that I'd put into them.

Most importantly, I was dealing with one of the most active and reputable music publishers in Nashville. Judy was great and helpful, and when I finally met Charlie Monk he was equally nice and gave me some advice that I'll always be thankful for. So it wasn't that anyone took advantage of me. It was merely a situation where my own lack of knowledge put me at a disadvantage.

After a writer and publisher have developed a rapport

over the years, the publisher may start volunteering different things, but right out of the box, the novice writer has to be assertive and know what to ask for and what he or she is entitled to. Of course, you always need to maintain a good balance between being a pain in the neck and looking out for Number One. Otherwise, by being too difficult to work with or by attempting to tilt the scales too much in your own favor, you can easily alienate a publisher.

Remember, after a publisher has given you and your material the once-over, you have every right to interview him. Ask about the company's latest hit. Ask what kind of material the publisher is used to working with. Similarly, what kind of contacts does the publisher have with regard to the kind of song you have? Also, size up your feelings about the publisher as a person and businessperson. Personally, I'm always a little leery of the hypeman. I've come to find that the people who are competent and confident about what they do don't feel the need to pressure you. They'll be open to making you an offer and letting you take the time to contemplate it.

Once you've garnered all the information you can, the only thing left to do is to proceed on gut instinct. But remember, there are no guarantees. Unfortunately, no matter which publisher you sign with, you never know how successful the outcome will be, whether anyone will want to record your songs. Although do keep in mind that if someone is anxious to sign your song, they're doing so for a good reason.

So when you sign with one publisher over another, you always take a chance. Still, you have to in order to have the possibility of getting results. But it's still important to protect yourself and your songs by investigating a publisher and knowing what to negotiate for in your contract.

# Recommended Contract Terms

The contracts used to sign a songwriter's tune will vary from publisher to publisher, but there are basic provisions that a songwriter is entitled to and can ask for if these are missing from the contract that's offered. For the most part, these provisions center around money and what means you have to get your song returned to you. You'll note that many of the following terms are further explained in Chapter 8, "Wheeling and Dealing," and that chapter should also be reviewed for more information.

## The Money Angle

You'll want to know when to ask for money, what portion of the revenue is rightfully yours, and how and when your money will be distributed to you. So keep the following in mind when reviewing a contract.

**Demo Costs.** From the personal experience I previously relayed, I'm sure you realize by now that if you'd like to be reimbursed for your demo costs, you'd better speak up and ask. Sharp businesspeople aren't in the practice of giving away money that isn't requested of them, but they usually will when asked in order to develop a good business relationship.

**Advances.** Most often, a songwriter will have to request an advance from a publisher, although some publishers will offer advances based on their relationship with a writer or the success of the writer. In any case, advances are normally deducted from royalties generated by a song.

Writers will want to be sure that their advances are viewed individually per song. In other words, if a publisher signs more than one of your songs, make sure the advance on one song isn't recoupable from the earnings of another song. This is termed "cross-collateralization" and is discussed below and in Chapter 8.

**Royalty Percentages.** Although it's true that the writer and publisher should split each dollar made fifty-fifty, many times that's on the net receipts. So be aware of what royalty percentage terms are outlined in your contract.

You may try to negotiate for 50 percent of the gross receipts, but don't be too frustrated if it doesn't come through. Most publishers will be reluctant to agree to this because they feel that the writer who enjoys a share of the profits should also be willing to share in the expenses, meaning the costs the publisher has incurred on phone calls, travel, and promotion while working your song. If you do deal with a publisher that pays on net rather than gross receipts, make certain there is a clear understanding of what expenses are deductible and get those items down on paper.

Whether your contract is based on net or gross receipts, the contract should provide that you receive 50 percent of revenues derived from mechanical royalties, synchronization licenses, and income earned for unspecified uses—"unspecified uses" being compulsory license fees from mediums such as jukeboxes and cable television. In negotiating sheet music income, you'll want to receive 10 percent of the retail selling price of each copy of sheet music sold.

**Time Limit for Payment.** Look for a defined payment period in your contract so you'll know when to expect payments. Most often, publishers pay semiannually and contracts normally state that at the end of the pay period the publisher has a ninety-day grace period in which to pay the songwriter.

For example, with semiannual royalty payments, the payment period would end on January 1 and July 1. However, the publisher then has ninety days to prepare his statements, so you may not receive payment until March 31 and September 30, respectively. The reason for the ninety-day grace period is that the process of money changing hands is extremely time-consuming. The record company that releases your song first pays a mechanical rights organization on the number of records sold. The mechanical rights organization then has to prepare their statements and draft a check to the music publisher. The music publisher then takes out his percentage and pays the writer. All of which can take some time to compute and complete.

**Cross-Collateralization.** Never stand for a cross-collateralization clause to be included in your contract. Cross-collateralization means that if a publisher picks up more than one of your songs at the same time or comes to acquire more than one over a period of time, he can deduct earnings from one song to pay for the expenses he has incurred on another.

For example, the songwriter could have one song that does quite well and one that does absolutely nothing. When the writer finally receives a check, it may be considerably less than what he or she has envisioned. Upon questioning the publisher, the writer will discover that the publisher deducted numerous expenses incurred while working the song that didn't do well from earnings from the one that did. For this reason, you can see why it's a necessity for each of your songs to be viewed individually.

**Subpublishing Advances.** Say that your song "Making You Mine" is signed to Moxie Music Publishing in the

United States, and Moxie Music subpublishes the song to Frankly Music Publishing in France. Moxie says that Frankly can have the right to publish your song and be its proprietor in France, but for that right they must pay Moxie a subpublishing advance of $1,000. This advance is recoupable against the monies that the song will earn in that territory.

Many contracts state that the writer doesn't get his or her 50 percent of the subpublishing advance until there are actually earnings from the song in the subpublisher's territory. That means that if Frankly gives Moxie the $1,000 advance and the song never earns a franc, the publisher retains the entire advance and the writer never sees his or her $500. If this clause appears in your contract, you'll definitely want to try to have it changed. The revision should state that the publisher must split any and all subpublishing advances with the writer as that money comes in.

### Getting Your Songs Back

The following are various provisions you can negotiate which will provide you with a means of getting your songs back if the publisher is unable to produce results.

**Time Reversion Clause.** With a time reversion clause, the songwriter's tune reverts back to him or her if the publisher hasn't been able to get the song recorded and released within an agreed-upon period of time. This time frame is usually set at one to two years, or in other words, a fair amount of time for the publisher to get results.

**Reversions with Bumpers.** The bumper specifies the time period in which the publisher must get the songwriter's tune recorded and released, but once the time period expires it allows the publisher to pay the writer an agreed-upon sum of money in order to retain the song for an additional amount of time. This money provides a show of good faith in the event that the publisher has a deal in the works at the date of expiration and needs extra time to see the deal through.

The amount of money is negotiable, but to give you an idea of where to start in your negotiations, SGA sets a $250 minimum in this instance.

**Minimum Earnings Clause.** The minimum earnings clause adds an extra ingredient of protection over the time reversion clause. Not only does it state that a song reverts back to the writer if the publisher hasn't gotten the song recorded and released within a specific time frame, but it also states that the writer must earn a specific amount of money from that song within that time frame.

However, if the song has been recorded and released within the set amount of time, yet hasn't generated the agreed-upon sum of money for the writer, the publisher may pay the writer that sum out of his own pocket in order to retain ownership of that song.

**Buybacks.** A buyback clause in your contract will give you the option of buying back your songs from a publisher at a certain point in time for a certain sum of money. Overall, because you're buying back your songs, the clause allows the writer to reap revenues from his or her songs instead of having the publisher accrue that future income himself.

In Chapter 8, other types of buyback situations are discussed.

## Other Conditions

The following are additional conditions that you'll want to look for in your contract, and ones you'll want to negotiate for if you find they're missing.

**The Right to Audit the Publisher.** All contracts should state that the songwriter has the right to audit the publisher's books and should further stipulate that in the event that publisher does not allow the songwriter to do so, the copyright ownership returns to the songwriter. This is known as a reversion of ownership for noninspection.

Most often the songwriter will only be permitted to conduct an audit during normal business hours after giving the publisher reasonable notice.

The songwriter may either conduct the audit personally or hire a certified public accountant to do so. But the writer cannot hire an auditor to work on a contingency basis—that is, where the auditor's payment is scaled according to the amount of money he finds is owed the writer during the audit.

**Reversion of Ownership for Reassignment Without Consent.** Simply put, a publisher can't sell or reassign your song to another publisher without your permission, and if he does, you'll be able to reclaim ownership of your song. The only instance when a publisher is able to sell or reassign your song without your consent is if he sells or reassigns his entire catalog to another publisher.

**Content Changes.** Most publishing contracts will allow for the publisher to make any changes to a song which he feels are necessary to make the song more commercial.

Ideally, this is a provision which you'd rather not have in your contract, but the chances are slim (yet never hesitate to try) that you'll be able to get it retracted. The reason is, major publishing outfits own thousands of songs. And they can't logistically track down each and every one of their writers on the spur of the moment to request permission to change a word, note, or line in a song. If they did, there wouldn't be enough time left in the day to work the material.

Looking at it from the publisher's side, suppose Cher wants to make a lyric change and is scheduled to go into the studio on Tuesday morning. The publisher tries all day Monday to contact the songwriter, with no luck. So what happens? Does the publisher say, "Forget about singing Tuesday, Cher"? To which Cher might reply, "Then forget about it altogether, Mr. Publisher." Or does the publisher allow Cher to make the lyric change and take his chances that the writer won't sue his company and Cher as a result?

As you can see, tying the publisher's hands with regard to content changes places a heavy and time-consuming burden on the publisher. So you might have to fight mighty hard to have this type of clause eliminated from your contract.

## Contract Samples

The AGAC songwriter contract was originally devised by the American Guild of Authors and Composers. However, that organization is now called SGA (Songwriters Guild of America; see Appendix D), so you may hear this contract referred to as either the AGAC songwriter contract or the SGA songwriter contract. Either way, it's one and the same, and is known to be the most equitable contract available to songwriters and offers writers optimum protection.

There are some music publishers who are signatories to the SGA contract, but it would be misleading to imply that almost any publisher you come across is going to offer you an SGA contract. More often than not, you're going to have to ask for this contract—and you still might not get it. Many publishers feel that the SGA contract ties their hands too much, and they don't always have the time or the money to bend over backwards for each of their writers.

The Passantino form contract is one that's been around the industry for years. Many publishers use this contract in its original form or a variation of it, such as the variation you'll find on the pages that follow, titled Standard Songwriters Contract. The Passantino was designed to leave space where provisions can be typed in once the writer and publisher have come to agreeable terms.

## Exclusive Songwriter Contracts

If a publisher feels a writer shows promise and wishes to invest in the writer's talent, he'll usually ask that the writer sign an exclusive songwriter agreement.

The advantage of an exclusive agreement is that the songwriter is placed on salary with the publisher. But what could be viewed as a negative is that the writer will be bound to the publisher for an initial period of one year, with one-year renewal options for up to a total of five years. These renewals are made at the publisher's discretion.

Since the songwriter who signs an exclusive songwriter agreement could be headed for a lengthy relationship with a publisher, he or she should give the contract careful

**THE SONGWRITERS
GUILD OF AMERICA**

NOTE TO SONGWRITERS: (A) DO NOT SIGN THIS CONTRACT IF IT HAS
ANY CHANGES UNLESS YOU HAVE FIRST DISCUSSED SUCH CHANGES
WITH THE GUILD; (B) FOR YOUR PROTECTION PLEASE SEND A FULLY
EXECUTED COPY OF THIS CONTRACT TO THE GUILD.

# POPULAR SONGWRITERS CONTRACT
© Copyright 1978 AGAC

AGREEMENT made this     day of        , 19   , between
. . . . . . . . . . . . . . . . . . . . . . . . . . . . . . . . . . . . . . . . . . . . . . . . . . . . . . . . .
(hereinafter called "Publisher") and . . . . . . . . . . . . . . . . . . . . . . . . .
. . . . . . . . . . . . . . . . . . . . . . . . . . . . . . . . . . . . . . . . . . . . . . . . . . . . . . . . .
. . . . . . . . . . . . . . . . . . . . . . . . . . . . . . . . . . . . . . . . . . . . . . . . . . . . . . . . .
(Jointly and/or severally hereinafter collectively called "Writer");
WITNESSETH:

Composition      1. The Writer hereby assigns, transfers and delivers to the Publisher a certain heretofore unpublished original musical composi-
**(Insert title of** tion, written and/or composed by the above-named Writer now
**composition** entitled . . . . . . . . . . . . . . . . . . . . . . . . . . . . . . . . . . . . . . . . . . . . . . . . . .
**here)**
(hereinafter referred to as "the composition"), including the title,
words and music thereof, and the right to secure copyright therein
**(Insert** throughout the entire world, and to have and to hold the said copy-
**number of** right and all rights of whatsoever nature thereunder existing, for
**years here)** . . . . . . . . . . . . . . . . . . . . years from the date of this contract or 35
not more than 40

years from the date of the first release of a commercial sound recording of the composition, whichever term ends earlier, unless this
contract is sooner terminated in accordance with the provisions
hereof.

Performing      2. In all respects this contract shall be subject to any existing
Rights   agreements between the parties hereto and the following small per-
Affiliation   forming rights licensing organization with which Writer and Pub-
lisher are affiliated:

**(Delete Two)**   (ASCAP, BMI, SESAC). Nothing contained herein shall, or shall
be deemed to, alter, vary or modify the rights of Writer and Publisher to share in, receive and retain the proceeds distributed to them
by such small performing rights licensing organization pursuant to
their respective agreement with it.

Warranty     3. The Writer hereby warrants that the composition is his sole,
exclusive and original work, that he has full right and power to make
this contract, and that there exists no adverse claim to or in the
composition, except as aforesaid in Paragraph 2 hereof and except
such rights as are specifically set forth in Paragraph 23 hereof.

Royalties    4. In consideration of this contract, the Publisher agrees to pay the Writer as follows:

**(Insert amount of advance here)**

(a) $........ as an advance against royalties, receipt of which is hereby acknowledged, which sum shall remain the property of the Writer and shall be deductible only from payments hereafter becoming due the Writer under this contract.

Piano Copies Sliding Scale

**(Insert percentage here)**

(b) In respect of regular piano copies sold and paid for in the United States and Canada, the following royalties per copy:

........% (in no case, however, less than 10%) of the wholesale selling price of the first 200,000 copies or less; plus

........% (in no case, however, less than 12%) of the wholesale selling price of copies in excess of 200,000 and not exceeding 500,000; plus

........% (in no case, however, less than 15%) of the wholesale selling price of copies in excess of 500,000.

Foreign Royalties **(Insert percentage here)**

(c) ........% (in no case, however, less than 50%) of all net sums received by the Publisher in respect of regular piano copies, orchestrations, band arrangements, octavos, quartets, arrangements for combinations of voices and/or instruments, and/or other copies of the composition sold in any country other than the United States and Canada, provided, however, that if the Publisher should sell such copies through, or cause them to be sold by, a subsidiary or affiliate which is actually doing business in a foreign country, then in respect of such sales, the Publisher shall pay to the Writer not less than 5% of the marked retail selling price in respect of each such copy sold and paid for.

Orchestrations and Other Arrangements, etc.

**(Insert percentage here)**

(d) In respect of each copy sold and paid for in the United States and Canada, or for export from the United States, of orchestrations, band arrangements, octavos, quartets, arrangements for combinations of voices and/or instruments, and/or other copies of the composition (other than regular piano copies) the following royalties on the wholesale selling price (after trade discounts, if any):

........% (in no case, however, less than 10%) on the first 200,000 copies or less; plus

........% (in no case, however, less than 12%) on all copies in excess of 200,000 and not exceeding 500,000; plus

........% (in no case, however, less than 15%) on all copies in excess of 500,000.

Publisher's Song Book, Folio, etc.

(e) (i) If the composition, or any part thereof, is included in any song book, folio or similar publication issued by the Publisher containing at least four, but not more than twenty-five musical compositions, the royalty to be paid by the Publisher to the Writer shall be an amount determined by dividing 10% of the wholesale selling price (after trade discounts, if any) of the copies sold, among the total number of the Publisher's copyrighted musical compositions included in such publication. If such publication contains more than twenty-five musical compositions, the said 10% shall be increased by an additional ½% for each additional musical composition.

Licensee's
Song Book,
Folio, etc.

(ii) If, pursuant to a license granted by the Publisher to a licensee not controlled by or affiliated with it, the composition, or any part thereof, is included in any song book, folio or similar publication, containing at least four musical compositions, the royalty to be paid by the Publisher to the Writer shall be that proportion of 50% of the gross amount received by it from the licensee, as the number of uses of the composition under the license and during the license period, bears to the total number of uses of the Publisher's copyrighted musical compositions under the license and during the license period.

(iii) In computing the number of the Publisher's copyrighted musical compositions under subdivisions (i) and (ii) hereof, there shall be excluded musical compositions in the public domain and arrangements thereof and those with respect to which the Publisher does not currently publish and offer for sale regular piano copies.

(iv) Royalties on publications containing less than four musical compositions shall be payable at regular piano copy rates.

Professional
Material and
Free Copies

(f) As to "professional material" not sold or resold, no royalty shall be payable. Free copies of the lyrics of the composition shall not be distributed except under the following conditions: (i) with the Writer's written consent; or (ii) when printed without music in limited numbers for charitable, religious or governmental purposes, or for similar public purposes, if no profit is derived, directly or indirectly; or (iii) when authorized for printing in a book, magazine or periodical, where such use is incidental to a novel or story (as distinguished from use in a book of lyrics or a lyric magazine or folio), provided that any such use shall bear the Writer's name and the proper copyright notice; or (iv) when distributed solely for the purpose of exploiting the composition, provided, that such exploitation is restricted to the distribution of limited numbers of such copies for the purpose of influencing the sale of the composition, that the distribution is independent of the sale of any other musical compositions, services, goods, wares or merchandise, and that no profit is made, directly or indirectly, in connection therewith.

Mechanicals,
Electrical
Transcription,
Synchroni-
zation, All
Other Rights
**(Insert
percentage
here)**

(g) . . . . . . . . . % (in no case, however, less than 50%) of:
All gross receipts of the Publisher in respect of any licenses (including statutory royalties) authorizing the manufacture of parts of instruments serving to mechanically reproduce the composition, or to use the composition in synchronization with sound motion pictures, or to reproduce it upon electrical transcription for broadcasting purposes; and of any and all gross receipts of the Publisher from any other source or right now known or which may

hereafter come into existence, except as provided in paragraph 2.

**Licensing Agent's Charges**

(h) If the Publisher administers licenses authorizing the manufacture of parts of instruments serving to mechanically reproduce said composition, or the use of said composition in synchronization or in timed relation with sound motion pictures or its reproduction upon electrical transcriptions, or any of them, through an agent, trustee or other administrator acting for a substantial part of the industry and not under the exclusive control of the Publisher (hereinafter sometimes referred to as licensing agent), the Publisher, in determining his receipts, shall be entitled to deduct from gross license fees paid by the Licensees, a sum equal to the charges paid by the Publisher to said licensing agent, provided, however, that in respect to synchronization or timed relation with sound motion pictures, said deduction shall in no event exceed $150.00 or 10% of said gross license fee, whichever is less; in connection with the manufacture of parts of instruments serving to mechanically reproduce said composition, said deductions shall not exceed 5% of said gross license fee; and in connection with electrical transcriptions, said deduction shall not exceed 10% of said gross license fee.

**Block Licenses**

(i) The Publisher agrees that the use of the composition will not be included in any bulk or block license heretofore or hereafter granted, and that it will not grant any bulk or block license to include the same, without the written consent of the Writer in each instance, except (i) that the Publisher may grant such licenses with respect to electrical transcription for broadcasting purposes, but in such event, the Publisher shall pay to the Writer that proportion of 50% of the gross amount received by it under each such license as the number of uses of the composition under each such license during each such license period bears to the total number of uses of the Publisher's copyrighted musical compositions under each such license during each such license period; in computing the number of the Publisher's copyrighted musical compositions for this purpose, there shall be excluded musical compositions in the public domain and arrangements thereof and those with respect to which the Publisher does not currently publish and offer for sale regular piano copies; (ii) that the Publisher may appoint agents or representatives in countries outside of the United States and Canada to use and to grant licenses for the use of the composition on the customary royalty fee basis under which the Publisher shall receive not less than 10% of the marked retail selling price in respect of regular piano copies, and 50% of all other revenue; if, in connection with any such bulk or block license, the Publisher shall have received any advance, the Writer shall not be entitled to share therein, but no part of said advance shall be deducted in computing the composition's earnings under said bulk or block license. A bulk or block license shall be deemed to mean any license or agreement, domestic or foreign, whereby rights are granted in respect of two or more musical compositions.

Television and New Uses

(j) Except to the extent that the Publisher and Writer have heretofore or may hereafter assign to or vest in the small performing rights licensing organization with which Writer and Publisher are affiliated, the said rights or the right to grant licenses therefor, it is agreed that no licenses shall be granted without the written consent, in each instance, of the Writer for the use of the composition by means of television, or by any means, or for any purposes not commercially established, or for which licenses were not granted by the Publisher on musical compositions prior to June 1, 1937.

Writer's Consent to Licenses

(k) The Publisher shall not, without the written consent of the Writer in each case, give or grant any right or license (i) to use the title of the composition, or (ii) for the exclusive use of the composition in any form or for any purpose, or for any period of time, or for any territory, other than its customary arrangements with foreign publishers, or (iii) to give a dramatic representation of the composition or to dramatize the plot or story thereof, or (iv) for a vocal rendition of the composition in synchronization with sound motion pictures, or (v) for any synchronization use thereof, or (vi) for the use of the composition or a quotation or excerpt therefrom in any article, book, periodical, advertisement or other similar publication. If, however, the Publisher shall give to the Writer written notice by certified mail, return receipt requested, or telegram, specifying the right or license to be given or granted, the name of the licensee and the terms and conditions thereof, including the price or other compensation to be received therefor, then, unless the Writer (or any one or more of them) shall, within five business days after the delivery of such notice to the address of the Writer hereinafter designated, object thereto, the Publisher may grant such right or license in accordance with the said notice without first obtaining the consent of the Writer. Such notice shall be deemed sufficient if sent to the Writer at the address or addresses hereinafter designated or at the address or addresses last furnished to the Publisher in writing by the Writer.

Trust for Writer

(l) Any portion of the receipts which may become due to the Writer from license fees (in excess of offsets), whether received directly from the licensee or from any licensing agent of the Publisher, shall, if not paid immediately on the receipt thereof by the Publisher, belong to the Writer and shall be held in trust for the Writer until payment is made; the ownership of said trust fund by the Writer shall not be questioned whether the monies are physically segregated or not.

Writer Participation

(m) The Publisher agrees that it will not issue any license as a result of which it will receive any financial benefit in which the Writer does not participate.

Writer Credit    (n) On all regular piano copies, orchestrations, band or other arrangements, octavos, quartets, commercial sound recordings and other reproductions of the composition or parts thereof, in whatever form and however produced, Publisher shall include or cause to be included, in addition to the copyright notice, the name of the Writer, and Publisher shall include a similar requirement in every license or authorization issued by it with respect to the composition.

Writers'
Respective
Shares    5. Whenever the term "Writer" is used herein, it shall be deemed to mean all of the persons herein defined as "Writer" and any and all royalties herein provided to be paid to the Writer shall be paid equally to such persons if there be more than one, unless otherwise provided in Paragraph 23.

Release of
Commercial
Sound
Recording
**(Insert period
not exceeding
12 months)**    6. (a)    (i) The Publisher shall, within . . . . . . . . . . months from the date of this contract (the "initial period"), cause a commercial sound recording of the composition to be made and released in the customary form and through the customary commercial channels. If at the end of such initial period a sound recording has not been made and released, as above provided, then, subject to the provisions of the next succeeding subdivision, this contract shall terminate.

**(Insert amount
to be not less
than $250)**

**(Insert period
not exceeding
six months)**    (ii) If, prior to the expiration of the initial period, Publisher pays the Writer the sum of $. . . . . . . (which shall not be charged against or recoupable out of any advances, royalties or other monies theretofor paid, then due, or which thereafter may become due the Writer from the Publisher pursuant to this contract or otherwise), Publisher shall have an additional . . . . . . . . . . months (the "additional period") commencing with the end of the initial period, within which to cause such commercial sound recording to be made and released as provided in subdivision (i) above. If at the end of the additional period a commercial sound recording has not been made and released, as above provided, then this contract shall terminate.

(iii) Upon termination pursuant to this Paragraph 6(a), all rights of any and every nature in and to the composition and in and to any and all copyrights secured thereon in the United States and throughout the world shall automatically re-vest in and become the property of the Writer and shall be reassigned to him by the Publisher. The Writer shall not be obligated to return or pay to the Publisher any advance or indebtedness as a condition of such re-assignment; the said re-assignment shall be in accordance with and subject to the provisions of Paragraph 8 hereof, and, in addition, the Publisher shall pay to the Writer all gross sums which it has theretofor or may thereafter receive in respect of the composition.

Writer's
Copies    (b) The Publisher shall furnish, or cause to be furnished, to the Writer six copies of the commercial sound recording referred to in Paragraph 6(a).

Piano Copies,
Piano
Arrangement
or Lead Sheet
**(Select (i) or
(ii)**    (c) The Publisher shall

☐    (i) within 30 days after the initial release of a commercial sound recording of the composition, make, publish and offer for sale regular piano copies of the composition in the form and through the channels customarily employed by it for that purpose;

☐     (ii) within 30 days after execution of this contract make a piano arrangement or lead sheet of the composition and furnish six copies thereof to the Writer.

In the event neither subdivision (i) nor (ii) of this subparagraph (c) is selected, the provisions of subdivision (ii) shall be automatically deemed to have been selected by the parties.

**Foreign Copyright**      7. (a) Each copyright on the composition in countries other than the United States shall be secured only in the name of the Publisher, and the Publisher shall not at any time divest itself of said foreign copyright directly or indirectly.

**Foreign Publication**      (b) No rights shall be granted by the Publisher in the composition to any foreign publisher or licensee inconsistent with the terms hereof, nor shall any foreign publication rights in the composition be given to a foreign publisher or licensee unless and until the Publisher shall have complied with the provisions of Paragraph 6 hereof.

**Foreign Advance**      (c) If foreign rights in the composition are separately conveyed, otherwise than as a part of the Publisher's current and/or future catalog, not less than 50% of any advance received in respect thereof shall be credited to the account of and paid to the Writer.

**Foreign Percentage**      (d) The percentage of the Writer on monies received from foreign sources shall be computed on the Publisher's net receipts, provided, however, that no deductions shall be made for offsets of monies due from the Publisher to said foreign sources; or for advances made by such foreign sources to the Publisher, unless the Writer shall have received at least 50% of said advances.

**No Foreign Allocations**      (e) In computing the receipts of the Publisher from licenses granted in respect of synchronization with sound motion pictures, or in respect of any world-wide licenses, or in respect of licenses granted by the Publisher for use of the composition in countries other than the United States, no amount shall be deducted for payments or allocations to publishers or licensees in such countries.

**Termination or Expiration of Contract**      8. Upon the termination or expiration of this contract, all rights of any and every nature in and to the composition and in and to any and all copyrights secured thereon in the United States and throughout the world, shall re-vest in and become the property of the Writer, and shall be re-assigned to the Writer by the Publisher free of any and all encumbrances of any nature whatsoever, provided that:

(a) If the Publisher, prior to such termination or expiration, shall have granted a domestic license for the use of the composition, not inconsistent with the terms and provisions of this contract, the re-assignment may be subject to the terms of such license.

(b) Publisher shall assign to the Writer all rights which it may have under any such agreement or license referred to in subdivision (a) in respect of the composition, including, but not limited to, the right to receive all royalties or other monies earned by the composition thereunder after the date of termination or expiration of this contract. Should the Publisher thereafter receive or be credited with any royalties or other monies so earned, it shall pay the same to the Writer.

(c) The Writer shall not be obligated to return or pay to the Publisher any advance or indebtedness as a condition of the re-assignment provided for in this Paragraph 8, and shall be entitled to receive the plates and copies of the composition in the possession of the Publisher.

(d) Publisher shall pay any and all royalties which may have accrued to the Writer prior to such termination or expiration.

(e) The Publisher shall execute any and all documents and do any and all acts or things necessary to effect any and all re-assignments to the Writer herein provided for.

**Negotiations for New or Unspecified Uses**

9. If the Publisher desires to exercise a right in and to the composition now known or which may hereafter become known, but for which no specific provision has been made herein, the Publisher shall give written notice to the Writer thereof. Negotiations respecting all the terms and conditions of any such disposition shall thereupon be entered into between the Publisher and the Writer and no such right shall be exercised until specific agreement has been made.

**Royalty Statements and Payments**

10. The Publisher shall render to the Writer, hereafter, royalty statements accompanied by remittance of the amount due at the times such statements and remittances are customarily rendered by the Publisher, provided, however, that such statements and remittances shall be rendered either semi-annually or quarterly and not more than forty-five days after the end of each such semi-annual or quarterly period, as the case may be. The Writer may at any time, or from time to time, make written request for a detailed royalty statement, and the Publisher shall, within sixty days, comply therewith. Such royalty statements shall set forth in detail the various items, foreign and domestic, for which royalties are payable thereunder and the amounts thereof, including, but not limited to, the number of copies sold and the number of uses made in each royalty category. If a use is made in a publication of the character provided in Paragraph 4, subdivision (e) hereof, there shall be included in said royalty statement the title of said publication, the publisher or issuer thereof, the date of and number of uses, the gross license fee received in connection with each publication, the share thereto of all the writers under contract with the Publisher, and the Writer's share thereof. There shall likewise be included in said statement a description of every other use of the composition, and if by a licensee or licensees their name or names, and if said use is upon a part of an instrument serving to reproduce the composition mechanically, the type of mechanical reproduction, the title of the label thereon, the name or names of the artists performing the same, together with the gross license fees received, and the Writer's share thereof.

**Examination of Books**

11. (a) The Publisher shall from time to time, upon written demand of the Writer or his representative, permit the Writer or his representative to inspect at the place of business of the Publisher, all books, records and documents relating to the composition and all licenses granted, uses had and payments made therefor, such right of inspection to include, but not by way of limitation, the right to examine all original accountings and records relating to uses and payments by manufacturers of commercial sound recordings and music rolls; and the Writer or his representative may appoint an accountant who shall at any time during usual business hours have

access to all records of the Publisher relating to the composition for the purpose of verifying royalty statements rendered or which are delinquent under the terms hereof.

(b) The Publisher shall, upon written demand of the Writer or his representative, cause any licensing agent in the United States and Canada to furnish to the Writer or his representative, statements showing in detail all licenses granted, uses had and payments made in connection with the composition, which licenses or permits were granted, or payments were received, by or through said licensing agent, and to permit the Writer or his representative to inspect at the place of business of such licensing agent, all books, records and documents of such licensing agent, relating thereto. Any and all agreements made by the Publisher with any such licensing agent shall provide that any such licensing agent will comply with the terms and provisions hereof. In the event that the Publisher shall instruct such licensing agent to furnish to the Writer or his representative statements as provided for herein, and to permit the inspection of the books, records and documents as herein provided, then if such licensing agent should refuse to comply with the said instructions, or any of them, the Publisher agrees to institute and prosecute diligently and in good faith such action or proceedings as may be necessary to compel compliance with the said instructions.

(c) With respect to foreign licensing agents, the Publisher shall make available the books or records of said licensing agents in countries outside of the United States and Canada to the extent such books or records are available to the Publisher, except that the Publisher may in lieu thereof make available any accountants' reports and audits which the Publisher is able to obtain.

(d) If as a result of any examination of books, records or documents pursuant to Paragraphs 11(a), 11(b) or 11(c) hereof, it is determined that, with respect to any royalty statement rendered by or on behalf of the Publisher to the Writer, the Writer is owed a sum equal to or greater than five percent of the sum shown on that royalty statement as being due to the Writer, then the Publisher shall pay to the Writer the entire cost of such examination, not to exceed 50% of the amount shown to be due the Writer.

(e)  (i) In the event the Publisher administers its own licenses for the manufacture of parts of instruments serving to mechanically reproduce the composition rather than employing a licensing agent for that purpose, the Publisher shall include in each license agreement a provision permitting the Publisher, the Writer or their respective representatives to inspect, at the place of business of such licensee, all books, records and documents of such licensee relating to such license. Within 30 days after written demand by the Writer, the Publisher shall commence to inspect such licensee's books, records and documents and shall furnish a written report of such inspection to the Writer within 90 days following such demand. If the Publisher fails, after written demand by the Writer, to so inspect the licensee's books, records and documents, or fails to furnish such report, the Writer or his representative may inspect such licensee's books, records and documents at his own expense.

(ii) In the further event that the Publisher and the licensee referred to in subdivision (i) above are subsidiaries or affiliates of the same entity or one is a subsidiary or affiliate of the other, then, unless the Publisher employs a licensing agent to administer the licenses referred to in subdivision (i) above, the Writer shall have the right to make the inspection referred to in subdivision (i) above without the necessity of making written demand on the Publisher as provided in subdivision (i) above.

(iii)  If as a result of any inspection by the Writer pursuant to subdivisions (i) and (ii) of this subparagraph (e) the Writer recovers additional monies from the licensee, the Publisher and the Writer shall share equally in the cost of such inspection.

**Default in Payment or Prevention of Examination**

12.  If the Publisher shall fail or refuse, within sixty days after written demand, to furnish or cause to be furnished, such statements, books, records or documents, or to permit inspection thereof, as provided for in Paragraphs 10 and 11 hereof, or within thirty days after written demand, to make the payment of any royalties due under this contract, then the Writer shall be entitled, upon ten days' written notice, to terminate this contract. However if the Publisher shall:

(a)  Within the said ten-day period serve upon the Writer a written notice demanding arbitration; and

(b)  Submit to arbitration its claim that it has complied with its obligation to furnish statements, books, records or documents, or permitted inspection thereof or to pay royalties, as the case may be, or both, and thereafter comply with any award of the arbitrator within ten days after such award or within such time as the artibrator may specify;

then this contract shall continue in full force and effect as if the Writer had not sent such notice of termination. If the Publisher shall fail to comply with the foregoing provisions, then this contract shall be deemed to have been terminated as of the date of the Writer's written notice of termination.

**Derivative Works**

13.  No derivative work prepared under authority of Publisher during the term of this contract may be utilized by Publisher or any other party after termination or expiration of this contract.

**Notices**

14.  All written demands and notices provided for herein shall be sent by certified mail, return receipt requested.

**Suits for Infringement**

15.  Any legal action brought by the Publisher against any alleged infringer of the composition shall be initiated and prosecuted at its sole cost and expense, but if the Publisher should fail, within thirty days after written demand, to institute such action, the Writer shall be entitled to institute such suit at his cost and expense. All sums recovered as a result of any such action shall, after the deduction of the reasonable expense thereof, be divided equally between the Publisher and the Writer. No settlement of any such action may be made by either party without first notifying the other; in the event that either party should object to such settlement, then such settlement shall not be made if the party objecting assumes the prosecution of the action and all expenses thereof, except that any sums thereafter recovered shall be divided equally between the Publisher and the Writer after the deduction of the reasonable expenses thereof.

**Infringement Claims**

16.  (a)  If a claim is presented against the Publisher alleging that the composition is an infringement upon some other work or a

violation of any other right of another, and because therof the Publisher is jeopardized, it shall forthwith serve a written notice upon the Writer setting forth the full details of such claim. The pendency of said claim shall not relieve the Publisher of the obligation to make payment of the royalties to the Writer hereunder, unless the Publisher shall deposit said royalties as and when they would otherwise be payable, in an account in the joint names of the Publisher and the Writer in a bank or trust company in New York, New York, if the Writer on the date of execution of this contract resides East of the Mississippi River, or in Los Angeles, California, if the Writer on the date of execution of this contract resides West of the Mississippi River. If no suit be filed within nine months after said written notice from the Publisher to the Writer, all monies deposited in said joint account shall be paid over to the Writer plus any interest which may have been earned thereon.

(b) Should an action be instituted against the Publisher claiming that the composition is an infringement upon some other work or a violation of any other right of another, the Publisher shall forthwith serve written notice upon the Writer containing the full details of such claim. Notwithstanding the commencement of such action, the Publisher shall continue to pay the royalties hereunder to the Writer unless it shall, from and after the date of the service of the summons, deposit said royalties as and when they would otherwise be payable, in an account in the joint names of the Publisher and the Writer in a bank or trust company in New York, New York, if the Writer on the date of execution of this contract resides East of the Mississippi River, or in Los Angeles, California, if the Writer on the date of execution of this contract resides West of the Mississippi River. If the said suit shall be finally adjudicated in favor of the Publisher or shall be settled, there shall be released and paid to the Writer all of such sums held in escrow less any amount paid out of the Writer's share with the Writer's written consent in settlement of said action. Should the said suit finally result adversely to the Publisher, the said amount on deposit shall be released to the Publisher to the extent of any expense or damage it incurs and the balance shall be paid over to the Writer.

(c) In any of the foregoing events, however, the Writer shall be entitled to payment of said royalties or the money so deposited at and after such time as he files with the Publisher a surety company bond, or a bond in other form acceptable to the Publisher, in the sum of such payments to secure the return thereof to the extent that the Publisher may be entitled to such return. The foregoing payments or deposits or the filing of a bond shall be without prejudice to the rights of the Publisher or Writer in the premises.

Arbitration    17. Any and all differences, disputes or controversies arising out of or in connection with this contract shall be submitted to arbitration before a sole arbitrator under the then prevailing rules of the American Arbitration Association. The location of the arbitration shall be New York, New York, if the Writer on the date of execution of this contract resides East of the Mississippi River, or Los Angeles, California, if the Writer on the date of execution of this contract resides West of the Mississippi River. The parties hereby individually and jointly agree to abide by and perform any award rendered in such arbitration. Judgment upon any such award rendered may be entered in any court having jurisdiction thereof.

**Assignment** 18. Except to the extent herein otherwise expressly provided, the Publisher shall not sell, transfer, assign, convey, encumber or otherwise dispose of the composition or the copyright or copyrights secured thereon without the prior written consent of the Writer. The Writer has been induced to enter into this contract in reliance upon the value to him of the personal service and ability of the Publisher in the exploitation of the composition, and by reason thereof it is the intention of the parties and the essence of the relationship between them that the rights herein granted to the Publisher shall remain with the Publisher and that the same shall not pass to any other person, including, without limitations, successors to or receivers or trustees of the property of the Publisher, either by act or deed of the Publisher or by operation of law, and in the event of the voluntary or involuntary bankruptcy of the Publisher, this contract shall terminate, provided, however, that the composition may be included by the Publisher in a bona fide voluntary sale of its music business or its entire catalog of musical compositions, or in a merger or consolidation of the Publisher with another corporation, in which event the Publisher shall immediately give written notice thereof to the Writer; and provided further that the composition and the copyright therein may be assigned by the Publisher to a subsidiary or affiliated company generally engaged in the music publishing business. If the Publisher is an individual, the composition may pass to a legatee or distributee as part of the inheritance of the Publisher's music business and entire catalog of musical compositions. Any such transfer or assignment shall, however, be conditioned upon the execution and delivery by the transferee or assignee to the Writer of an agreement to be bound by and to perform all of the terms and conditions of this contract to be performed on the part of the Publisher.

**Subsidiary Defined** 19. A subsidiary, affiliate, or any person, firm or corporation controlled by the Publisher or by such subsidiary or affiliate, as used in this contract, shall be deemed to include any person, firm or corporation, under common control with, or the majority of whose stock or capital contribution is owned or controlled by the Publisher or by any of its officers, directors, partners or associates, or whose policies and actions are subject to domination or control by the Publisher or any of its officers, directors, partners or associates.

**Amounts** 20. The amounts and percentages specified in this contract shall be deemed to be the amounts and percentages agreed upon by the parties hereto, unless other amounts or percentages are inserted in the blank spaces provided therefor.

**Modifications** 21. This contract is binding upon and shall enure to the benefit of the parties hereto and their respective successors in interest (as hereinbefore limited). If the Writer (or one or more of them) shall not be living, any notices may be given to, or consents given by, his or their successors in interest. No change or modification of this contract shall be effective unless reduced to writing and signed by the parties hereto.

The words in this contract shall be so construed that the singular shall include the plural and the plural shall include the singular where the context so requires and the masculine shall include the feminine and the feminine shall include the masculine where the context so requires.

Paragraph   22. The paragraph headings are inserted only as a matter of conve-
Headings   nience and for reference, and in no way define, limit or describe the
scope or intent of this contract nor in any way affect this contract.

Special   23.
Provisions

Witness:                          Publisher . . . . . . . . . . . . . . . . . .

. . . . . . . . . . . . . . . . . . . . . . . .   By . . . . . . . . . . . . . . . . . . . . . .

Witness:                          Address . . . . . . . . . . . . . . . . . .

. . . . . . . . . . . . . . . . . . . . . . . .   Writer . . . . . . . . . . . . . . (L.S.)

Witness:                          Address . . . . . . . . . . . . . . . . . .

. . . . . . . . . . . . . . . . . . . . . . . .   Soc. Sec. # . . . . . . . . . . . . . . .

Witness:                          Writer . . . . . . . . . . . . . . (L.S.)

. . . . . . . . . . . . . . . . . . . . . . . .   Address . . . . . . . . . . . . . . . . . .

Soc. Sec. # . . . . . . . . . . . . . . .

Writer . . . . . . . . . . . . . . (L.S.)

Address . . . . . . . . . . . . . . . . . .

Soc. Sec. # . . . . . . . . . . . . . . .

## FOR YOUR PROTECTION, SEND A COPY OF THE FULLY SIGNED CONTRACT TO THE GUILD.

******

Special Exceptions to apply only if filled in and initialed by the parties.
☐ The composition is part of an original score (not an interpolation) of

☐ Living Stage Production        ☐ Motion Picture        ☐ Night Club
Revue
☐ Televised Musical Production

which is the subject of an agreement between the parties dated          , a copy
of which is hereto annexed. Unless said agreement requires compliance with Paragraph 6 in respect of a greater number of musical compositions, the Publisher shall
be deemed to have complied with said Paragraph 6 with respect to the composition
if it fully performs the terms of said Paragraph 6 in respect of any one musical
composition included in said score.

# STANDARD SONGWRITERS CONTRACT

𝔄𝔤𝔯𝔢𝔢𝔪𝔢𝔫𝔱 made this                  day of                    1992, between

(hereinafter called the Publisher) and

jointly and/or severally (hereinafter called "Writer(s)"):

## 𝔚𝔦𝔱𝔫𝔢𝔰𝔰𝔢𝔱𝔥:

In consideration of the agreement herein contained and of the sum of One (1.00) Dollar and other good and valuable consideration in hand paid by the Publisher to the Writer(s), receipt of which is hereby acknowledged, the parties agree as follows:

1. The Writer(s) hereby sells, assigns, transfers and delivers to the Publisher, its successors and assigns, a certain heretofore unpublished original musical composition, written and/or composed by the above named writer(s), now entitled:

including the title, words and music, and all copyrights thereof, including but not limited to the copyright registration thereof No. (pending), and all rights, claims and demands in any way relating thereto, and the exclusive right to secure copyright therein throughout the entire world, and to have and to hold the said copyrights and all rights of whatsoever nature now and hereafter thereunder existing and/or existing under any agreements or licenses relating thereto, for and during the full terms of all of said copyrights. In consideration of the agreement herein contained and the additional sum of One (1.00) Dollar and other good and valuable consideration in hand paid by the Publisher to the Writer(s), receipt of which is hereby acknowledged, the Writer(s) hereby sells, assigns, transfers and delivers to the Publisher, its successors and assigns, all renewals and extensions of the copyrights of said musical composition(s) to which the Writer(s) may be entitled hereafter, and all registrations thereof, and all rights of any and every nature now and hereafter existing, for the full terms of all such renewals and extensions of copyrights.

2. The Writer(s) hereby warrants that the said composition is his sole, exclusive and original work, and that he has full right and power to make the within agreement, and that there exists no adverse claims to or in the said composition.

3. The Writer(s) hereby warrant(s) that the foregoing musical composition is new and original and does not infringe any other copyrighted work and has been created by the joint collaboration of the Writer(s) named herein and that said composition, including the title, words and music thereof, has been, unless herein otherwise specifically noted, the result of the joint efforts of all the undersigned Writers and not by way of any independent or separable activity by any of the Writers.

4. In consideration of this agreement, the Publisher agrees to pay the Writer(s) as follows:

(a) In respect of regular piano copies sold and paid for at wholesale in the United States of America, royalties of 50% of all net earned proceeds per copy;

(b) A royalty of 50% of all net earned proceeds per copy of dance orchestrations thereof sold and paid for in the United States of America;

(c) A royalty of 50% of all net earned sums received by the Publisher in respect of regular piano copies and/or orchestrations thereof sold and paid for in any foreign country by a foreign publisher;

(d) The sum of One Dollar as and when the said composition is published in any folio or composite work or lyric magazine by the Publisher or licensees of the

Publisher. Such publication may be made at any time in the discretion of the Publisher;

(e) In respect of the copies sold and rights licensed or sold in the Dominion of Canada, the royalties to be paid to the Writer(s) shall be on the same royalty basis as herein provided for sales or licenses in the United States.

(f) As to "professional material"—Not sold or resold, no royalty shall be payable;

(g) An amount equal to 50% of all net earned proceeds received and actually retained by the Publisher arising out of (1) the manufacture of phonograph records and other parts of instruments serving to mechanically reproduce said composition, or (2) the use of said composition in synchronization with sound motion pictures;

(h) Except as herein expressly provided, no other royalties shall be paid with respect to the said composition.

(i) Notwithstanding anything contained in this agreement, the Publisher shall deduct ten percent of all net receipts from all licenses issued by it to licensees in the United States and elsewhere, as collection charges for the collection of the proceeds of such licenses, before computing the royalties payable under paragraph 4 of this agreement.

5. It is understood and agreed by and between all the parties hereto that all sums hereunder payable jointly to the Writer(s) shall be paid to and divided amongst them respectively as follows:

NAME                                                      SHARE

6. The Publisher shall render the Writer(s), as above, on or before each September 30th covering the six months ending June 30th; and each March 31st covering the six months ending December 31st, royalty statements accompanied by remittance for any royalties due thereunder.

7. Anything to the contrary notwithstanding, nothing in this agreement contained shall obligate the Publisher to print copies of said composition or shall prevent the Publisher from authorizing publishers, agents and representatives in countries inside and outside of the United States from exercising exclusive publication and all other rights in said foreign countries in said composition on the customary royalty basis; and nothing in this agreement shall prevent the Publisher from authorizing publishers in the United States from exercising exclusive publication rights and other rights in the United States in said composition, provided the Publisher shall pay the Writer(s) the royalties herein stipulated.

8. All statements and payments made hereunder, in the absence of written objection thereto by Writer(s) within one (1) year from receipt thereof, shall constitute an account stated as to all royalties due for the period covered by such statement and/or payment. Within such time, the Writer(s) may appoint a certified public accountant who shall, upon written request therefor and at a mutually convenient time, have access to all records of the Publisher during business hours relating to said composition for the purpose of verifying royalty statemants hereunder, but not more than once for every royalty period.

9. The Writer(s) hereby consent to such changes, adaptations, dramatizations, transpositions, editing and arrangements of said composition, and the setting of words to the music and of music to the words, and the change of title as the Publisher

deems desirable. The Writer(s) hereby waive any and all claims which they have or may have against the Publisher and/or associated, affiliated and subsidiary corporations by reason of the fact that the title of said composition may be the same or similar to that of any musical composition or compositions heretofore or hereafter acquired by the Publisher and/or its associated, affiliated and subsidiary corporations. The Writer(s) consents to the use of his (their) name and likeness and the title to the said composition on the music, folios, recordings, performances, player rolls and in connection with publicity and advertising concerning the Publisher, its successors, assigns and licensees, and said composition, and agrees that the use of such name, likeness and title may commence prior to publication and may continue so long as the Publisher shall own and/or exercise any rights in said composition.

10. Written demands and notices other than royalty statements provided for herein shall be sent by registered mail.

11. Any legal actions brought by the Publisher against any alleged infringer of said composition shall be initiated and prosecuted at the Publisher's sole expense, and of any recovery made by it as a result thereof, after deduction of the expense of the litigation, a sum equal to thirty-three and one-third ($33\frac{1}{3}$) percent shall be paid to the Writer(s).

(a) If a claim is presented against the Publisher in respect of said composition and because thereof the Publisher is jeopardized, it shall thereupon serve written notice upon the Writer(s), containing the full details of such claim known to the Publisher and thereafter until the claim has been adjudicated or settled shall hold any moneys coming due the Writer(s) in escrow pending the outcome of such claim or claims. The Publisher shall have the right to settle or otherwise dispose of such claims in any manner as it in its sole discretion may determine. In the event of any recovery against the Publisher, either by way of judgement of settlement, all of the costs, charges, disbursements, attorney fees, and the amount of the judgement or settlement, may be deducted by the Publisher or by its associated, affiliated or subsidiary corporations.

(b) From and after the service of summons in a suit for infringement filed against the Publisher with respect to said composition, any and all payments thereafter coming due the Writer(s) shall be held by the Publisher in trust until the suit has been adjudicated and then be disbursed accordingly, unless the Writer(s) shall elect to file an acceptable bond in the sum of payments, in which event the sums due shall be paid to the Writer(s).

12. "Writer" as used herein shall be deemed to include all authors and composers signing this agreement.

13. The Writer(s), each for himself, hereby irrevocably, constitute and appoint the Publisher or any of its officers, directors, or general manager, his (their) attorney and representative, in the name(s) of the Writer(s), or any of them, or in the name of the Publisher, its successors and assigns, to make, sign, execute, acknowledge and deliver any and all instruments which may be desirable or necessary in order to vest in the Publisher, its successors and assigns, any of the rights hereinabove referred to, may be desirable or necessary in order to vest in the Publisher, its successors and assigns, any of the rights hereinabove referred to.

14. The Publisher shall have the right to sell, assign, transfer, license or otherwise dispose of any of its rights in whole or in part under this agreement to any person, firm or corporation, but said disposition shall not affect the right of the Writer(s) to the royalties hereinabove set forth.

15. This agreement shall be construed only under the laws of the State of New York. If any part of this agreement shall be invalid or unenforceable, it shall not affect the validity of the balance of this agreement.

16. This agreement shall be binding upon and shall inure to the benefit of the respective parties hereto, their respective successors in interest, legal representatives and assigns, and represents the entire understanding between the parties.

17. Any and all advances made to writers are fully recoupable, under this or any other agreement between Writer(s) and Publisher(s), their affiliates, subsidiaries, and assigns.

IN WITNESS WHEREOF, the parties hereto have hereunto set their hands and seals the day and year first above written.

By _____

Writer _____

Address _____

**PLEASE SHOW**
**PERMANENT**                Writer _____
**MAILING ADDRESS**

Address _____

Writer _____

Address _____

# SESAC, INC.
# WRITER AFFILIATION AGREEMENT

**AGREEMENT** made                    , by and between

whose address is

("WRITER") and SESAC, INC., a New York corporation whose address is 156 West 56th Street, New York, New York 10019 ("SESAC").

## RECITALS

A. SESAC is a performing rights licensing organization engaged in the business of licensing certain rights under copyright to PERFORM PUBLICLY certain musical and/or dramatico-musical WORKS.

B. WRITER desires to engage SESAC to license such rights to PERFORM PUB-LICLY WRITER'S WORKS.

NOW THEREFORE, in consideration of the mutual promises contained herein, WRITER and SESAC hereby agree as follows (capitalized terms shall have the meanings set forth in this Agreement):

## 1. WRITER'S GRANT OF RIGHTS TO SESAC

Effective as of                    , WRITER grants SESAC:

(a) all of WRITER'S rights to PERFORM PUBLICLY and to license others to PERFORM PUBLICLY, WRITER'S WORKS throughout the world; and

(b) the non-exclusive right to record, and to license others to record, WRITER'S WORKS, in whole or in part, by any means now known or hereafter invented, in connection with SESAC'S exercise of its rights under paragraph 1(a) of this Agreement; provided, however, that any such recording shall be solely for the purpose of delayed transmission of "live" programs (as such term is commonly understood in the United States broadcasting industry) or for archival or audition purposes; and

(c) the non-exclusive right, in connection with SESAC'S exercise of its rights under paragraphs 1(a) and 1(b) of this Agreement, to make new adaptations and arrangements of any of WRITER'S WORKS and to license or authorize others to do the same; and

(d) the non-exclusive right to use the names (real and assumed), image, likeness, signature and biography, or any portion thereof, of WRITER in connection with the exercise of the rights granted by WRITER to SESAC under this Agreement.

## 2. SESAC'S RIGHT TO GRANT LICENSES TO THIRD PERSONS

(a) During the term of this Agreement, SESAC shall have the right to grant to third PERSONS licenses of the rights granted by WRITER to SESAC under this Agreement, and shall have the right to include WRITER'S WORKS in BLANKET LICENSES in effect as of the date set forth in paragraph 1 of this Agreement. SESAC may do all such things and take all such actions as in SESAC'S judgment may be reasonable and proper in order to enter into such licenses, and SESAC may enter into such licenses in its own name or in the name of WRITER. Such licenses may authorize the use of any or all of WRITER'S WORKS, either separately or in BLANKET LICENSES. As between WRITER and SESAC, SESAC shall determine, fix, regulate and enforce all of the terms of any and all such licenses.

(b) Notwithstanding anything in this Agreement to the contrary, SESAC shall not have the right to grant licenses:

    (i) to PERFORM PUBLICLY any of WRITER'S WORKS as part of a performance of the musical play or other dramatico-musical WORK for which such WRITER'S WORKS were written originally, if such performance is of the complete musical play or dramatico-musical WORK and uses dramatic action, scenery and/or costumes, such rights being reserved, as between WRITER and SESAC, to WRITER for such use; and

    (ii) to synchronize any of WRITER'S WORKS in any production in any audio-visual medium, including without limitation, motion pictures, prerecorded television programs and home video devices, or to record and distribute for sale to the public, recordings in any medium of any of WRITER'S WORKS, except as provided in paragraph 1(b) of this Agreement.

(c) Notwithstanding WRITER'S grant of rights to SESAC in paragraph 1 of this Agreement:

    (i) WRITER reserves the right to issue directly to any third PERSON, other than another performing right licensing organization, non-exclusive licenses to PERFORM PUBLICLY any of WRITER'S WORKS (each such license being hereinafter referred to as a "DIRECT LICENSE"), provided that any DIRECT LICENSE must be issued prior to the first public performance given under that DIRECT LICENSE. Within ten (10) days after the issuance of a DIRECT LICENSE, WRITER shall provide SESAC with written notice thereof, which notice shall contain the titles of WRITER'S WORKS being licensed, the names of any co-writers and publishers of each such WRITER'S WORK, the name of the licensee and the location at which each performance will be given, the nature of the performance(s) (e.g., radio, television, live concert) so licensed, and the duration of the license. WRITER shall also provide SESAC with such other information concerning any DIRECT LICENSE as SESAC may reasonably request within ten (10) days of such request. In no event shall SESAC make any payments to WRITER in connection with any performance given under a DIRECT LICENSE granted by WRITER hereunder.

    (ii) WRITER reserves the right to enter into publishing agreements with respect to any or all of WRITER'S WORKS provided that any and all such publishing agreements shall be subject to this Agreement.

    (iii) WRITER reserves the right to enter into agreements to create WORKS that are owned by another PERSON as "works made for hire" as defined under the United States Copyright Law, Title 17 U.S.C., as amended from time to time, subject to paragraph 7(e) of this agreement.

(d) The parties acknowledge that SESAC has heretofore entered into and may during the Term of this Agreement enter into agreements with foreign performing rights licensing organizations for the licensing in territories outside the United States, its territories and possessions, of the rights granted by WRITER to SESAC under this Agreement.

### 3. REPORTING OF WORKS

(a) With respect to each of WRITER'S WORKS, WRITER shall promptly:

    (i) upon execution of this Agreement, provide SESAC with a completed "index form," in the form supplied by SESAC, for each of WRITER'S WORKS and "supplemental forms" if any WRITER'S WORK is thereafter recorded, synchronized in any production in any audio-visual medium, or otherwise is exploited in a manner designed to increase the likelihood that such WRITER'S WORK will be PERFORMED PUBLICLY; provided, however, that if WRITER shall fail to provide an index form as to any WRITER'S WORK, SESAC shall be entitled to rely on the information, including without limitation, the royalty recipients and their respective shares, stated on any index form covering such WRITER'S WORK, which has been provided by any other SESAC AFFILIATE, provided such other SESAC AFFILIATE is either a co-writer, publisher, co-publisher or administrator of, or otherwise has a financial interest in, that WRITER'S WORK; and

(ii) upon completion of creation of each of WRITER'S WORK following the execution of this Agreement, provide SESAC with a completed index form and supplemental form if needed; and

(iii) cause SESAC to be furnished with cue sheets for any production in any audio-visual medium, including without limitation, motion pictures and pre-recorded television programs, in which any of WRITER'S WORKS are synchronized and, in the case of radio and television advertisements and commercials, copies of the advertiser's logs of stations and times of broadcasts; and

(iv) upon request, cause SESAC to be furnished with any phonorecords or audio-visual devices embodying any of WRITER'S WORKS; and

(v) upon request, provide SESAC with a printed copy in the best edition available; and

(vi) upon request, provide SESAC with the copyright date, registration number and renewal number, if any, and copies of any certificate of copyright registration and renewal, if any; and

(vii) upon request, provide SESAC with true and complete copies of any and all agreements, assignments, instruments and documents of any kind by which WRITER obtained, recorded or registered rights in any of WRITER'S WORKS.

(b) Upon request, WRITER shall secure, execute and deliver to SESAC such additional documents and other material, and shall do such things and take such actions as SESAC in its judgment shall deem reasonable and proper in order for SESAC to exercise fully the rights granted by WRITER to SESAC under this Agreement.

## 4. WRITER'S WARRANTIES AND REPRESENTATIONS

(a) WRITER warrants and represents that all of the information provided on WRITER'S SESAC Writer Application form, and each and every index form and supplemental form, if any, is and shall remain true and correct.

(b) With respect to each and every one of WRITER'S WORKS, WRITER warrants and represents that:

(i) WRITER does presently and, during the Term of this Agreement, will own or control all rights to PERFORM PUBLICLY granted to SESAC under this Agreement, and there are, and during the Term of this Agreement there will be, no adverse claims against any of WRITER'S WORKS;

(ii) WRITER has the right to enter into this Agreement and to grant the rights granted to SESAC under this Agreement, and WRITER is not bound by any prior contracts, agreements or obligations which conflict with this Agreement;

(iii) no other PERSON has or will have any right, title or interest in any of WRITER'S WORKS, except as may be expressly set forth in the index form submitted by WRITER for each of WRITER'S WORKS;

(iv) each and every WRITER'S WORK is and shall remain WRITER'S original composition, or WRITER'S authorized arrangement of an original composition by WRITER or by another PERSON or PERSONS, or WRITER'S original arrangement of a WORK in the public domain, and that each and every such WRITER'S WORK shall not infringe upon the copyright in any other WORK or otherwise violate any right of any other PERSON; and

(v) WRITER has complied or shall timely comply with all required domestic and international copyright or other legal formalities, including registration, notice, renewal and recordation of any agreements, assignments, instruments or documents of any kind.

### 5. WORKS EXCLUDED; BREACHES OF WARRANTY; DISPUTES; FRACTIONAL ALLOCATIONS

(a) At any time during the term of this Agreement, SESAC shall have the right to exclude from this Agreement any of WRITER'S WORKS which, in SESAC'S judgment, may

(i) be substantially or confusingly similar to any other then-existing WORK; or

(ii) infringe the copyright in any other then-existing WORK; or

(iii) violate any other right of any PERSON; or

(iv) be offensive or immoral; or

(v) tend to bring SESAC or any of its AFFILIATES into disrepute for any reason.

(b) If WRITER shall breach any of WRITER's warranties and representations contained in this Agreement, then, in addition to any remedies available to SESAC under this Agreement or at law, SESAC shall have the right to exclude any or all of WRITER'S WORKS from this Agreement, and shall have the right to withhold payment of all monies which may be or become due to WRITER, until SESAC receives written notice which in SESAC'S judgment is satisfactory evidence of a cure of each and every such breach.

(c) If any claim, demand, litigation or proceeding involving any of WRITER'S WORKS (each being hereinafter referred to as a "DISPUTE") arises, SESAC shall have the right to exclude those of WRITER'S WORKS involved in such DISPUTE from this Agreement, and shall have the right to withhold payment of all monies which may be or become due to WRITER until SESAC receives written notice which in SESAC'S judgment is satisfactory evidence of a final resolution of the DISPUTE binding on all parties thereto.

(d) If, in SESAC'S judgment, any of WRITER'S WORKS are based on WORKS in the public domain, SESAC shall have the right, upon written notice to WRITER, either (i) to exclude any such WRITER'S WORKS from this Agreement; or (ii) to pay royalties for any such WRITER'S WORKS at a fraction, to be determined by SESAC in SESAC'S judgment, of the rate at which WRITER would be paid for performances of that WRITER'S WORK if such WRITER'S WORK were a completely original WRITER'S WORK.

(e) If SESAC exercises its right to exclude any of WRITER'S WORKS from this Agreement, all rights in and to each such WRITER'S WORK granted to SESAC under this Agreement shall revert to WRITER upon SESAC'S notification to WRITER of such determination. If any of WRITER'S WORKS are assigned a fractional royalty rate pursuant to paragraph 5(d) of this Agreement, WRITER may notify SESAC of WRITER'S determination to withdraw that WRITER'S WORK from this Agreement within ten (10) days of SESAC'S notification, such withdrawal to be effective as of the date of SESAC'S notification to WRITER.

## 6. ROYALTY DISTRIBUTION

(a) SESAC shall remit to WRITER such monies as may be payable to WRITER under this Agreement in respect of uses of WRITER'S WORKS in the United States, its territories and possessions, in distributions to be made within ninety (90) days following the end of each calendar quarter.

(b) SESAC shall remit to WRITER such monies as may be payable to WRITER under this Agreement in respect of uses of WRITER'S WORKS in all territories other than the United States, its territories and possessions, in distributions to be made within one hundred eighty (180) days following the end of the calendar quarter in which SESAC shall have received payment from a foreign performing rights licensing organization with respect to such uses.

(c) Each remittance shall be accompanied by a statement setting forth in reasonable detail the source and nature of the income received, the amounts payable to WRITER, and for which of WRITER'S WORKS such payments are being made, it being understood that in the case of monies received from a foreign performing rights licensing organization, such statement shall only set forth the name of such foreign performing rights licensing organization and the amount of monies payable to WRITER.

(d) Notwithstanding the foregoing, SESAC shall not be required to remit to WRITER in respect of any distribution in which the total sum due to WRITER for that distribution is less than twenty ($20.00) dollars; however, SESAC shall distribute all monies so withheld at least once in each calendar year.

(e) If SESAC shall make a payment to WRITER under this Agreement and such payment is returned to SESAC as undeliverable for any reason whatsoever, SESAC shall hold such payment until the last day of the eighth calendar quarter following the calendar quarter in which the first undeliverable payment is returned to SESAC (the "CLAIM DEADLINE"). Any further payments which become due to WRITER under this Agreement will be held until WRITER notifies SESAC of WRITER'S new address. If WRITER does not notify SESAC of WRITER'S new address by the first day of the sixth calendar quarter following the calendar quarter in which the first payment is returned to SESAC as undeliverable, SESAC shall send notice to the WRITER at the last address of WRITER of which SESAC was notified, that WRITER is required to claim all such payments by the CLAIM DEADLINE. If said payments remain unclaimed after the CLAIM DEADLINE, they shall be considered new monies for the calendar quarter in which the CLAIM DEADLINE occurs, and shall be reallocated and distributed in the distribution for that calendar quarter in accordance with this Agreement.

(f) If because of a breach of any of WRITER'S warranties and representations contained in this Agreement, SESAC elects to withhold payment pursuant to paragraph 5(b) of this Agreement, SESAC shall be entitled to withhold such monies for a period ending on the last day of the calendar quarter in which SESAC receives written notice which in SESAC'S judgment is satisfactory evidence of a cure of each such breach, in which event SESAC shall pay out to WRITER all withheld monies in the distribution for the calendar quarter in which SESAC received such notification.

(g) If because of a DISPUTE, SESAC elects to withhold payment pursuant to paragraph 5(c) of this Agreement, SESAC shall be entitled to withhold such monies for a period ending on the earlier of (i) the last day of the calendar quarter in which SESAC receives written notice which in SESAC'S judgment is satisfactory evidence of a final resolution of the DISPUTE binding on all parties thereto, in which event

SESAC shall pay out all withheld monies in accordance with that resolution in the distribution for the calendar quarter in which SESAC received notification thereof; or (ii) the last day of the fourth calendar quarter following the quarter in which SESAC received notice of the DISPUTE (the "WITHHOLDING DEADLINE"). If no litigation has commenced by the WITHHOLDING DEADLINE, SESAC may release all monies withheld in connection with such DISPUTE to the AFFILIATES listed on the index form which was in effect when SESAC received notice of the DISPUTE. If litigation has been commenced prior to the WITHHOLDING DEADLINE, SESAC shall be entitled to withhold all such monies pending notification to SESAC of a final, non-appealable judgment, a settlement binding upon all parties, dismissal of the DISPUTE with prejudice, or such other information which in SESAC's judgment is satisfactory evidence of a final resolution of the DISPUTE, following which SESAC shall pay out all withheld monies in accordance with such judgment, settlement, dismissal or final resolution in the distribution for the calendar quarter in which SESAC received notification thereof.

## 7. ROYALTY DETERMINATION

As full consideration for the rights granted to SESAC under this Agreement, SESAC shall make the following payments to WRITER in respect of each of WRITER'S WORKS:

(a) <u>Blanket Licenses</u>. SESAC shall pay to WRITER an amount equal to WRITER'S share of the monies allocated by SESAC for distribution in the relevant calendar quarter in respect of BLANKET LICENSES entered into by SESAC with users in the United States. All such amounts shall be calculated in accordance with SESAC'S then-current standard practices and shall reflect the then-current performance rates generally paid by SESAC to its AFFILIATES in respect of similar performances of similar WORKS. SESAC shall have the right to modify such practices and performance rates from time to time without prior notice to WRITER.

(b) <u>Licenses of WRITER'S WORKS only</u>. SESAC shall pay to WRITER, any SESAC AFFILIATE co-writer and the SESAC AFFILIATE publisher or publishers of the relevant WRITER'S WORK or WORKS, an amount equal to their respective share of the monies allocated by SESAC for distribution in the relevant calendar quarter in respect of licenses of one or more of WRITER'S WORKS only (as distinguished from BLANKET LICENSES). All such amounts shall be calculated in accordance with SESAC's then-current standard practices and shall reflect the then-current performance rates generally paid by SESAC to its AFFILIATES in respect of similar licenses of similar performances of similar WORKS.

(c) <u>Foreign Performing Rights Licensing Organization Income</u>. SESAC shall pay to WRITER an amount equal to WRITER's share of monies allocated by SESAC for distribution in the relevant calendar quarter out of monies actually received from any foreign performing rights licensing organization by SESAC and designated by such foreign performing rights licensing organization as the WRITER's share of monies in respect of uses of WRITER's WORKS in the relevant territory. SESAC shall have the right, in respect of monies received from a foreign performing rights licensing organization, to deduct such amounts as SESAC is entitled to retain for its own account under the then-current agreement between SESAC and such foreign performing rights licensing organization.

(d) As to any WRITER'S WORKS which were written by WRITER with any other PERSON, SESAC shall pay WRITER a share of royalties equal in amount to the royalties payable to WRITER if such WRITER'S WORKS were written solely by WRITER, multiplied by a fraction, the numerator of which shall be one (1) and the denominator of which shall be the number of writers of such WRITER'S WORK. If the WRITER and the other co-writers agree to a different division of royalties, WRITER shall submit to SESAC a copy of a written agreement signed by WRITER and all other co-writers specifying such division. Following receipt of such written agreement, SESAC shall pay WRITER a share of royalties in accordance with that agreement, beginning with the distribution for the calendar quarter in which such instructions are received by SESAC.

(e) WRITER shall not be entitled to any payment under this Agreement for any WORK written by WRITER that is owned by another PERSON as a "work made for hire" as defined under the United States Copyright Law, Title 17 U.S.C., as amended from time to time, unless the PERSON who is the copyright owner of such WORK authorizes SESAC in writing to collect and pay to WRITER the share of royalties which would have been payable to WRITER had such WORKS not been a "work made for hire."

(f) SESAC shall have no obligation to make payment to WRITER under this Agreement as to (i) any performance of any of WRITER'S WORKS which occurs prior to the date on which SESAC receives an index form from any AFFILIATE with respect to that WRITER'S WORK; and (ii) any performance of any of WRITER'S WORKS of which SESAC receives notice more than one (1) year following the date of such performance.

(g) If, as to any of WRITER'S WORKS, the index form and supplemental form or forms, if any, filed by WRITER with respect to that WRITER'S WORK do not indicate that the publishing rights in such WRITER'S WORK have been granted to a publisher, SESAC shall pay to WRITER all such monies as may have been payable to a SESAC AFFILIATE publisher under the then-current SESAC Publisher Affiliation Agreement in respect of uses of that WRITER'S WORK. If such publishing rights are subsequently granted to a SESAC AFFILIATE publisher, WRITER shall notify SESAC of such assignment and SESAC shall pay to that SESAC AFFILIATE publisher such monies as publisher shall be entitled to receive under its SESAC Publisher Affiliation Agreement with respect to performances of that WRITER'S WORK, commencing with the distribution for the calendar quarter in which notice is received by SESAC. In no event shall SESAC make any retroactive payments to any SESAC AFFILIATE publisher of any monies paid to WRITER under this paragraph 7(g) prior to SESAC's receipt of such notice.

(h) Except as expressly provided for in this Agreement, WRITER shall not be entitled to any share whatsoever of any monies received by SESAC from any source.

## 8. TERM OF AGREEMENT; TERMINATION

(a) The term of this Agreement shall be for a period of three (3) years commencing as of the date set forth in paragraph 1 of this Agreement and shall automatically be renewed for successive consecutive periods of three (3) years each upon all of the same terms and conditions (the initial three (3)-year period and each three (3)-year renewal period being hereinafter referred to individually and in the aggregate as the "TERM").

(b) Either party may terminate the TERM of this Agreement upon written notice to the other party received not less than ninety (90) days, nor greater than one hundred eighty (180) days prior to the expiration of the then-current TERM. Such termination shall be effective at the end of the then-current TERM during which notice of termination is given.

(c) SESAC may also terminate this Agreement at any time upon thirty (30) days' prior written notice if:

    (i) WRITER shall make an assignment for the benefit of creditors, or a voluntary or involuntary petition in bankruptcy shall be filed by or against WRITER; or

    (ii) WRITER, during any eight (8) consecutive quarters has not been entitled to receive any monies under this Agreement; or

(iii) SESAC, during any eight (8) consecutive quarters, is unable to contact WRITER by giving notice in accordance with paragraph 15(d) of this Agreement; or

(iv) WRITER shall, without the written consent of SESAC, purport to assign to any other PERSON any of the rights granted by WRITER to SESAC under this Agreement, except as expressly provided in this Agreement; or

(v) WRITER shall engage in the business of printing or publishing lyrics or music for other writers on any financial basis whereby such writers pay WRITER for those services prior to publication, it being understood that nothing in this Agreement shall preclude WRITER from obtaining employment by or establishing a bona fide music publishing company.

## 9. RETENTION OF RIGHTS

(a) In the event the TERM of this Agreement is terminated under paragraph 8 of this Agreement, WRITER'S WORKS shall continue to be subject to this Agreement for a period ending on the last day of the fourth calendar quarter following the calendar quarter in which such termination is effective (the "RETENTION PERIOD"). At the end of the RETENTION PERIOD, any of WRITER'S WORKS which are not then published by a SESAC AFFILIATE publisher shall no longer be subject to the Agreement. Those of WRITER'S WORKS which are then published by a SESAC AFFILIATE publisher shall continue to be subject to this Agreement for the duration and pursuant to the terms of the Publisher Affiliation Agreement between SESAC and that SESAC AFFILIATE publisher, including any renewals or extensions of that agreement. During that period, WRITER shall continue to receive any and all payments to which WRITER may become due under paragraph 7 of this Agreement as if this Agreement were still in full force and effect.

(b) Notwithstanding any other provision of this Agreement to the contrary, it is expressly acknowledged by WRITER that any grant of rights by SESAC under any and all licenses for use of WRITER'S WORKS (including BLANKET LICENSES) issued by SESAC to any PERSON pursuant to this Agreement shall be valid and binding upon WRITER for the full term of each and every such license and that each and every such license shall survive the termination of this Agreement in accordance with the respective terms of such licenses.

## 10. INDEMNITY

(a) WRITER shall and hereby does indemnify, protect, defend, save and hold SESAC, its shareholders, directors, officers, employees, and agents, and SESAC's subsidiaries and affiliated companies and their respective assignees, nominees, licensees, the advertisers of its licensees, and their respective shareholders, directors, officers, employees, and agents free and harmless of and from any and all liability, loss, damage, cost or expense, including without limitation attorneys' fees, arising out of (i) any claim arising out of any breach or alleged breach of any of WRITER'S warranties, representations, undertakings or covenants contained in this Agreement, or by reason of any action, suit or other proceeding, (each being hereinafter referred to as an "ACTION") asserted or instituted as a result of such breach; or (ii) any claim by any third PERSON arising out of SESAC's exercise of the rights granted by WRITER to SESAC under this Agreement (any such claim being hereinafter referred to as a "CLAIM"). WRITER shall reimburse SESAC, on demand, for any payment made by SESAC at any time after the effective date of this Agreement with regard to any liability to which the foregoing indemnity applies. This indemnity shall survive the termination of the TERM of this Agreement for any reason.

(b) If SESAC is entitled to indemnification under paragraph 10(a) of this Agreement, SESAC shall give WRITER prompt written notice of the CLAIM or CLAIMS subject to indemnification. WRITER shall cooperate with SESAC by making available all necessary records and other data and by performing such other acts as SESAC may reasonably require. WRITER shall have the right to (i) participate in the defense or disposition of any CLAIM and (ii) to the extent WRITER desires to do so, to assume the defense of any CLAIM by giving prompt written notice of such election to SESAC (provided that SESAC, at its option, shall have the right to continue to participate in the defense), and in either case the fees and expenses of attorneys and others retained by WRITER shall be borne exclusively by WRITER.

## 11. SESAC'S RIGHT TO PROTECT WRITER'S WORKS

(a) WRITER grants to SESAC the non-exclusive right, without any obligation on the part of SESAC to exercise such right, to enforce, protect and defend all rights granted to SESAC under this Agreement in WRITER'S WORKS including, without limitation, the right to prevent and enjoin infringement of the copyright in any of WRITER'S WORKS. SESAC may exercise or refrain from the exercise of the rights granted to it under this paragraph 11(a) as SESAC in its judgment may determine. If SESAC exercises such right, SESAC may join such others, including WRITER, as SESAC in its judgment may deem advisable as parties plaintiff or defendant in any ACTION in connection with such exercise. WRITER, at WRITER'S sole expense, shall have the right to participate with SESAC in the prosecution or defense (as the case may be) of any ACTION.

(b) If there is any recovery from any ACTION under paragraph 11(a), SESAC, after deducting all of SESAC'S expenses of the ACTION (including without limitation, attorneys' fees, attorneys' expenses and court costs), shall pay fifty (50%) percent of the amount recovered in respect of WRITER'S WORKS to WRITER, WRITER'S SESAC AFFILIATE co-writers, if any, and WRITER'S SESAC AFFILIATE publisher or publishers in the same proportion as the shares of royalties payable to those parties as set forth on the index form covering that WRITER'S WORK. If SESAC's expenses in any ACTION shall exceed the amount of recovery from that ACTION, or if SESAC is unsuccessful in any ACTION, then, without limiting any of SESAC's other rights and remedies, any expenses of that ACTION not so recovered may be recouped, in the same proportion as set forth in the preceding sentence, from monies due or which become due to WRITER, WRITER'S SESAC AFFILIATE co-writers, if any, and WRITER'S SESAC AFFILIATE publisher or publishers. If the ACTION which gave rise to the recovery involved WRITER'S WORKS and the WORKS of other writers, then the recovery as to each WORK (including each WRITER'S WORK) shall be prorated such that each WORK (including each WRITER'S WORK) is allocated an equal amount of the recovery and the costs of the ACTION.

## 12. POWER OF ATTORNEY

WRITER irrevocably constitutes and appoints SESAC, or its nominee, as WRITER'S true and lawful attorney to do all acts and things, and to make, sign, execute, acknowledge and deliver any and all licenses, instruments, papers, documents, process or pleadings which in SESAC's judgment may be desirable to exploit, enforce, protect or defend any of the rights granted by WRITER to SESAC under this Agreement, to restrain infringements, or to recover damages or to settle, compromise and give a release in respect of any infringement or violation of any such rights upon such terms and conditions as SESAC shall in its judgment deem reasonable and proper.

## 13. SESAC'S JUDGMENT OR DETERMINATION

The judgment or determination of SESAC as to all matters stated in this Agreement to be within SESAC's judgment or determination shall be sole, absolute, final and non-appealable.

## 14. DEFINITIONS

(a) "AFFILIATE" shall mean any PERSON who is a party to a SESAC Writer Affiliation Agreement or to a SESAC Publisher Affiliation Agreement.

(b) "BLANKET LICENSE" shall mean a license issued by SESAC to any PERSON which allows such PERSON to PERFORM PUBLICLY any or all of the WORKS, including WRITER'S WORKS, as to which SESAC has been granted the right to PERFORM PUBLICLY.

(c) "PERFORM PUBLICLY" shall mean to render, play, or display a WORK, either directly or by means of any device or process now known or hereafter invented or discovered, at a place open to the public or at any place where a substantial number of persons outside of a normal circle of a family and its social acquaintances is gathered, or to transmit or otherwise communicate a rendition, playing or display of any WORK to such a place or to the public, by means of any device or process, now known or hereafter invented or discovered, whether the members of the public capable of receiving such rendition, playing or display receive it in the same place or in separate places and at the same time or at different times, it being the intention of the parties that this term shall at all times have the full meaning given to it under the United States Copyright Act, Title 17 U.S.C., as amended from time to time.

(d) "PERSON" shall mean any individual, corporation, partnership, association, joint-stock company, trust, unincorporated organization, governmental unit or political subdivision thereof, or any other legal entity.

(e) "WORKS" shall include all musical works, musical compositions and other works with music, dramatico-musical works, individual selections, fragments and arrangements from dramatico-musical works, and all arrangements, adaptations, versions, editions and translations of any or all of the foregoing whether published or unpublished, printed or in manuscript or any other form, mechanical or otherwise, and whether or not statutory United States copyright has been secured in same, including the titles, texts, librettos, words and music of each.

(f) "WRITER'S WORKS" shall include all WORKS which (i) WRITER, now and hereafter during the Term of this Agreement, either alone, jointly or in collaboration with any other PERSON, writes, composes, creates, in whole or in part, under WRITER'S name or any other name; and (ii) WRITER, prior to the effective date of this Agreement has, either alone, jointly or in collaboration with any other PERSON, written, composed, created, in whole or in part, under WRITER'S name or any other name, except those WORKS, if any, as to which there is an outstanding grant of the right to PERFORM PUBLICLY to a person other than a SESAC AFFILIATE publisher, it being understood that at the expiration of such grant as to each such WORK, the right to PERFORM PUBLICLY such WORK shall be deemed granted to SESAC under this Agreement, and WRITER shall cause each such WORK to be published by a SESAC AFFILIATE publisher.

## 15. MISCELLANEOUS

(a) <u>Binding Agreement; Assignment</u>. This Agreement shall be binding upon and inure to the benefit of the respective parties hereto, their legal representatives, successors and assigns; provided however, that the assignment by WRITER of this Agreement or any interest in this Agreement, or of any monies due or to become due under this Agreement, without the prior written consent of SESAC, shall be void.

(b) <u>Entire Agreement</u>. This Agreement sets forth the entire agreement of the parties with respect to its subject matter and supersedes any and all prior understandings between the parties regarding its subject matter, whether oral or written. This Agreement may not be canceled, modified, altered or amended except in a writing signed by both parties. No waiver by either party of any provision of, or default under, this Agreement shall affect that party's rights thereafter to enforce such provision or to exercise any right or remedy in the event of any other default whether or not similar. All rights and remedies of either party contained in this Agreement shall be cumulative and none shall be in limitation of any other right or remedy of either party.

(c) Governing Law; Jurisdiction. This Agreement shall be governed by and construed in accordance with the laws of the State of New York applicable to agreements made and to be performed wholly in that State without regard to that State's internal conflicts of law. The state and federal courts having jurisdiction over New York County, New York shall have exclusive jurisdiction over this Agreement and any controversies arising out of this Agreement shall be brought by the parties to the Supreme Court of the State of New York, County of New York or to the United States District Court to the Southern District of New York and they hereby grant jurisdiction to such court(s) and to any appellate courts having jurisdiction over appeals from such courts.

(d) Notices. Any and all notices which either party may be required or may wish to give to the other under this Agreement shall be in writing and shall be sent to the party to be notified at their address first set forth above, by certified mail, return receipt requested. Notices shall be deemed received three (3) business days following the date of mailing. Each party shall notify the other in writing of any change of address. Any notification sent by SESAC to WRITER'S address set forth above or in the notification of change of address last received by SESAC prior to the mailing of such notification shall be deemed sufficient and effective.

(e) Survival of Warranties. All of WRITER'S warranties, representations, undertakings and covenants contained in this Agreement shall survive the termination of the TERM of this Agreement.

(f) Severability. If any provision of this Agreement shall be deemed invalid or illegal for any reason whatsoever by a court of competent jurisdiction then, notwithstanding such invalidity or illegality, the remaining provisions of this Agreement shall remain in full force and effect in the same manner as if the invalid or illegal provisions had not been contained in this Agreement.

(g) Captions. Captions and paragraph headings are for convenience only and shall not affect or control the meaning or construction of the provisions of this Agreement.

(h) Acceptance. This Agreement shall not be valid until executed by SESAC's President, SESAC's Vice President or other authorized signatory of SESAC.

IN WITNESS WHEREOF, the parties have caused this Agreement to be executed as of the date and year first above written.

SESAC, INC.

By: _____

Title: _____


WRITER _____

Social Security Number: _____

consideration before agreeing to it. Besides the recommended contract terms mentioned previously in this
chapter, the songwriter should also be certain to check on
these other conditions:

- Once the contract is terminated, will any of your
  songs revert back to you? (As a general rule, the
  songs will remain with the publisher, since over the
  years he has, in essence, paid for them by giving the
  writer a salary.)
- Does your salary remain the same, or does it increase (as it should) with each renewal period?
- If you're given a quota of twelve songs to write for
  the publisher each year and you write twenty, what
  happens to the other eight? May you take those
  tunes to other publishers after you've given your
  publisher first refusal?
- Does the agreement state that the publisher owns all
  of your former songs, meaning those songs that
  were written prior to your signed agreement?
- Can you collaborate with anyone you choose?
  And how is your collaborator's portion of the publishing handled? (Many exclusive agreements state
  that if you're working with a collaborator you
  must make every effort to have your collaborator
  sign his or her publishing over to your publisher.
  Or sometimes the agreement will disallow collaboration with anyone who isn't already signed to your
  publisher.)
- Are options renewed automatically? Or does the
  publisher have to write you a letter prior to the
  actual renewal date informing you of the renewal
  status?
- Does the publisher have the right to sell or assign
  your agreement to a third party?

## Entertainment Attorneys

If you needed a lawyer to handle a divorce case, you wouldn't retain one who was schooled in real estate law. In the same way, when you're seeking an attorney to handle your music business affairs, it behooves you to find an attorney who is knowledgeable about music industry standards and astute at handling contract negotiations for you.

Be aware that an entertainment attorney's clientele will consist of many other music industry personnel. So, many times these attorneys will act in the capacity of an agent by linking songwriters with producers, publishers, artists, and A & R executives. As a result, the songwriter not only retains a legal expert, but often secures a source of influential contacts as well.

# 8

# Wheeling and Dealing

There's no way I'd ever want to be the one to burst anyone's idealistic bubble, but it is a true fact that most people in the music industry are more interested in making money than they are in making music. What's more, they're concerned about making that money for themselves.

So if, through your creative talents, you also plan to accumulate stacks of greenbacks, you should definitely be cognizant of the type of wheeling and dealing you'll have to do and how to scrutinize deals to make the most profitable decisions.

## The Songwriter's Bargaining Tools

When songwriters shop their wares to anyone in the industry, they take along a song and the song's publishing. These are the things that songwriters have to offer, and both can and should be used as bargaining tools.

Some songwriters tend to forget that they have to get

started somewhere, and quite often it takes some heavy bargaining on their part to get that start. As with any other profession, there's little room for hefty demands from the voice of an unknown. And really, why should the songwriter be any different from the A & R executive, producer, artist, manager, or publisher who had to scrape, crawl, and claw their way to the top?

But even while all songwriters do possess the same bargaining tools, it should be noted that every writer's personal situation is different and every writer will be dealing with a different set of people. So songwriters can only go forward armed with information, and then decide on their own whether to turn down or agree to a deal.

To help make that decision an easier one, first evaluate the conditions of a deal and then analyze your own position by asking yourself:

- Where am I in my career?
- Do I need a foot in the door somewhere or have I had a couple of hits?
- Do I have money in the bank to live on?
- Can I really afford to nix this deal and take my chances that someone else will want to cut my song?
- How big is the artist? How big is the producer? Will I be able to place more songs with them in the future?
- Is the record company really behind this project?
- Who needs whom more? Whose name, mine or theirs, carries more weight?
- Has my song been sitting in my desk drawer for five years?
- Will a chance like this ever come around again?

## A Great Song—Bargaining Tool Number 1

As I've mentioned before, there are good songs and then there are great songs. And if you should be clever enough to write a tune that could possibly be one of the top songs of the year, there's a good chance you won't have to endure any bargaining whatsoever.

That's because when most people hear a great song, they know it. It's the sound reminiscent of a Jaguar purring down the boulevard or a fifty-foot yacht starting its engine. In other words, it sounds like a tune that will handsomely increase their income through record sales. And that in itself might be enough of an enticement for them not to get greedy about the song's publishing.

## The Publishing—Bargaining Tool Number 2

A song's publishing is the mega-bargaining tool.

Needless to say, most publishers are going to expect 100 percent of your publishing right off. And if you're in a situation where you can bypass the publisher and head straight for the artist, manager, or producer, you should know that they're apt to actively pursue your publishing, too.

From their side it looks like this: Your song can only go so far without the strength of their names and expertise. For example, if your song is recorded by an unknown artist and produced by an unknown producer, it's unlikely to stride up the charts as far and as quickly as it could with an established artist and producer. That's because along with a known artist and producer come immediate access to radio and an established market and audience. And, in their eyes, that should certainly be worth something to you. Besides, if you're not willing to barter, they can always opt to leave you in a cloud of dust and turn their attentions to a host of other writers who are willing to spread the wealth.

Don't be appalled if any of these individuals asks for 100 percent of your publishing when the bargaining ensues, but do know that most of them will be willing to settle for 50 percent, which is considered a fair and typical arrangement.

If at first you're dead set on retaining your publishing, look at things in black and white before you waive the deal. Sometimes your calculations will prove to you that you can actually make more money by giving up something—as hard as that may be to believe. For instance, say you do relinquish 50 percent of your publishing to a major artist instead of keeping 100 percent and letting an unknown artist take a shot at it. Many times the major artist will sell ten times the amount of records that an unknown would, and in the final analysis that equals more money for you.

The last entity that might try to negotiate with you for publishing is the record company. Here, you have to understand that when a label spends thousands of dollars to make and break a record, it's always a gamble. So they may want a part of the publishing as a way of hedging their risk and securing a nice return on their ante.

But the rule of thumb is that the larger the label, the less likely that they will be interested in the publishing. Many major labels are content with sticking to one thing—selling records—and the publishing won't enter the picture. However, in some instances where the major label has their own affiliated publishing company, they may strongly recommend that a new singer/songwriter work out an in-house deal and give up 50 percent of the publishing to their affiliate. If that situation arises, you'll find that the writer will usually be given a sizeable publishing advance.

Conversely, at an independent label where everything is done under one roof and where there is less capital and consequently fewer records are released, it wouldn't hurt to be prepared to discuss your publishing.

# Writing Credit

It may be somewhat unethical, but it's certainly not unusual that along the way someone will change one line of your song and feel entitled to a part of the writing credit. Remember, though, that if you do turn over a percentage of the writing credit to someone, you're automatically giving that person an equal share of the publishing, too, since he or she is now entitled to it as a co-creator of the song.

# Publishing Administration

The person or company maintaining the publishing administration is responsible for filing the copyright forms, making foreign deals with subpublishers, and handling the day-to-day business of the copyright.

If someone has 100 percent of the publishing, they automatically become the administrator of the publishing. However, if the publishing is split up, an administrator will be designated (usually from among the copyright owners) and will normally receive an extra 10 percent for the work involved.

Some administration deals state that the administrator receives 10 percent of the entire publishing deal (which would be 10 percent of 100 percent), meaning that if you negotiate for a fifty-fifty split with someone who asks for the administration, he'll then be receiving 60 percent, and you'll be left with 40 percent. Therefore, a more typical and fairer resolution, and what you want to aim for, is for the administrator to receive 10 percent of your portion of the publishing. So that, in this case, you only give up another 5 percent (or 10 percent of 50 percent) instead of a full 10 percent.

Along with the administration comes many benefits. First off, the administrator, having full control of the copyright, has the right to grant or to disallow first usage of that particular song. (Remember, the original artist must obtain permission and a license to record a song. Once the song has been released, anyone may record it.) Plus, the proprietor of the administration receives the mechanical royalty money and in turn pays the other publisher and the writer their appropriate percentages. However, if the administrator has incurred telephone or traveling expenses during the administration process, he may take the opportunity to be reimbursed for those costs by taking them from the top of the royalty payments.

Many well-known songwriters who retain the publishing on their songs merely hire the administrative services of a publishing company to handle their administration for an agreed-upon percentage of the writer's gross receipts.

## Advances

If a publisher, producer, artist, or record label has a pretty good idea that they're going to be able to either place or use your song, you may be able to secure an advance from them. But let it be known that 99 percent of the time you're going to have to use the "ask and you might receive" technique. There are few saints out there wanting to give you money that you haven't even asked for. The only time when you might get an advance without requesting it is if you're an established writer. And by that time, you probably won't need the money anyway. Any advances that a songwriter might receive are recoupable against future royalties.

The amount of an advance varies with the songwriter's stature and the quality of the song, so they can commonly range anywhere from $100 to well over $1,000. The "well over $1,000" sector is usually reserved for the songwriter who has had some commercial success in the past.

In a sense, an advance actually makes a deal more binding, and it gives a feeling of security to the parties seated on both sides of the table.

When a publisher hands a songwriter $1,000, the writer feels more certain that the publisher is going to work diligently to see that the song is recorded and released so that the advance money can be recouped.

An advance can also be protection for the publisher in the event that the songwriter becomes displeased with the publisher's effort to work the song. For instance, some writers will attempt to take a publisher to court in an effort to get their song back, saying that they never received money for it and that the publisher didn't give it a decent effort. If the songwriter has been given an advance, there's not much of an argument there.

## Demo Costs

During the time that I was making demos of my songs and handing them over to publishing companies, I was so elated that someone was actually interested that I let that elation pad my ego, while my wallet kept getting thinner and thinner. But after a while I realized that I was spending my hard-to-come-by money on something that was actually the publisher's responsibility. After all, the publisher was using my demos to shop my material, so I was actually saving him the money that he would normally have to lay out on demos. Needless to say, I should have been reimbursed, but going without reimbursement was no one's fault but my own, since I didn't make the move to ask for it.

A good publisher really doesn't expect a songwriter to have funds to go out and make a superior demo. However, if you should make an excellent demo, it is an added incentive for the publisher.

Most commonly, when a songwriter brings demo costs to the attention of the publisher, he or she will negotiate for one of the following arrangements:

1. When the writer takes a demo to the publisher, he or she asks for reimbursement, preferably for 100 percent of the expenses. It's likely that the publisher will view this money as an advance that will enable the writer to move on to demoing his or her next tune. Whatever the case, the publisher will want to recoup that money from any future song earnings, but the writer can always attempt to receive it free and clear.

2. If a writer takes a demo to a publisher and the publisher uses that demo when shopping the song, the writer should certainly be reimbursed for the demo costs. In this instance, it may be that the publisher gives the writer 100 percent of the charges and recoups 50 percent from future song earnings. Or he may try to give the writer only 50 percent of the costs up front by saying that no demo charges will be recouped against the royalties. However, songwriters are wise to work toward getting 100 percent of their costs right off so that in

the event the song never earns any money, they've still gotten their money out of it.

3. It's true that up front the demo is the sole responsibility of the publisher, so if any publisher asks you for 50 percent of the money needed to go into the studio and make a demo, consider it a shady proposition. But you will find that many contracts state that once a song starts making money, the publisher is allowed to recoup 50 percent of the money outlaid to make the demo from those earnings. This is because most publishers feel that if the writer is going to share in the profits, he or she should also be obliged to share in the expenses. However, before the publisher recoups that 50 percent he should present you with an invoice summarizing all of the demo costs so that you can see for yourself just what your half of the debt is.

## Time Reversion Clauses

No matter what, a songwriter should always try to safeguard his or her song by requesting that some type of reversion clause be included in the contract.

A time reversion clause limits the time a publisher has to get your song recorded and released. During that time period, the publisher retains all of the publishing and the rights that go with it. If the song is not recorded and released within the specified time frame, the song reverts back to you, the songwriter. It should be noted that most time reversion clauses deal with a term of one to two years.

There are also variations that stem from the time reversion clause. For example, you could make a deal where you turn over 100 percent of your publishing with the stipulation that 50 percent will come back to you after a designated period of time. Yet another possibility is to make a deal where publishing revenue is extended to someone for their specific version of the song and not for any subsequent versions. This is normally done when the original publisher is asked for a piece of the publishing by another individual.

## Reversions with Bumpers

There's another angle on the time reversion clause which is called a bumper, and it seems to cover everyone's best interests.

The bumper is outlined in the SGA songwriter contract and others as well, and states that the publisher has a specified number of years to get a song recorded and released. After that time has expired, he has the option of giving the songwriter an agreed-upon sum of money in order to be able to retain the song for an additional period of time.

To a songwriter, a year may seem like forever, but in all honesty one and a half to two years is fair, and according to most publishers is a short amount of time to get a song recorded and released. Besides, a publisher may get a song recorded right off the bat, but because of a record company's schedule or the artist's wishes, the record may not be released promptly or as planned. Since the publisher has no control over the record's release date, he shouldn't be penalized.

From a producer's standpoint, I could see that if a publisher brought me a song today and I really wanted to record that song, I couldn't possibly fit it into my schedule for the next six months. Now if the publisher was bound to a contract containing a one-year time reversion clause and had already used up four months shopping the tape before he stumbled upon me, there'd only be two months left to get the song recorded and released—which is cutting it close. But with a bumper, the publisher could buy more time, if needed, in order to complete the deal.

## Minimum Earnings Clause

If a songwriter has a good reputation, or has a great song and a lot of guts, he or she may try to go one step beyond the time reversion clause and request that a minimum earnings clause also be included in the contract.

Like the time reversion clause, the minimum earnings clause states that a song reverts back to a writer if the publisher doesn't get the song recorded and released within a certain period of time. But additionally, this clause provides that the writer must earn a certain amount of money from the tune within the specified time period.

Using arbitrary numbers, let's say a contract states that the publisher must get a song recorded and released in two and a half years and the songwriter must earn $5,000 from the song during that time frame. Now, if the song is released, yet doesn't generate that much income within two and half years, the publisher may either pay the writer $5,000 of his own money (if he really wants to hang on to the song), or he must return the ownership of the song to the writer.

You'll note that the time period that's agreed upon in a minimum earnings clause is usually longer than that in a simple time reversion clause. This is because not only does the publisher have to get the song recorded and released, but there also has to be enough time for the song to generate income. Remember that when a song is played on the radio, no one sees any money the very next day.

Performance royalties are paid to writers quarterly, and mechanical royalties are normally paid semiannually by publishers. Considering the delays and all the things that could possibly go wrong, it's easy to see that it could be some time before the writer sees his or her first check.

Basically, the minimum earnings clause gives added protection to the writer. With a simple reversion clause, the publisher is only bound to get a song recorded and released within a designated period of time. So to live up to that condition and beat the deadline, he could essentially go about things halfheartedly and have the song recorded by a bunch of amateurs. Once the song was released, it probably wouldn't do so well or generate much money, but the publisher could still keep the song and get it recorded at a later date. With the minimum earnings clause, the songwriter is guaranteed a sum of money or has the recourse of taking the song back.

## Buybacks

When John Lennon was alive, he and Paul McCartney, as you've probably heard or read about, were trying to buy back ownership of the songs they wrote together. Over the years, McCartney has been fairly successful in getting some of his songs back, but because of the high revenues these songs generate, he has had to pay some exorbitant prices.

If you're a prolific writer or a singer/songwriter who plans to follow in the footsteps of talents like Lennon and McCartney, protect your future at the inception of your career. Ask that your publishing contract include an option that will allow you to buy back your songs, if you choose, in an agreed-upon number of years for an agreed-upon amount of money. In the beginning, when no money has been earned, the publisher is more likely to agree to this option and set a more reasonable buyback price on your songs.

Buybacks come in other forms, too. For example, if a publisher has had your song for two to three years and hasn't been able to generate any interest in it, yet you locate an interested party, you may be able to buy your song back. The price will probably be determined by the total expenses the publisher has incurred in phone calls, travel, tape costs, and so forth while working your song over that period of time.

So let's say the publisher's expenses come to $3,000. You can then go back to your interested party and tell him that the song and publishing can be his if he pays that sum to the publisher. This party might figure that even if the song is used as an album cut, it will generate more than that amount in mechanical royalties and he will, therefore, agree to pay that price.

If you have a major artist interested in your song, you may even want to put up the $3,000 yourself, figuring that even if the artist demands 50 percent of the publishing, you could still come out ahead.

## Cross-Collateralization

One sunny day you take two songs to a publisher. The first is entitled "Nowhere Highway," the other "Soaring Love." The publisher is crazy about both of them and gives you $500 advances for each of your songs. So, in your delight, you eagerly sign the contracts. But once you get home, you notice something in the contracts about "cross-collateralization." You also notice that your world is clouding over.

Cross-collateralization means that the publisher has

the right to recoup monies spent on your lost-cause song from the earnings of your successful song. Say the publisher pours $10,000 into "Nowhere Highway" while working the song, yet it never gets anywhere and doesn't earn a nickel. "Soaring Love," on the other hand, gets recorded and released and starts zooming up the charts without much help or money from the publisher. With the cross-collateralization clause, you won't see a penny from "Soaring Love" until the day that the publisher has recouped the $10,000 that he lost on "Nowhere Highway."

Songwriters should always have their eyes open for a clause of this nature in their contracts, because it's something they never want to agree to. If you're dealing with master tapes, you should be aware that record companies, too, may try to slip in a cross-collateralization clause in order to recoup monies lost on one record against the earnings of another record.

## Finding Financial Backing

Although this chapter has dealt with how to get the most money out of a deal, I realize that there may also be times when you need to find some money to complete a project, or just to live on in between projects.

There are a couple of sources the songwriter can attempt to tap for cash.

### Investors

There are always people who want to invest their money or find a tax shelter, though it may not seem that way when you set out looking for them. Most often, songwriters will try to find this type of investor when they plan to make a master recording, which usually runs into thousands of dollars.

But why would someone want to give you $4,000 or so to make a master? Because in return you're going to give them a piece of the publishing or a point on your record. (A point is equal to one percent of the suggested retail list price of a record.) Of course, none of that is going to make any sense to someone unfamiliar with the record industry, so it's up to you to explain it thoroughly and convincingly. Dust off your calculator and show them just what their $4,000 investment could possibly yield over the years to come.

By using your publishing as bait, you may be able to lure a publisher into putting up enough money to finance a master of your song, too. In order to do so, you'll have to have all of your ducks in a row. The publisher will certainly want to hear a tape so he can evaluate the artist's potential. Likewise, he'll want to know about the producer and his track record. Regarding the material, is this the only song you're planning to record, or are there others? What about the musicians? Have they ever played on a hit record before? What studio do you plan to book and what do you foresee as the total expenditure? If the publisher likes the answers you give him and believes the song has great potential, then he might take you up on it.

## Banks

Just like a car or home, a song's copyright can actually be put up as collateral in order to obtain a loan. For example, if you're the copyright owner of a song that consistently generates $100,000 in publishing income each year, there are banks that will gladly allow you to secure a loan. If you renege on the loan, the copyright ownership will transfer to the bank.

The problem is, most banks aren't knowledgeable about song copyrights and publishing, and don't always realize their worth. Banks in major music cities like New York, Los Angeles, or Nashville might be more inclined to secure a loan based on a song's copyright. However, at many banks across America, you'll probably have to be prepared to educate the loan officers, or give them enough time to research the matter for themselves.

# 9

# How Your Songs Earn Money

Now that you're aware of who's involved in getting your song recorded and released, it's time to get down to the nitty-gritty and find out how your song can earn you money.

A musical copyright has four basic sources of income. Once your song has been recorded and released, it can generate money from: performance royalties, mechanical royalties, synchronization, and printed editions royalties, all of which are discussed in this chapter. As an aside, you should also know that a song might earn money from grand rights (theatrical licensing) and specific rights such as use in a jingle, greeting card, or pinball machine.

## Performance Royalties

### What Is a Performing Right?

Under the U.S. Copyright Act, a performing right is a right granted to copyright owners of musical works which allows them to license their works for public performance. In other words, since the right to publicly perform a musical work is exclusive to the copyright owner, anyone who wishes to publicly perform that work must obtain the copyright owner's permission, called a license. In most cases, failure to obtain licensing would constitute an infringement of the copyright.

## The Performing Rights Organizations

The three performing rights organizations in the United States—also referred to as clearance agencies—are the American Society of Composers, Authors and Publishers (ASCAP), Broadcast Music, Incorporated (BMI), and SESAC., Inc., formerly called the Society of European Stage Authors and Composers. These organizations license copyrighted musical works for their members or affiliates (the copyright owners) to those music users who wish to publicly perform the copyrighted compositions.

Since the term "public performance" encompasses live and broadcast performances, music users may include radio stations, network TV, cable TV, hotels, restaurants, airlines, discos, spas, roller-skating rinks, concert halls, wired music services—in short, wherever music is being performed live or broadcast in some manner.

Basically, what happens is this: The performing rights organizations acquire certain rights from songwriters and music publishers which permit them, in turn, to license a nondramatic public performance of a composition to music users. Because of the broad number of songs and music users, individual tunes and performances aren't licensed separately. Rather, the music user pays the performing rights organization a blanket license fee which entitles them to use the organization's entire repertory of songs as often as they wish.

The amount of a license fee is negotiable and is usually

tailored to a music user's particular circumstances and intentions for use. Overall, though, the fees for radio and TV broadcasters are generally based on gross income, while the fees for nightclubs, hotels, restaurants, and so on are determined by such factors as the facility's seating capacity, cover charge, and yearly entertainment budget. Theoretically, all of the license fees paid to a performing rights organization are pooled, and it's from that central fund that monies are broken down and performance royalties are distributed to the organization's publisher and writer affiliates.

In general, performance royalty payments are based on how often a song is performed. However, because of the vast number of music users, it's virtually impossible for the performing rights organizations to monitor each user individually on a daily basis. As a result, the organizations have been forced to develop intricate sampling techniques to determine the number of performances. The sampling techniques utilized are unique to each organization and will be discussed below.

But just to give you a basic idea of how some performances are monitored, let's say that in order to determine radio performances, a performing rights organization chooses a cross section of stations to represent the entire country. What's more, these stations might be further weighed according to whether the broadcast was AM or FM, network or local. That means a songwriter–publisher team with a national Top 10 hit could split more than $100,000 in performance royalties, that figure being higher or lower depending on the longevity of the song's popularity. Yet if the same team had a song that was only considered a hit on local stations, it might not generate any performance royalties whatsoever because those local stations might not ever turn up in the performing rights organizations' samples.

## Affiliation with a Performing Rights Organization

Performing rights organizations are voluntary organizations; publishers and songwriters are not compelled to join. But you can easily see that with over 8,000 radio stations and 750 TV stations, not to mention an enormous list of hotels, nightclubs, roller-skating rinks, restaurants, and so forth, an individual who is not affiliated with a performing rights organization could have an impossible time trying to license music users, collect license fees, and monitor a song's performances.

Songwriters may only affiliate with one of the three performing rights organizations at a time, but are permitted to collaborate with writers who are affiliated with either of the other organizations.

On the other hand, publishers may and usually do have multiple affiliations. However, each affiliation must be set up under a different company name, and these companies are usually operated as subsidiaries of the parent company. For example, Shapiro, Bernstein & Co., Inc., is known throughout the industry by that name, and that company happens to be their ASCAP-affiliated enterprise. Yet they've also established a company known as Painted Desert for their BMI affiliation. With multiple affiliations, the publisher can readily accept songs from writers who are affiliated with either ASCAP, BMI, or SESAC. And this is something they must do, since in order to receive performance royalties both the publisher and writer must be affiliated with the same performing rights organization.

Performance royalties are divided fifty-fifty between the publisher and songwriter. The performing rights organization sends checks for the respective shares directly to the writer and publisher.

These organizations are always on the lookout for new

writers, and you'll find they'll even engage in recruitment campaigns at certain times. They can be an invaluable source of information for writers, but before signing a contract with any of the three organizations, you should call or write to each to obtain literature and answers to your specific questions. Most importantly, if it's at all possible, you should visit their offices and meet the people who work there. Find out on a firsthand basis where you'll be the most contented and which organization seems better equipped to meet your individual needs and aspirations as a songwriter.

## ASCAP

Headquarters:    1 Lincoln Plaza
New York, NY 10023
(212) 621-6000

Membership       7920 Sunset Boulevard
Offices:         Los Angeles, CA 90046
(213) 883-1000

2 Music Square West
Nashville, TN 37203
(615) 742-5000

Kingsbury Center
350 West Hubbard Street
Chicago, IL 60610
(312) 527-9775

52 Haymarket
London SW1 Y4RP England
011-44-71-973-0069

First National Bank Building
1519 Ponce De Leon Avenue
Santurce, Puerto Rico 00910
(809) 725-1688

The American Society of Composers, Authors and
Publishers (ASCAP) was formed in 1914 by a group of
songwriters (two of whom were John Philip Sousa and
Victor Herbert) so that "creators of music would be paid
for the public performances of their works, and users
(licensees) could comply with the Federal Copyright
Law."

ASCAP's distinction lies not only in being the oldest
performing rights licensing organization in the United
States, but also in standing alone as the only performing
rights organization owned and operated solely by its
writer and publisher members. All members with ASCAP
earnings are given the opportunity to elect the organization's Board of Directors, which, needless to say, consists only of composers, lyricists (authors), and music
publishers.

ASCAP has been a leader in protecting the interests of
American songwriters both at home and abroad, and as a
part of their regular services they provide seminars, workshops, and showcases for their writers.

ASCAP functions as a nonprofit organization, meaning that, after collecting licensing fees, money is deducted
for the organization's operating expenses, and the balance
is distributed to its writers and publishers. The organization provides full financial disclosure to its members and
to the public on an annual basis. And it's estimated that
approximately eighty cents out of every dollar ASCAP
receives is paid out to members each year. Additionally,
ASCAP's annual revenues from licensing of music users

are greater than those of any other performing rights organization.

Performance royalty checks from ASCAP are issued
seven times a year for writer members. Four of these
distributions cover domestic performances, and the other
three distributions cover foreign performances. There are
also seven distributions for publishers.

To determine how revenues will be distributed to its
members, ASCAP surveys all licensees (radio, television,
wired music services, and other music users) and notes
and logs the number of performances of a song. Each
licensee is placed into a particular music-user category,
and revenues from each category are distributed based on
the performances by licensees within each category. Thus
local television revenues are distributed on the basis of
local television performances, local radio revenues are
based on local radio performances, and so on.

ASCAP uses a census survey to get a full count of all
performances on network television (namely, ABC, NBC,
CBS, plus HBO), some wired music services, and some
nonbroadcast, nonconcert licensees. Sample surveys are
used to determine performances on radio stations, local
television stations, cable stations, Muzak, and public
broadcasting services.

When an ASCAP performance is picked up in an
ASCAP survey, a certain number of credits are generated.
Basically, for broadcast surveys, the number of credits
will vary as to the medium in which the work is performed
(local radio, network television, etc.), the type of use (featured, background, etc.), and the station weight of the
station airing the performance. These credits are then
given a dollar value which is determined by dividing the
total number of ASCAP credits being processed into the
total number of dollars available for distribution.

More specifically, ASCAP surveys performances

made by broadcasters, who represent the largest category of their music users, as follows:

**Network Television.** ASCAP is able to count all music performances on network television (ABC, NBC, CBS, plus HBO) with program logs (lists of performances) and cue sheets (which represent music used in film) furnished by the networks and program producers. Additionally, ASCAP makes its own audio- and videotapes of the network television performances to verify the accuracy of this information.

**Local Television.** With over 126,000 hours of local commercial television performances, ASCAP must sample cue sheets, tapes, and regional issues of *TV Guide* to determine what ASCAP works are being performed.

**Radio Stations.** Because of the great number of radio stations, ASCAP uses a sampling technique to track song performances aired on radio. This is done by taping sixty thousand hours of radio play each year from a representative class of both AM and FM stations which are ASCAP licensees. This amount, considered to be statistically representative by their independent survey experts, has been approved by the U.S. Department of Justice. The performances of ASCAP works are then identified by specialists at the New York headquarters.

The entire process of monitoring performances is carried out confidentially, and neither the stations nor any ASCAP board member or management member has prior knowledge as to which stations are being taped and monitored.

Songwriters may join ASCAP as either full writer members or associate members. For a full writer membership, a writer needs to have a copyrighted work that's been either commercially recorded or performed in a medium licensed by ASCAP, or a musical composition for which sheet music has been made available. Associate writer memberships are open to those writers who have had at least one work registered with the Copyright Office. Publisher memberships are available to any firm or individual regularly engaged in the publishing business. No initiation fees are required. Annual dues for full writer members are $10, and $50 for publishers.

## BMI

| | |
|---|---|
| Main Office: | 320 West 57th Street<br>New York, NY 10019<br>(212) 586-2000 |
| Major Offices: | 8730 Sunset Boulevard<br>Third Floor West<br>Los Angeles, CA 90069<br>(213) 659-9109 |
| | 10 Music Square East<br>Nashville, TN 37203<br>(615) 259-3625 |
| | 79 Harley House<br>Marylebone Road<br>London NW1 5HN England<br>011-44-71-935-8517 |

About six hundred enterprises, most of which are engaged in broadcasting, came together to form Broadcast Music, Incorporated (BMI) in 1940. Their purpose in

**1986–1995**
**ASCAP**

### Agreement Between

**AND**

### American Society

OF

### Composers, Authors & Publishers
### 1 LINCOLN PLAZA
### NEW YORK, N.Y. 10023

AGREEMENT made between the Undersigned (for brevity called *"Owner"*) and the AMERICAN SOCIETY OF COMPOSERS, AUTHORS AND PUBLISHERS (for brevity called *"Society"*), in consideration of the premises and of the mutual covenants hereinafter contained, as follows:

1. The *Owner* grants to the *Society* for the term hereof, the right to license non-dramatic public performances (as hereinafter defined), of each musical work:

Of which the *Owner* is a copyright proprietor; or

Which the *Owner,* alone, or jointly, or in collaboration with others, wrote, composed, published, acquired or owned; or

In which the *Owner* now has any right, title, interest or control whatsoever, in whole or in part; or

Which hereafter, during the term hereof, may be written, composed, acquired, owned, published or copyrighted by the *Owner,* alone, jointly or in collaboration with others; or

In which the *Owner* may hereafter, during the term hereof, have any right, title, interest or control, whatsoever, in whole or in part.

The right to license the public performance of every such musical work shall be deemed granted to the *Society* by this instrument for the term hereof, immediately upon the work being written, composed, acquired, owned, published or copyrighted.

The rights hereby granted shall include:

(a) All the rights and remedies for enforcing the copyright or copyrights of such musical works, whether such copyrights are in the name of the *Owner* and/or others, as well as the right to sue under such copyrights in the name of the *Society* and/or in the name of the *Owner* and/or others, to the end that the *Society* may effectively protect and be assured of all the rights hereby granted.

(b) The non-exclusive right of public performance of the separate numbers, songs, fragments or arrangements, melodies or selections forming part or parts of musical plays and dramatico-musical compositions, the *Owner* reserving and excepting from this grant the right of performance of musical plays and dramatico-musical compositions in their entirety, or any part of such plays or dramatico-musical compositions on the legitimate stage.

(c) The non-exclusive right of public performance by means of radio broadcasting, telephony, "wired wireless," all forms of synchronism with motion pictures, and/or any method of transmitting sound other than television broadcasting.

(d) The non-exclusive right of public performance by television broadcasting; provided, however, that:

(i) This grant does not extend to or include the right to license the public performance by television broadcasting or otherwise of any rendition or performance of (a) any opera, operetta, musical comedy, play or like production, as such, in whole or in part, or (b) any composition from any opera, operetta, musical comedy, play or like production (whether or not such opera, operetta, musical comedy, play or like production was presented on the stage or in motion picture form) in a manner which recreates the performance of such composition with substantially such distinctive scenery or costume as was used in the presentation of such opera, operetta, musical comedy, play or like production (whether or not such opera, operetta, musical comedy, play or like production was presented on the stage or in motion picture form): provided, however, that the rights hereby granted shall be deemed to include a grant of the right to license non-dramatic performances of compositions by television broadcasting of a motion picture containing such composition if the rights in such motion picture other than those granted hereby have been obtained from the parties in interest.

(ii) Nothing herein contained shall be deemed to grant the right to license the public performance by television broadcasting of dramatic performances. Any performance of a separate musical composition which is not a dramatic performance, as defined herein, shall be deemed to be a non-dramatic performance. For the purposes of this agreement, a dramatic performance shall mean a performance of a musical composition on a television program in which there is a definite plot depicted by action and where the performance of the musical composition is woven into and carries forward the plot and its accompanying action. The use of dialogue to establish a mere program format or the use of any non-dramatic device merely to introduce a performance of a composition shall not be deemed to make such performance dramatic.

(iii) The definition of the terms "dramatic" and "non-dramatic" performances contained herein are purely for the purposes of this agreement and for the term thereof and shall not be binding upon or prejudicial to any position taken by either of us subsequent to the term hereof or for any purpose other than this agreement.

(e) The *Owner* may at any time and from time to time, in good faith, restrict the radio or television broadcasting of compositions from musical comedies, operas, operettas and motion pictures, or any other composition being excessively broadcast, only for the purpose of preventing harmful effect upon such musical comedies, operas, operettas, motion pictures or compositions, in respect of other interests under the copyrights thereof; provided, however, that the right to grant limited licenses will be given, upon application, as to restricted compositions, if and when the *Owner* is unable to show reasonable hazards to his or its major interests likely to result from such radio or television broadcasting; and provided further that such right to restrict any such composition shall not be exercised for the purpose of permitting the fixing or regulating of fees for the recording or transcribing of such composition, and provided further that in no case shall any charges, "free plugs", or other consideration be required in respect of any permission granted to perform a restricted composition; and provided further that in no event shall any composition, after the initial radio or television broadcast thereof, be restricted for the purpose of confining further radio or television broadcasts thereof to a particular artist, station, network or program. The *Owner* may also at any time and from time to time, in good faith, restrict the radio or television broadcasting of any composition, as to which any suit has been brought or threatened on a claim that such composition infringes a composition not contained in the repertory of *Society* or on a claim by a non-member of *Society* that *Society* does not have the right to license the public performance of such composition by radio or television broadcasting.

2. The term of this agreement shall be for a period commencing on the date hereof and expiring on the 31st day of December, 1995.

3. The *Society* agrees, during the term hereof, in good faith to use its best endeavors to promote and carry out the objects for which it was organized, and to hold and apply all royalties, profits, benefits and advantages arising from the exploitation of the rights assigned to it by its several members, including the *Owner*, to the uses and purposes as provided in its Articles of Association (which are hereby incorporated by reference), as now in force or as hereafter amended.

4. The *Owner* hereby irrevocably, during the term hereof, authorizes, empowers and vests in the *Society* the right to enforce and protect such rights of public performance under any and all copyrights, whether standing in the name of the *Owner* and/or others, in any and all works copyrighted by the *Owner*, and/or by others; to prevent the infringement thereof, to litigate, collect and receipt for damages arising from infringement, and in its sole judgment to join the *Owner* and/or others in whose names the copyright may stand, as parties plaintiff or defendants in suits or proceedings; to bring suit in the name of the *Owner* and/or in the name of the *Society*, or others in whose name the copyright may stand, or otherwise, and to release, compromise, or refer to arbitration any actions, in the same manner and to the same extent and to all intents and purposes as the *Owner* might or could do, had this instrument not been made.

5. The *Owner* hereby makes, constitutes and appoints the *Society*, or its successor, the *Owner's* true and lawful attorney, irrevocably during the term hereof, and in the name of the *Society* or its successor, or in the name of the *Owner*, or otherwise, to do all acts, take all proceedings, execute, acknowledge and deliver any and all instruments, papers, documents, process and pleadings that may be necessary, proper or expedient to restrain infringements and recover damages in respect to or for the infringement or other violation of the rights of public performance in such works, and to discontinue, compromise or refer to arbitration any such proceedings or actions, or to make any other disposition of the differences in relation to the premises.

6. The *Owner* agrees from time to time, to execute, acknowledge and deliver to the *Society*, such assurances, powers of attorney or other authorizations or instruments as the *Society* may deem necessary or expedient to enable it to exercise, enjoy and enforce, in its own name or otherwise, all rights and remedies aforesaid.

7. It is mutually agreed that during the term hereof the Board of Directors of the *Society* shall be composed of an equal number of writers and publishers respectively, and that the royalties distributed by the Board of Directors shall be divided into two (2) equal sums, and one (1) each of such sums credited respectively to and for division amongst (a) the writer members, and (b) the publisher members, in accordance with the system of distribution and classification as determined by the Classification Committee of each group, in accordance with the Articles of Association as they may be amended from time to time, except that the classification of the *Owner* within his class may be changed.

8. The *Owner* agrees that his classification in the *Society* as determined from time to time by the Classification Committee of his group and/or The Board of Directors of the *Society*, in case of appeal by him, shall be final, conclusive and binding upon him.

The *Society* shall have the right to transfer the right of review of any classification from the Board of Directors to any other agency or instrumentality that in its discretion and good judgment it deems best adapted to assuring to the *Society's* membership a just, fair, equitable and accurate classification.

The *Society* shall have the right to adopt from time to time such systems, means, methods and formulae for the establishment of a member's status in respect of classification as will assure a fair, just and equitable distribution of royalties among the membership.

9. **"Public Performance" Defined.** The term *"public performance"* shall be construed to mean vocal, instrumental and/or mechanical renditions and representations in any manner or by any method whatsoever, including transmissions by radio and television broadcasting stations, transmission by telephony and/or "wired wireless"; and/or reproductions of performances and renditions by means of devices for reproducing sound recorded in synchronism or timed relation with the taking of motion pictures.

10. **"Musical Works" Defined.** The phrase *"musical works"* shall be construed to mean musical compositions and dramatico-musical compositions, the words and music thereof, and the respective arrangements thereof, and the selections therefrom.

11. The powers, rights, authorities and privileges by this instrument vested in the *Society,* are deemed to include the World, provided, however, that such grant of rights for foreign countries shall be subject to any agreements now in effect, a list of which are noted on the reverse side hereof.

12. The grant made herein by the owner is modified by and subject to the provisions of (a) the Amended Final Judgment (Civil Action No. 13-95) dated March 14, 1950 in U. S. A. v. ASCAP as further amended by Order dated January 7, 1960, (b) the Final Judgment (Civil Action No. 42-245) in U. S. A. v. ASCAP, dated March 14, 1950, and (c) the provisions of the Articles of Association and resolutions of the Board of Directors adopted pursuant to such judgments and order.

SIGNED, SEALED AND DELIVERED, on this . . . . . day of . . . . . . . . . . . . . ,
19. . . . . . . . .

*Society*  {  AMERICAN SOCIETY
OF COMPOSERS,
AUTHORS AND
PUBLISHERS

By . . . . . . . . . . . . . . . . . .          *Owner*  {  . . . . . . . . . . . . . . . . . . . . . . . .
President                                      . . . . . . . . . . . . . . . . . . . . . . . .

## FOREIGN AGREEMENTS AT THIS DATE IN EFFECT
(See paragraph 11 of the within agreement)

| COUNTRY | WITH (Name of Firm) | EXPIRES | REMARKS |
|---------|---------------------|---------|---------|
|         |                     |         |         |
|         |                     |         |         |
|         |                     |         |         |
|         |                     |         |         |
|         |                     |         |         |
|         |                     |         |         |
|         |                     |         |         |
|         |                     |         |         |
|         |                     |         |         |
|         |                     |         |         |
|         |                     |         |         |
|         |                     |         |         |
|         |                     |         |         |
|         |                     |         |         |
|         |                     |         |         |
|         |                     |         |         |

25M-3/91-CH

**BMI · 320 West 57th Street, New York, NY 10019 · 212-586-2000 · Telex 127823**

Dear

The following shall constitute the agreement between us:

1. As used in this agreement:

(a) The word "period" shall mean the term from                    to

, and continuing thereafter for additional terms of two years each unless terminated by either party at the end of said initial term or any additional term, upon notice by registered or certified mail not more than six months or less than sixty (60) days prior to the end of any such term.

(b) The word "works" shall mean:

(i) All musical compositions (including the musical segments and individual compositions written for a dramatic or dramatico-musical work) composed by you alone or with one or more collaborators during the period; and

(ii) All musical compositions (including the musical segments and individual compositions written for a dramatic or dramatico-musical work) composed by you alone or with one or more collaborators prior to the period, except those in which there is an outstanding grant of the right of public performance to a person other than a publisher affiliated with BMI.

2. You agree that:

(a) Within ten (10) days after the execution of this agreement you will furnish to us two copies of a completed clearance sheet in the form supplied by us with respect to each work heretofore composed by you which has been published in printed copies or recorded commercially or which is being currently performed or which you consider as likely to be performed.

(b) In each instance that a work for which clearance sheets have not been submitted to us pursuant to sub-paragraph (a) hereof is published in printed copies or recorded commercially or in synchronization with film or tape or is considered by you as likely to be performed, whether such work is composed prior to the execution of this agreement or hereafter during the period, you will promptly furnish to us two copies of a completed clearance sheet in the form supplied by us with respect to each such work.

(c) If requested by us in writing, you will promptly furnish to us a legible lead sheet or other written or printed copy of a work.

3. The submission of clearance sheets pursuant to paragraph 2 hereof shall constitute a warranty by you that all of the information contained thereon is true and correct and that no performing rights in such work have been granted to or reserved by others except as specifically set forth therein in connection with works heretofore written or co-written by you.

4. Except as otherwise provided herein, you hereby grant to us for the period:

(a) All the rights that you own or acquire publicly to perform, and to license others to perform, anywhere in the world, any part or all of the works.

(b) The non-exclusive right to record, and to license others to record, any part or all of any of the works on electrical transcriptions, wire, tape, film or otherwise, but only for the purpose of performing such work publicly by means of radio and television or for archive or audition purposes and not for sale to the public or for synchronization (i) with motion pictures intended primarily for theatrical exhibition or (ii) with programs distributed by means of syndication to broadcasting stations.

(c) The non-exclusive right to adapt or arrange any part or all of any of the works for performance purposes, and to license others to do so.

5. (a) The rights granted to us by sub-paragraph (a) of paragraph 4 hereof shall not include the right to perform or license the performance of more than one song or aria from a dramatic or dramatico-musical work which is an opera, operetta, or musical show or more than five minutes from a dramatic or dramatico-musical work which is a ballet if such performance is accompanied by the dramatic action, costumes or scenery of that dramatic or dramatico-musical work.

(b) You, together with the publisher and your collaborators, if any, shall have the right jointly, by written notice to us, to exclude from the grant made by sub-paragraph (a) of paragraph 4 hereof performances of works comprising more than thirty minutes of a dramatic or dramatico-musical work, but this right shall not apply to such performances from (i) a score originally written for and performed as part of a theatrical or television film, (ii) a score originally written for and performed as part of a radio or television program, or (iii) the original cast, sound track or similar album of a dramatic or dramatico-musical work.

(c) You retain the right to issue non-exclusive licenses for performances of a work or works (other than to another performing rights licensing organization), provided that within ten (10) days of the issuance of such license we are given written notice of the titles of the works and the nature of the performances so licensed by you.

6. (a) As full consideration for all rights granted to us hereunder and as security therefor, we agree to pay to you, with respect to each of the works in which we obtain and retain performing rights during the period:

(i) For performances of a work on broadcasting stations in the United States, its territories and possessions, amounts calculated pursuant to our then current standard practices upon the basis of the then current performance rates generally paid by us to our affiliated writers for similar performances of similar compositions. The number of performances for which you shall be entitled to payment shall be estimated by us in accordance with our then current system of computing the number of such performances.

It is acknowledged that we license the works of our affiliates for performance by non-broadcasting means, but that unless and until such time as feasible methods can be devised for tabulation of and payment for such performances, payment will be based solely on broadcast performances. In the event that during the period we shall establish a system of separate payment for non-broadcasting performances, we shall pay you upon the basis of the then current performance rates generally paid by us to our other affiliated writers for similar performances of similar compositions.

(ii) In the case of a work composed by you with one or more collaborators, the sum payable to you hereunder shall be a pro rata share, determined on the basis of the number of collaborators, unless you shall have transmitted to us a copy of an agreement between you and your collaborators providing for a different division of payment.

(iii) All monies received by us from any performing rights licensing organization outside of the United States, its territories and possessions, which are designated by such performing rights licensing organization as the author's share of foreign performance royalties earned by your works after the deduction of our then current handling charge applicable to our affiliated writers.

(b) We shall have no obligation to make payment hereunder with respect to (i) any performance of a work which occurs prior to the date on which we have received from you all of the information and material with respect to such work which is referred to in paragraphs 2 and 3 hereof, or (ii) any performance as to which a direct license as described in sub-paragraph (c) of paragraph 5 hereof has been granted by you, your collaborator or publisher.

7. We will furnish statements to you at least twice during each year of the period showing the number of performances as computed pursuant to sub-paragraph (a) (i) of paragraph 6 hereof and at least once during each year of the period showing the monies due pursuant to sub-paragraph (a) (iii) of paragraph 6 hereof. Each statement shall be accompanied by payment to you, subject to all proper deductions for advances, if any, of the sum thereby shown to be due for such performances.

8. (a) Nothing in this agreement requires us to continue to license the works subsequent to the termination of this agreement. In the event that we continue to license any or all of the works, however, we shall continue to make payments to you for so long as you do not make or purport to make directly or indirectly any grant of performing rights in such works to any other licensing organization. The amounts of such payments shall be calculated pursuant to our then current standard practices upon the basis of the then current performance rates generally paid by us to our affiliated writers for similar performances of similar compositions. You agree to notify us by registered or certified mail of any grant or purported grant by you directly or indirectly of performing rights to any other performing rights organization within ten (10) days from the making of such grant or purported grant and if you fail so to inform us thereof and we make payments to you for any period after the making of any such grant or purported grant, you agree to repay to us all amounts so paid by us promptly on demand. In addition, if we inquire of you by registered or certified mail, addressed to your last known address, whether you have made any such grant or purported grant and you fail to confirm to us by registered or certified mail within thirty (30) days of the mailing of such inquiry that you have not made any such grant or purported grant, we may, from and after such date, discontinue making any payments to you.

(b) Our obligation to continue payment to you after the termination of this agreement for performances outside of the United States, its territories and possessions shall be dependent upon our receipt in the United States of payments designated by foreign performing rights organizations as the author's share of foreign performance royalties earned by your works. Payment of such foreign royalties shall be subject to deduction of our then current handling charge applicable to our affiliated writers.

(c) In the event that we have reason to believe that you will receive or are receiving payment from a performing rights licensing organization other than BMI for or based on United States performances of one or more of your works during a period when such works were licensed by us pursuant to this agreement, we shall have the right to withhold payment for such performances from you until receipt of evidence satisfactory to us of the amount so paid to you by such other organization or that you have not been so paid. In the event that you have been so paid, the monies payable by us to you for such performances during such period shall be reduced by the amount of the payment from such other organization. In the event that you do not supply such evidence within eighteen (18) months from the date of our request therefor, we shall be under no obligation to make any payment to you for performances of such works during such period.

9. In the event that this agreement shall terminate at a time when, after crediting all earnings reflected by statements rendered to you prior to the effective date of such termination, there remains an unearned balance of advances paid to you by us, such termination shall not be effective until the close of the calendar quarterly period

during which (a) you shall repay such unearned balance of advances, or (b) you shall notify us by registered or certified mail that you have received a statement rendered by us at our normal accounting time showing that such unearned balance of advances has been fully recouped by us.

10.  You warrant and represent that you have the right to enter into this agreement; that you are not bound by any prior commitments which conflict with your commitments hereunder; that each of the works, composed by you alone or with one or more collaborators, is original; and that exercise of the rights granted by you herein will not constitute an infringement of copyright or violation of any other right of, or unfair competition with, any person, firm or corporation. You agree to indemnify and hold harmless us and our licensees from and against any and all loss or damage resulting from any claim of whatever nature arising from or in connection with the exercise of any of the rights granted by you in this agreement. Upon notification to us or any of our licensees of a claim with respect to any of the works, we shall have the right to exclude such work from this agreement and/or to withhold payment of all sums which become due pursuant to this agreement or any modification thereof until receipt of satisfactory written evidence that such claim has been withdrawn, settled or adjudicated.

11.  (a) We shall have the right, upon written notice to you, to exclude from this agreement, at any time, any work which in our opinion (i) is similar to a previously existing composition and might constitute a copyright infringement, or (ii) has a title or music or lyric similar to that of a previously existing composition and might lead to a claim of unfair competition, or (iii) is offensive, in bad taste or against public morals, or (iv) is not reasonably suitable for performance.

(b) In the case of works which in our opinion are based on compositions in the public domain, we shall have the right, upon written notice to you, either (i) to exclude any such work from this agreement, or (ii) to classify any such work as entitled to receive only a fraction of the full credit that would otherwise be given for performances thereof.

(c) In the event that any work is excluded from this agreement pursuant to paragraph 10 or subparagraph (a) or (b) of this paragraph 11, all rights in such work shall automatically revert to you ten (10) days after the date of our notice to you of such exclusion. In the event that a work is classified for less than full credit under sub-paragraph (b) (ii) of this paragraph 11, you shall have the right, by giving notice to us, within ten (10) days after the date of our letter advising you of the credit allocated to the work, to terminate our rights therein, and all rights in such work shall thereupon revert to you.

12.  In each instance that you write, or are employed or commissioned by a motion picture producer to write, during the period, all or part of the score of a motion picture intended primarily for exhibition in theaters, or by the producer of a musical show or revue for the legitimate stage to write, during the period, all or part of the musical compositions contained therein, we agree to advise the producer of the film that such part of the score as is written by you may be performed as part of the exhibition of said film in theaters in the United States, its territories and possessions, without compensation to us, or to the producer of the musical show or revue that your compositions embodied therein may be performed on the stage with living artists as part of such musical show or revue, without compensation to us. In the event that we notify you that we have established a system for the collection of royalties for performance of the scores of motion picture films in theaters in the United States, its territories and possessions, we shall no longer be obligated to take such action with respect to motion picture scores.

13.  You make, constitute and appoint us, or our nominee, your true and lawful attorney, irrevocably during the term hereof, in our name or that of our nominee, or in your name, or otherwise, to do all acts, take all proceedings, execute, acknowledge

and deliver any and all instruments, papers, documents, process or pleadings that may be necessary, proper or expedient to restrain infringement of and/or to enforce and protect the rights granted by you hereunder, and to recover damages in respect to or for the infringement or other violation of the said rights, and in our sole judgment to join you and/or others in whose names the copyrights to any of the works may stand; to discontinue, compromise or refer to arbitration, any such actions or proceedings or to make any other disposition of the disputes in relation to the works, provided that any action or proceeding commenced by us pursuant to the provisions of this paragraph shall be at our sole expense and for our sole benefit.

14. You agree that you, your agents, employees or representatives will not, directly or indirectly, solicit or accept payment from writers for composing music for lyrics or writing lyrics to music or for reviewing, publishing, promoting, recording or rendering other services connected with the exploitation of any composition, or permit use of your name or your affiliation with us in connection with any of the foregoing. In the event of a violation of any of the provisions of this paragraph 14, we shall have the right, in our sole discretion, by giving you at least thirty (30) days' notice by registered or certified mail, to terminate this agreement. In the event of such termination no payments shall be due to you pursuant to paragraph 8 hereof.

15. No monies due or to become due to you shall be assignable, whether by way of assignment, sale or power granted to an attorney-in-fact, without our prior written consent. If any assignment of such monies is made by you without such prior written consent, no rights of any kind against us will be acquired by the assignee, purchaser or attorney-in-fact.

16. In the event that during the period (a) mail addressed to you at the last address furnished by you pursuant to paragraph 19 hereof shall be returned by the post office, or (b) monies shall not have been earned by you pursuant to paragraph 6 hereof for a period of two consecutive years or more, or (c) you shall die, BMI shall have the right to terminate this agreement on at least thirty (30) days' notice by registered or certified mail addressed to the last address furnished by you pursuant to paragraph 19 hereof and, in the case of your death, to the representative of your estate, if known to BMI. In the event of such termination no payments shall be due you pursuant to paragraph 8 hereof.

17. You acknowledge that the rights obtained by you pursuant to this agreement constitute rights to payment of money and that during the period we shall hold absolute title to the performing rights granted to us hereunder. In the event that during the period you shall file a petition in bankruptcy, such a petition shall be filed against you, you shall make an assignment for the benefit of creditors, you shall consent to the appointment of a receiver or trustee for all or part of your property, or you shall institute or shall have instituted against you any other insolvency proceeding under the United States bankruptcy laws or any other applicable law, we shall retain title to the performing rights in all works for which clearance sheets shall have theretofore been submitted to us and shall subrogate your trustee in bankruptcy or receiver and any subsequent purchasers from them to your right to payment of money for said works in accordance with the terms and conditions of this agreement.

18. Any controversy or claim arising out of, or relating to, this agreement or the breach thereof, shall be settled by arbitration in the City of New York, in accordance with the Rules of the American Arbitration Association, and judgment upon the award of the arbitrator may be entered in any Court having jurisdiction thereof. Such award shall include the fixing of the expenses of the arbitration, including reasonable attorney's fees, which shall be borne by the unsuccessful party.

19. You agree to notify our Department of Performing Rights Administration promptly in writing of any change in your address. Any notice sent to you pursuant to the terms of this agreement shall be valid if addressed to you at the last address so furnished by you.

20. This agreement cannot be changed orally and shall be governed and construed pursuant to the laws of the State of New York.

21. In the event that any part or parts of this agreement are found to be void by a court of competent jurisdiction, the remaining part or parts shall nevertheless be binding with the same force and effect as if the void part or parts were deleted from this agreement.

Very truly yours,
BROADCAST MUSIC, INC.

ACCEPTED AND AGREED TO:

By . . . . . . . . . . . . . . . . . . . . . . . . . . . . . . . .
                    Vice President
. . . . . . . . . . . . . . . . . . . . . . . . . . . . . . . .

5/81

founding the organization was to "provide a competitive source of music licensing in the United States."

At the time that BMI was founded, the combined works of approximately 150 publishers and 1,000 writers were the only works available in the U.S. through the existing performing rights organizations, and this reper-tory was almost entirely exclusive of music genres like country and rhythm and blues, which were growing in popularity around the country. So when BMI proclaimed an "open door" policy to all types of music, writers and publishers of all types of works felt encouraged to join the organization and were finally able to receive royalties for the performances of their works. Thus BMI has grown quickly over the past five decades and now has a larger number of publisher and writer affiliates than any other performing rights organization.

BMI does not operate for profit; all BMI income is distributed to its affiliates, except for monies set aside for minimal operating expenses and a small general reserve. From this income, performance royalties for broadcast performances in the U.S. are remitted to affiliates four times a year, and foreign royalty statements are rendered semiannually.

At the time of affiliation, affiliates are given a copy of the BMI payment schedule which describes how royalties are computed, and if there are any revisions made to the payment structure, a revised schedule will follow.

Basically, the money is distributed according to per-formance credits, as reflected in logs which are submitted to BMI from their licensed broadcasting stations. The logs are fed into an elaborate computer system which multi-plies each performance listed by a "factor" which reflects the ratio of the number of stations logged to the number licensed. So if BMI licenses five hundred stations of a certain kind and ten of them were logged during a given time period, every performance of a song listed would be multiplied by fifty performances every time the work appeared in a log.

In monitoring BMI-licensed broadcasters, the organization uses the following sampling techniques:

**Network Television.** The networks provide BMI with daily logs of all music performed.

**Local Television.** To determine performances of BMI works here, the organization has access to cue sheets as well as to computerized data.

**Radio Stations.** Each quarter, a certain number of stations are asked to keep an accurate log of the music they use, hour-by-hour and day-by-day, for a duration of one week. These stations are chosen using scientific measures and represent a cross section of broadcasting activity and geographic area. Once this information has been delivered to BMI from the stations, it's checked, and the song titles and names of writers and publishers are identified by computer.

Communication with the stations to be logged is handled by an independent accounting firm, so until the logs actually arrive at BMI from the stations, BMI personnel have no clue as to which stations will be providing the information.

Writers are welcome to apply for affiliation with BMI if they have a work which is either commercially published or recorded, or is likely to be performed. And writers aren't charged an initiation fee or any dues. Publisher applicants should have some musical compositions being performed or likely to be performed and are charged an application fee of $25. No annual dues are required.

## SESAC

Headquarters:          156 West 56th Street
                       New York, NY 10019
                       (212) 556-3450

Regional Office:       55 Music Square East
                       Nashville, TN 37203
                       (615) 320-0055

SESAC, Inc., established in 1930 by Paul Heinecke, was formerly called the Society of European Stage Authors and Composers because at the time of its founding its catalog consisted mainly of published works from European firms.

In the past, SESAC functioned more as a publisher-oriented organization and was known primarily for its activities in gospel and country music. However, in 1973 SESAC began to affiliate writers directly, and its repertory now includes a diversity of musical genres.

SESAC obtains information on performances of works in its repertory from the following sources, among others: radio playlists, *Billboard Information Network* (computer database), *Radio and Records EZI Street* (computer database), network and cable programming service logs, regional editions of *TV Guide*, *OnSat* (satellite programming guide), cue sheets from television and radio program syndicators, reports from affiliates, the *Neilson Report on Syndicated Television* programs, *TV Data* (computer database), and spot monitoring of radio and television stations.

Points for each type of performance are assigned, totaled, and translated into dollars, and payments are made quarterly to both writer and publisher affiliates. Performance points vary according to the place in which the work is performed, e.g., network television or local radio, the type of performance (is the song featured, background music, a theme or jingle), duration, and time of day (prime time or non–prime time). Payment for radio perform- ances of hit songs is made under SESAC's unique Chart Payment System. Under this system, points are allocated for the release of a song on a record and its progress up national music publication popularity charts.

Along with the consideration of performance and chart activities, royalty payments are also based on the overall growth and diversity of an affiliate's catalog, and bonuses are awarded for Grammy nominations and the like.

SESAC affiliation is open to any publisher who pub- lishes works written by SESAC writer affiliates. Writers seeking SESAC affiliation may either submit a demo tape of their material, which will be reviewed by the SESAC Screening Committee, or may be given a personal inter- view with a SESAC affiliations representative. In the sec- ond instance, the representative will review the writer's works and outline SESAC's procedures and payment methods, and both parties may determine at that point whether affiliation would be mutually beneficial. There are no initiation fees or dues charged to either writers or publishers.

## Mechanical Royalties

### What Is a Mechanical Right?

Under the U.S. Copyright Act, the copyright owner of a musical work has the right to profit from the mechanical reproduction (use of the song in records, tapes, CDs, electrical transcriptions, and audiotapes for broadcast and background music purposes) of the copyrighted work.

What this means is that for each record or tape sold at retail, the copyright owner is entitled to receive a license fee for the mechanical use of the song on that record or tape. The fees collected from that usage are termed mechanical royalties and are usually collected and distributed by a mechanical rights organization.

The mechanical right is guaranteed under the compulsory licensing provision of the U.S. Copyright Act, which stipulates that after a copyright owner has once given permission for a phonocord to be manufactured and distributed in the U.S., any other person may then obtain a compulsory license to make and distribute phonocords of that musical work. (In essence, this prevents the copyright owner from monopolizing recording of the copyrighted work.) The person who requests a mechanical license of a work must notify the copyright owner and pay the statutory royalty specified for each phonocord manufactured and distributed.

## The Mechanical Royalty Rate

Just to give you a little history, from 1909 to 1978 the mechanical royalty rate per song was two cents. Luckily, due to a provision in the 1976 Copyright Act, songwriters are now getting more than their two cents worth per song. The provision called for a Copyright Royalty Tribunal to review the rate, which they did in 1980 when it was decided that the royalty rate be increased in yearly increments. As it stands currently, the rate is 6.25 cents per song for each copy of a record, tape, or CD distributed or 1.2 cents per minute of playing time. This rate per song will be readjusted in relation to the Consumer Price Index (CPI) every two years until January 1, 1996, and most likely at that time provisions will be set for future readjustments.

In the everyday goings-on of the music industry, it's

common for the copyright owner and licensee to negotiate for a rate lower than the statutory rate. And although the law states that the copyright owners may be paid on copies of phonocords manufactured and distributed, in practice, mechanical royalties are only paid on copies of phonocords that are manufactured and sold. If it were otherwise, there wouldn't be too many record companies left in existence today.

Frequently, record companies (the licensees) only pay 75 percent of the statutory rate on each song. In fact, this is so common that songwriters will find that many publishing contracts will allow for the publisher to enter into a deal with a record company based on 75 percent of the statutory rate. However, if a songwriter with a lot of clout demands that 100 percent of the statutory rate be paid to him or her, then the publisher is bound to pay the writer 100 percent of the rate whether or not he receives that rate in his negotiations with a record label.

## Computing Your Mechanical Royalties

It's easy enough to estimate what your mechanical royalties will be by multiplying the agreed-upon mechanical rate by the number of records, tapes, and CDs sold and dividing by two. For instance, for the sake of simple computation, let's say that you're receiving the full statutory rate of 6.25 cents, and your song was on a record that sold 100,000 copies. The mechanical royalties will be $6,250 (6.25 × 100,000 = $6,250). Remember, though, you'll be splitting that amount in half with your publisher, so you're actually talking about $3,125. Additionally, if the publisher has incurred any expenses on the record or has given you an advance, it's likely he'll deduct these costs from the mechanical royalties before remitting your share to you.

On an album project, a record company is likely to negotiate for an overall mechanical rate rather than negotiating a rate on a per song basis. For example, the record company may say they'll pay 46 cents on each album, tape, or CD sold. If there are eight songs on the album, tape, or CD, this equals a 5 ¾-cent rate per song. So if a writer and publisher had one song on an album project and 100,000 albums, tapes, and CDs were sold, then there will be $5,750 to split before expenses. If the record sold 1,000,000 copies, you're looking at $57,500. And just think—if you have all eight songs on the album, that would come to $46,000 on the sale of 100,000 copies and $460,000 on 1,000,000 copies.

Songwriters are sometimes confused about mechanical royalties because in this difficult business it seems strange that you could actually get paid on a record no one has ever heard. But the fact is, you do receive mechanical royalties on any copy of your song that sells—no matter if it's a little-known cut on an album, tape, CD or not. So while it may hurt your pride to have a song that didn't make it on the airwaves, you can still doctor up your bank account with a nice, unexpected mechanical royalty check.

## Mechanical Rights Organizations

Basically, these organizations grant mechanical licenses to record companies and collect the license fees for the records, tapes, and CDs sold. After deducting their service charge, these fees are paid to their affiliated publishers, who, in turn, pay the writer his or her share of the mechanical royalty income.

Upon the request of affiliated publishers, the mechanical rights organization will also collect synchronization fees for the use of a copyrighted work in motion pictures, television films, and videotapes. (More on synchronization later.)

Like the performing rights organizations, the mechanical rights organizations are totally voluntary services for publishers. These organizations serve as the liaisons between the record manufacturers and publishers, provide for centralized bookkeeping, and relieve the publisher of the paperwork involved in compulsory licensing. Most importantly, with a mechanical rights organization involved, it's a surer bet that everyone is going to get whatever mechanical royalties are due them.

The mechanical rights organization that you'll hear mentioned most often is the Harry Fox Agency, Inc. (205 East 42nd Street, New York, New York 10017), the reason being that to date it represents over 9,700 publishers internationally and is one of the oldest and most creditable mechanical royalty collection agencies in the United States.

For their representation in handling mechanical licensing and collecting fees, the Harry Fox Agency still only charges a commission of $4\frac{1}{2}$ percent for mechanical licensing for records, tapes, and CDs. They'll also handle synchronization licensing upon the request of an affiliated publisher.

Since most record companies do accounts at three-month intervals, with periods ending on March 31, June 30, September 30, and December 31, the Harry Fox Agency remits quarterly royalty payments (around May 15, August 15, November 15, and February 15), but is allowed a forty-five-day period after each quarter in which to prepare statements and draft checks.

The Harry Fox Agency also audits record companies of all sizes at periodic intervals at no extra charge, and will take legal action against a record company, if necessary, after consulting with the publisher involved, as another part of their regular service.

It's a well-known fact that the Harry Fox Agency finds substantial amounts of money each year which record companies were holding in reserve and probably had no intention of paying out. Like a cop walking his beat, this type of agency keeps everyone honest and on their toes.

Other organizations that handle mechanical licensing include:


AMRA (American Mechanical Rights Agency, Inc.)
200 West 20th Street, Ste. 714
New York, NY 10011
(212)/877-4077

CMI (Copyright Management, Inc.)
1102 17th Avenue, South, Ste. 400
Nashville, TN 37212
(615)/327-1517

SESAC, Inc.
156 West 56th Street
New York, NY 10019
(212)/556-3450


# Synchronization

A synchronization right allows for a musical composition to be used in timed relation to a film or videotape. So if a television producer or a film producer wishes to use a previously composed musical work in the soundtrack of a TV show or a motion picture, a synchronization license must be obtained from the copyright owner.

The rate for synchronization licenses is negotiable. The music publisher usually determines this fee based upon such factors as the length of the use, the impact of the song's use (namely, is the song featured or used as background music? are the lyrics used or just the melody?), and the type of medium the song is being used in. Yet another consideration is the territories in which the film or video will appear. For example, if a film producer plans to merchandise his film worldwide, the publisher might restrict the license to the U.S. and Canada, so that the film producer has to acquire separate licenses for the foreign territories.

As mentioned previously, many publishers will enlist the services of their mechanical rights organization in issuing synchronization licenses. And, as discussed in Chapter 7, "Songwriter Contracts," songwriters will want to negotiate for 50 percent of the monies earned from synchronization licensing.

## Printed Editions Royalties

If a song has enjoyed great success, the publisher will attempt to further exploit the song's copyright by making it available to the public in printed editions. Printed editions include printing of the song for sheet music, songbooks, folios, and for stage and marching band arrangements.

If a publisher does put a deal together with an independent sheet music printer, the songwriter should receive the standard percentage of 10 to 15 percent of the retail selling price of each copy of the sheet music sold. If the publisher is able to have the song included in a songbook, the songwriter may either be paid a fixed onetime sum or be given a percentage of the retail selling price of each copy of the songbook that is sold.

# Foreign Subpublishing Deals

It could happen that once your record has been widely accepted in the U.S., or if it has foreign appeal, your publisher will be able to acquire subpublishing deals for the song in foreign territories.

Years ago, it was standard to subpublish a song on a fifty-fifty basis for the life of the copyright. However, that's seldom done today. Usually the original publisher (or U.S. publisher) will license a song to a subpublisher for three to five years, and more commonly the subpublisher will receive a 25 percent share of all income collected on the song in that particular territory. Yet there are still many instances where the division of the income between the original publisher and subpublisher will either increase or decrease depending on the relationship between the two companies and/or the circumstances surrounding the record.

For example, if the companies have an ongoing working relationship and the original publisher knows for a fact that the subpublisher always works material as best he can, the song might be licensed on a fifty-fifty basis. Sometimes, though, if a major artist is involved and the subpublisher needs only to collect income on the song and do little else, the song might be licensed to the subpublisher on a 15 percent basis. And in the extreme case, there are a few huge artists who can actually license a song on a zero-income basis. That is, the only money the subpublisher receives is the interest on the collected territorial income.

Regardless of the subpublishing rate, the original publisher should split the net foreign income equally with the songwriter. As with income earned in the U.S., the mechanical royalty money will be paid to the writer by the publisher, and the performance royalty money will be paid directly to the writer by his or her performing rights organization. In the event that another writer was brought in on the project to write foreign lyrics, it's considered fair for that writer to receive 15 to 25 percent of the writer's share of the performance royalties earned in that territory.

Songwriters should keep in mind that they'll want their publishing contracts to state that any advances the publisher receives from the subpublisher should be split equally with the writer as those advances come in. The advances should not be held until the song has actually earned money in the overseas territory.

# 10

# Starting Your Own Publishing Company

Many songwriters go on to head up their own publishing company, but often I've found that writers start a company for all of the wrong reasons. So I've chosen to list only the more sane and sound reasons for a writer to expand into publishing. They are:

+ The songwriter wishes to increase his or her revenue by retaining some of the publishing, or wishes to act as the sole negotiator when making a publishing deal for his or her tunes.
+ The songwriter is experienced in the music industry, has a wide range of contacts, and believes he or she can do just as well, if not better, on his or her own.
+ The songwriter wishes to control his or her own copyrights.
+ The songwriter has legitimately shopped material to a great number of publishers and has been rejected.
+ The songwriter is also a singer or a member of a band and, therefore, doesn't require an outlet (artist) for the material. Even if the singer/songwriter or

band is unknown, it's felt the middleman process of the outside publisher can be skipped, and the individual or band can act on their own behalf.

• The songwriter's tunes have been eagerly accepted in the past by outside publishers, or the writer is a performer of some stature. In either case, the songwriter or singer/songwriter's reputation will allow him or her the means of obtaining deals easily.

Like most other well-run businesses, the success of a publishing company depends on time, money, and contacts. When you look at all the publishers who handle publishing on a full-time basis, it's immediately apparent just how much time is involved in publishing material. I haven't met a person yet, although I'll admit there may be some, who can act as a full-time publisher—contacting people, keeping appointments, administering copyrights, checking out tip sheets and trade publications, making demos, and mailing out material—and still devote the time it takes to be a well-crafted songwriter. Unless a person has worked out some infallible formula or requires little to no sleep, one area or the other is bound to suffer. And as for money, launching and maintaining a publishing company takes plenty of it. I'll discuss that further in the next few pages.

The publishing business relies heavily on contacts, since material must be sifted through to artists, managers, producers, and A & R executives. And I mean honest-to-goodness contacts—the kind you can arrange to have a beer with, who are eager, or at least willing, to pick up the phone when they're told you're on the other end of the line. Developing these kinds of contacts doesn't happen overnight. Again, it takes money to withstand the time it takes.

The best advice I can give to any songwriter who is

thinking about starting a publishing company and plans to run it as well is to experience the business firsthand. That means taking a position at a publishing company and learning how publishing deals transpire on a daily basis. You can begin making contacts there, so that once you go out on your own, you'll have those names in your Rolodex. In time, those will multiply into more names.

## The Mechanics of Starting a Publishing Company

The first step in initiating your own publishing company is to call, write, or visit either ASCAP, BMI, or SESAC. Which one? you ask. Whichever performing rights organization you, as a songwriter, are already affiliated with. (If you're not affiliated, you cannot form a publishing company.) Understand that each performing rights organization only collects monies for the writers and publishers that are affiliated with their organization. So if you're an ASCAP writer, for instance, you'll have to register with ASCAP for your publishing membership. And if, at some point in time, you plan to publish the songs of other writers who are members of either BMI or SESAC, you'll then be required to start a different publishing company that's registered with either of these organizations.

For that reason, you'll often hear a major publishing company be called by one name, yet later come to learn of another name associated with it. For instance, April Music, Inc., is also known as April Blackwood. "April" is really the ASCAP-affiliated company, and "Blackwood" is this publisher's BMI-affiliated company.

Once you have your publishing registration form in

hand, the next thing you must do is choose names for your company. These forms will indicate spots for your first, second, and third choices in names. The reason for the multiple choice is that the performing rights organization wants to make certain that your name isn't already being used or that there are no company names which are similar. This will ensure against any confusion between companies in the distribution of monies.

In order to set up a publishing company years ago, you merely had to show that you had had songs published before, even if those songs had never been recorded or released. However, the criteria have changed, as noted in Chapter 9, "How Your Songs Earn Money," which outlines the requirements for publishing affiliations in the section under the name of each performing rights organization. Now you're usually required to give proof that your song has already been recorded and/or is in the process of being released, so that the performing rights organization knows there is a possibility that income will be generated from the song. You should also note that the performing rights organization will only administer copyrighted works, so you'll also have to register your songs with the U.S. Copyright Office. SGA will administrate your copyrights for you if you prefer not to do so yourself.

The performing rights organizations have changed their standards because in the past many people were starting their own publishing companies with songs that never ended up being recorded and released and, therefore, never produced revenue. In the meantime, the organizations were spending wasted time, effort, and money initiating paperwork, mailing out updates, and so forth for companies that were for all significant purposes inactive.

After you've submitted your completed form and

have shown proof that you have a song that will possibly generate income, the performing rights organization will then vote on whether or not to grant your publishing affiliation. This is usually an affirmative vote.

As mentioned in Chapter 9, ASCAP charges publisher members $50 in annual dues; BMI has a onetime application fee of $25 for publisher affiliates; and publishers aren't charged any fees by SESAC.

So now you've been voted in as a publishing member of a performing rights organization, and they've cleared the name of your company. Your next step is to file for a business permit. You do that by filing a DBA ("Doing Business As") form with the county clerk's office in the county where you'll be conducting business. The fee for the DBA will vary with each county. SGA can guide you in this process, or, if you have questions about incorporating, you should consult an attorney. Once you have your DBA, you can then open a bank account in your company name. You should also keep a file of all business-related receipts (lunches, postage, records, etc.) for tax purposes.

Lastly, you'll want to affiliate with a mechanical rights organization, like the Harry Fox Agency, that will take care of administering and collecting the mechanical royalties on your songs. (The functions and procedures of the mechanical rights organizations were discussed in Chapter 9.)

Note that the performing rights organizations and the mechanical rights organizations have affiliates overseas which will assist you in monitoring and collecting royalty monies internationally.

# The Day-to-Day Operation of a Publishing Company

In the day-to-day operation of your publishing company, you'll need all of those things normally required to maintain a small business. It's very important that you have a permanent mailing address and a phone—and someone to man it or at least an answering machine in your absence. A logo on your stationery is also a smart way to make your company stationery instantly identifiable.

As a publisher, you'll also have to subscribe to tip sheets and trade publications so that you can study these to determine what industry personnel are looking for material and how you can reach them.

Additionally, you can no longer get by with demos consisting of a voice accompanied by a guitar or piano. Now you'll be responsible for outlaying the cash that's required to refine a demo to make it presentable for the ears of other industry administrators. You'll also be purchasing cassettes in quantity, along with cassette cases, identification stickers, and large mailing envelopes.

Throughout your daily business routines, you'll want to keep photocopies of all of your correspondence. Plus you'll want to keep a record of your efforts to get each of your songs recorded. To do this, I used to use two sets of index cards and head the first set of cards with the songs' titles, then list which companies or individuals I had submitted a demo of the song to, along with the mailing date and their response. I would then use the second set to tabulate each month's activities, so I could gauge my efforts and have an overview of what songs, people, or direction I wanted to pursue. Of course, a small personal computer would also be ideal as a means of tracking your efforts.

# Ways to Increase Your Publishing Revenue

Once you're publishing songs that have been recorded and released, you should do everything in your power as a publisher to squeeze every last dime out of those songs. This is called exploiting the copyright, and it can be done by pursuing these standard publishing activities:

- Although sheet music doesn't sell like it used to, if you have a record that achieves a notable success, you should contact a sheet music publishing company to see if they'd like to print and distribute sheet music for that song. In most cases, the sheet music publishing company will offer you an advance for the printing rights on your song. This advance is then recouped from the sale of the sheet music. Again, the song must be of high acclaim to merit the printing and distribution of sheet music. A number-one dance record wouldn't warrant sheet music, but a Top 10 pop record most certainly would.
- Attempt to have songs rerecorded by artists other than the original one who recorded your song. This is called getting a cover version for your song. Send the original record to various artists and producers and see if they might be interested in covering the song, perhaps in a different genre of music. Do your utmost not to let the song die with the original artist; keep the song working for you.
- In the case of a widely successful record, make it a point to contact foreign publishers in an effort to acquire foreign subpublishing deals. In some cases, a foreign artist may even wish to rerecord the song and the lyrics will be translated to the native language. Your publishing company and the foreign

subpublisher will then split the earnings on the record for that specific territory according to the percentages that were agreed upon. Generally, your company will also receive advances for licensing the record to foreign subpublishers. This type of deal can prove to be lucrative because even if the record doesn't sell all that well in the foreign territories, you can still scoop up income from the advances.

# 11

# Mastering the Master

## Master vs. Demo

A demo is a representation of a song and displays the potential that the song might have as a record. But a master is the finished recording of a song from which records, tapes, or digital products are actually made. It doesn't demonstrate how things could be but is the final product.

So if you play a demo for someone and they have to ask if the recording is a demo or a master, you should be flattered. Just the same, if you go into the studio with the intent of making a master and, when finished, realize that your production isn't up to snuff, you should call that recording a demo and start the production of your master over again.

There are other differences between the demo and the master. When you shop a demo, you're selling a song. But when you peddle a master, you're selling the song, the artist, and the production, and the recording is expected to be flawless. The master, then, is where all the excuses end. No A & R director wants to hear all your "if only" stories about how the vocal could've been better if only the artist hadn't had a headache, or how the production could've been improved if only you'd had another couple thousand dollars to spend. When you say you have a master, the A & R executive listens to that tape as if it's finished. The performances of the artist and musicians and the overall production have to be right.

Getting that degree of perfection means lots of studio time, and as you well know by now, when you're talking studio time, you're talking big dollars. Demos can be made in approximately ten hours either at home or in a 4-, 8-, or 16-track studio. However, a master usually takes at least three times that number of hours, and you'll be scheduling time at a 16-, 24-, or even a 48-track studio. So instead of spending $300 as you might on a demo, you may be investing $4,000 or more to produce a master.

With stakes like that, plus the fact that there's no guarantee that you can sell your master, producing one is a real gamble. So why take a chance?

Well, there are several reasons. Sometimes writers have been rejected so many times they feel their only recourse is to record their song themselves in hopes that they'll be able to sell it as a master recording.

Another reason is that in today's economic climate, record companies are rarely anxious to spend money on artists and producers until they feel relatively certain that their investment is at least going to come back to them. The closer you are to presenting a finished product to a record company, the more comfortable they can be in accepting you and/or your song because there's less guess-work involved and less risk in giving you money for your master—versus giving someone money to go into a studio in hopes they'll come out with something decent. So quite often, it does seem they wait for someone to walk in their door with a finished product that they want to buy. Consequently, this forces a lot of people to take matters into their own hands, meaning they go out and produce a master in hopes of putting themselves in the position of landing a record deal.

Some songwriters are also producers at heart, waiting to come out of the closet, and the only way they can make any headway in that field is to have their names attached to masters—not demos.

Or sometimes a person just reaches that point in his or her career where he or she has the right song, the right artist, and some money, and they're ready to take the chance.

Whatever the reason, it's still quite a gamble, considering the amount of money and time involved in making and selling a master. But you'll be gambling for something worthwhile—your career.

## Making a Master

Before I get into what's involved in making a master, let me first tell you how not to go about making one. That's what I learned my first time around, an extremely speedy but costly lesson, to say the least.

While I was first writing songs, I cultivated a relationship with a man who, as it happened, was the president of a bank in a small nearby town. It doesn't really matter much how we met, but we got to be on good terms and somehow, with all of my talk, I got Dave to believe in my musical abilities.

Anyway, after I'd been living in New York City for a while and things just didn't seem to be happening quickly enough for me, I grew impatient and could think of nothing else but starting my own production company. Of course, that wasn't going to be too easy, I realized, on the nonsalary I was making. So I talked to Dave about a loan to get me started, and I was able to borrow $10,000 from his bank.

Within three weeks of the day that that money went into my checking account, I had $2,000 of it left and what were supposed to be two master recordings which in reality sounded more like two half-baked demos.

How did that happen? Well, after three whirlwind weeks of spending money and going into the studio, I took some time to ask myself that same question.

In retrospect, I can admit that I just wanted to do my own thing so badly that I didn't take the time to do things the right way. Not only that, but I wanted to be boss man, too, so I was the executive producer, the producer, the arranger—you name it, I was it—and I had absolutely no idea what I was doing or should've been doing in the studio.

I picked two noncommercial songs which to this day I still like. But also to this day, I find that I and the songwriter are the only two people who like those songs. Regretfully, I had also allowed the songwriter to be the artist—which was not a step in the right direction.

I hired the wrong musicians for the type of material I was doing and ended up firing them and bringing in an entirely new group of musicians who, as it turned out, made me wish I had stuck with the original crew. The engineer was good at what he did, but wasn't really the type of engineer that I needed for the kind of songs I was doing. Of course, I didn't realize that until it was too late.

Because of my lack of studio experience, it would've made sense (too much sense, I guess) for me to make another demo of the songs so I could get a better feel for where they should head. But I didn't. Nor did I rehearse the singer/songwriter or any of the musicians.

In short, I didn't approach this making a master business in the right way at all, and my diminished bank account, along with the mediocre recordings—which I couldn't sell for the life of me—were proof of that.

Do I consider that experience a mistake? Not really. I rationalize it by figuring that the real mistake would've been to go back into the studio and repeat my lousy performance, thereby not learning from my initial errors.

So, for those of you who would rather not make my mistakes, on your first master, I recommend the following:

**The Song.** If you're thinking of making a master, it goes without saying that you probably already feel you've written or latched on to a strong song. But step back a minute and give it a scrutinizing look. How commercial is the tune? Is it timely? Do people outside your immediate family and circle of friends like the song? Is the song good—or really good? If you have any doubts, then don't risk spending the money, because it's probably not the right tune.

**The Artist.** Whether you're producing a group or an individual artist, make sure these are people who are going to enhance the record. Remember, with a master you're not just selling a song, you're selling an artist, so you want someone who's an unbelievable singer, like Michael Bolton, or someone with a unique style, like Bob Dylan—overall, someone an A & R person will take notice of. Additionally, be certain that the artist and the song are compatible and that the artist adds to the song's impact.

**Who Do You Plan to Be?** When you're making a master, you can assume the role of executive producer, producer, coproducer, arranger, or all of the above. But if you're not too experienced in the studio, I wouldn't try to take on all of these roles as I did the first time out. Instead, you may want to hire other people to help you with the production. Remember that no A & R executive is going to care that you didn't do the master production all on your own, especially if he likes it. He's simply going to give you credit for being wise enough to hire the people who got those results. And if you should end up employing people with name value, all the better, because that may elevate the A & R person's interest, too.

By looking at the roles of the executive producer, producer, and arranger, you can get a clearer idea of how you want to cast yourself in this master production.

**The Executive Producer.** The executive producer isn't always directly involved with the creative aspects of the production, yet he's normally the person who's footing the bill. It's the role of the executive producer to see that the producer is doing a good job in overseeing all elements of the project.

**The Producer.** The producer is responsible for making the creative decisions. He's the boss and will be the one hiring and firing the people who work on the session.

A producer's fee can range from $200 to $20,000, depending on his reputation. A real heavy won't even work for $20,000, nor is it likely that he'll be willing to work with an unknown, so you can cross Quincy Jones from your list right off.

Besides putting the producer's fee in writing, your production agreement with the producer should also state the number of points, or the percentage, he'll receive in the event the master is sold to a label. His portion of the points will commonly range from two to four, and I'll be explaining more about points and production deals later on in this chapter.

If you're new at this master business or pretty green about the industry in general, hiring a producer can be advantageous. While he's going around hiring all the right people for the session and assuming full responsibility for the production, you can sit back and learn from what he does, and get indoctrinated into the studio at a comfortable pace. There's also the advantage of the producer's contacts. Through him you'll get to meet musicians who could be of value to you later on. And when you do go to sell the master, the producer might be open to giving you names of people he knows, or companies where his name value might add to the salability of the master.

It's unlikely that a well-known producer will shop the master for you—but it never hurts to ask. However, if he should, be prepared to give up an additional point on the deal because he'll certainly ask for it.

If you arrange to coproduce with someone, you might be able to equally split the two to four points which you'll receive. But again, a producer with a good track record may not find it to his benefit to coproduce with an unknown. If he agrees to do the project at all, he'll probably prefer to do it on his own.

The producer is also probably going to want a statement included in the production agreement that says if you do get a deal on the master, he'll have the option to produce any subsequent recordings the artist does on that label. This means that if the single does well and an album follows, he'll be the producer or coproducer of the artist on x number of songs, according to whatever agreement you make.

Also remember what your connection is with the artist. Are you the artist's manager, or is the artist being represented by someone else? Do you have any kind of contract with the artist? Before you bring more people into the picture, you and the artist have to decide what your deal is first. You can't go around giving away a piece of the artist and making promises to others about his or her future before all of that is resolved.

**The Arranger.** Many experienced producers do "head" arrangements, meaning that they plot out the song's course and parts as they go along in the production. But if you haven't hired a producer and are new at the role yourself, the arranger can chart the route of your song and at the same time will lend you a sense of security by his mere presence in the studio.

For a full rhythm arrangement, the arranger's fee can vary from $250 to $1,200, depending again on who the arranger is. Unlike the producer, the arranger only receives a fee and doesn't get points on the record.

**The Musicians.** Needless to say, you'll want to hire musicians who can be assets to your production and who can deliver the right sounds to fit your song. You'll also want to find musicians with whom you can communicate.

Always attempt to set the musicians' fees based on the entire length of the production rather than on an hourly rate. Whether you're using union or nonunion musicians, you can always find people who will play for reasonable rates and won't require that you pay union scale. Many times cash in hand is enough incentive to sway a musician into playing on your session, but there are also other measures you might consider if your funds are extremely low. Perhaps you can agree to exchange favors. Maybe you work for a publishing company and are in the position to get the musician's songs to your boss. Or it could be that you'll only be able to pay a musician $50 or so up front for the session, but promise that you'll pay him more money from the advance you receive from the label.

Once the master is sold, it's up to all nonunion musicians who played on the session to join the American

Federation of Musicians. The purchasing record company then makes sure all union musicians are paid union scale for the project.

## Making the Right Preparations

As the producer of a master recording, it's your responsibility to hire all musicians as well as select a studio.

Studio time makes up the bulk of your expenses, and studio hours rack up rapidly as your savings diminish quickly. (When you're spending $100 per hour, you don't need a calculator to see that it doesn't take too long to run up a $3,000 bill.) Keep in mind that you not only have to take the time to get all the parts you want down on tape, but then you also have to do a mix, which could easily run ten hours or more (some of ours last forty-eight!), and that has to fall within your budget, too. The point being, you should make an effort to do some preproduction work in order to curtail your studio expenses.

If you're using a live band, be sure the band is rehearsed, and in all instances make sure the artist knows the song well. Think about your song and its direction, and if you're going to be using synthesizers work out the song at home before you set foot in the studio.

With all of the advances in musical technology, you honestly can do a lot of preproduction work at home. That's because your ability to manipulate many synthesizers and samplers today can very closely approximate the feel and color of a final piece of product. In other words, the advent of multitimbral synthesis will now allow you to access a variety of different sounds out of a specific keyboard or module. And a sampler like the S1000, for example, will store as many sounds as the internal memory will hold (this is normally determined by the length of the sample to be loaded).

Depending on how many voices your module or keyboard has (a voice is how many notes the synthesizer will play at one time), you can have one voice be your kickdrum, one your snare drum, another your high hat, another your sidestick, and another a tom-tom. At that point, you've only eaten up five voices with your drum kit and you still have voices left over to do your keyboard pad, bass, and even a simple overdub or two (remember, with a multitimbral synthesizer that has enough voices, this can all be happening out of the same keyboard or module). So, realistically, you could have a very good picture of what your final product will be prior to your studio date.

By doing this sort of preproduction work, you'll also discover many things about your song—the most important being whether or not it's good enough to go into a big studio to make a master in the first place. If after a good listen you feel the song and arrangement are solid enough to go into the studio, you can now relax and concentrate your efforts on being more creative and will be freed up to try some of the other ideas floating around in your head.

If you feel you have your song exactly as you want it—with today's equipment it is possible to get a quality product at home—then you can go into the big studio with your own equipment and mix what you have. This will allow you to use a better, more flexible console (mixer), more outboard gear (gates, compressors, and so on), and a larger array of effects in a more critical listening environment. No matter how you look at it, you're likely to come out of your experience with better product—and save money in studio time as well.

So, remember to do your homework at home. Believe me, the studio owner doesn't care how many hours you spend in his studio or how much time you waste. In fact, he's hoping you come in totally unprepared and unrehearsed. I have a buddy who's a studio owner, and he says, with a smile on his face and dollar signs in his eyes, that the motto of his studio is, "There's no such thing as a waste of time," which I can appreciate and laugh at only because we are good friends. So when you're making a master, call on a motto of your own from Boy or Girl Scout training: "Be prepared."

### Spec Recording Time

You can try to lessen the up front cost of studio time by approaching a studio about a speculative recording deal.

From time to time, studios have cancellations or just aren't busy, yet they still have to pay to keep their equipment on. So, if you're without loads of money or financial backing, talk to the studio owner or manager about specing recording time. Tell him you want to make a master but don't have quite enough money to do so. Offer to work the weirdest hours of the night if he'll allow you to do that master in his studio. It could be that if the studio owner likes the song or knows you, the artist, or the producer (or if he just has a lot of downtime), he'll be glad to help you out. However, he'll expect payment from you if and when you sell the master. Normally, this payment will come from the advance the record company gives you when purchasing the master. Note, too, that over and above his book rate, the studio owner may request a bonus of $25 or so an hour or even a piece of the song's publishing.

You can also attempt to work out the same type of arrangement if you have a lump sum of money like $2,000 or so to spend on studio time, yet figure that amount might not be enough to finish your project. Let the studio owner know you only have $2,000 to spend, and ask if he'll take that amount and allow you to work on your master until it's completed—mix and all. If you give him cash in hand, it's a good bet that he'll go for it. The owner might permit you to finish your master on these terms alone, or he might do it on the basis that you pay the balance of what you owe him from your record advance.

If you make a spec recording deal and then sell your master, you may end up spending more money on studio time than you would have if you'd had the money to start with. But the studio is gambling along with you and doing you a favor, and the facts are that they're calling the shots. So while you may end up giving away a lot, it's still one way to get your own ball rolling.

## Selling Your Master

Where you do start?

Well, of course you'll want to cover all the bases and take your master to as many labels as you possibly can. But since certain labels project certain images and generally stick to one type of music, you'll have to single out the companies which would be interested in your type of master. You can do this by referring to Appendix B, making phone calls, and checking out the names of record companies on albums, tapes, and CDs which bear songs that typify your genre of music.

I strongly feel that if you're going to give yourself every chance you can to sell your master, you'll have to shop the master in an area where record companies are involved in your type of music. For a broad overview, New York is mostly known for rock, urban contemporary, and dance records. Los Angeles is geared toward traditional R & B, polished pop, and alternative music. Nashville is gospel, country, and country crossover like

Garth Brooks. You'll even find labels in Memphis, Muscle Shoals, and Atlanta. In fact, Atlanta has become a hotbed for R & B, with producers like L.A. and Babyface making it their home. So if you live outside these major music cities, do everything possible to dig up the plane fare or get behind the wheel of your car so you can go and see the people you need to get to. In many instances, if you don't, the money you've spent on your master is going to be wasted. Your tape is going to sit in your closet gathering dust while you're sitting in front of the radio thinking how much better your record is than the songs you're hearing on the airwaves.

If you're a newcomer, taking a master around in person allows you to start making some of your first real contacts. It links your face with your name, and your name with your product. Of course, it might be tough getting appointments in the beginning. But if you can push without being pushy, after a while people will realize that you're not going away and you're not giving up, so they may as well break down and make an appointment with you. Even more, it could be that you won't sell your first master, but these relationships will put you in a better position to sell your second and third ones.

When shopping a master, start at the top. Try for an appointment with the head administrator. If you can't get through to him, then work your way down. Just make sure that you get to the people who can really do something for you, those who have clout or are actively involved in getting records signed.

Sometimes you'll invariably wind up presenting your master to the wrong set of ears or to people who have no connections with your specific type of music. But nothing negative will result from a meeting with anyone if you've acted professionally and have a decent piece of product in tow. Since the people in the music industry are always playing musical chairs, every contact counts. As I've tried to stress, the person you face across the desk at one company in July can easily become the person who sits in an executive chair at another firm in October.

## Reaching the A & R Executive

Most likely, the person who will be reviewing your master is the A & R director at a record label. So after you've made up a list of the prospective record companies that might be interested in your product, you should then call each label and find out the name of the A & R director who handles your specific genre of music. This should be done even if you're submitting tapes by mail, so that you can direct your package to the right person's attention.

Whether you're submitting tapes by mail or wishing to present them in person, you should maintain either a written chart or a chart on your personal computer listing the contacts' names, the dates you called for an appointment or mailed your tapes, the dates you should try back for responses, and the responses themselves. Listing the secretaries' names or any other bits of information you glean from your calls will also be quite helpful. All in all, this chart eliminates much confusion and many mistakes. (You're going to get mighty mixed up when you're calling thirty people for appointments three and four times each. You'll be glad you have something to refer back to for names, dates, times and responses.)

If, after several calls, you haven't had any luck in getting an appointment with an A & R director and are asked to mail a tape of your master, say, "I'm going to be in the neighborhood," and ask if you may drop off a copy of the tape instead. The idea here, of course, is to show your face in the office—even if it's only to the secretary.

And who knows? The A & R executive might find a minute to see you once you're there.

While you're at the office, ask when a good time would be to call the A & R director for a response on your tape. If you're told they'll call you if they like the tape, let four or five days pass by, and if you haven't heard anything, call them. When you drop off the tape, also be sure that the front of your envelope clearly states: "TO (name of the A & R director)" and "FROM (your name)."

If you mail a tape, it's common for a month to slip by before you hear a response, and you might have to do some calling in between to prompt that response. However, if you have the opportunity to present your master in person, at least you'll be able to elicit some sort of response right then and there. Remember, though, that even if the A & R person has an extremely positive reaction, hold on to your hat while you're holding on to your hopes, because this doesn't always mean he has the authority to do anything for you. And that's how we get to our lesson on understanding the A & R executive.

## Understanding Where the A & R Executive Is Coming From

In the major label category you have names like MCA, Warner Brothers, Elektra, Atlantic, BMG, Capitol, Poly-Gram, Sony—and these labels all have affiliate labels. For example, Sony has Epic and Epic has Solar; Atlantic has Atco and Atco has East-West.

So when it comes down to deciding which records will get signed to a label, sometimes there might be a handful of people—or even one person at the helm of the parent company—who listens to all of the product being considered for deals on the subsidiary labels. Therefore, an A & R executive might jump up and down when you play him your cassette, but you should realize that he may still have to take your tape into a board meeting and get the feedback of nine other people (and keep your fingers crossed that it'll be on a day when all ten people happen to agree on the same thing), or his hands might be tied until he gets the go-ahead from a higher-up.

Sometimes, too, the A & R director will love the material while you're sitting in his office, but once you leave, he may play your cassette a dozen more times and decide against taking it to the board meeting at all.

However, don't misjudge the A & R executive. He's not fickle—he's human. After all, his ears listen to countless tapes every day of the week, and out of all of these recordings his budget only allows him to sign a few each year. Considering that it's not uncommon that an A & R director's job is on the line if he signs a few projects that fail, you can't really blame him if he has second thoughts about your master.

In fact, an A & R person passed on a song that I was shopping a few years ago, and before I left his office he said to me, "If you get a deal for this artist on another label, and it does well, we never had this meeting, okay?" I did get a deal for the record and the song went on to do a little damage—but not much. So, when push came to shove, the A & R executive really did make the right decision for his label. But you can see that if my record had gone on to be a number-one smash and the company president found out about our meeting, it's doubtful my contact would've been up for a promotion.

## Submitting and Presenting Your Master

If you're submitting a cassette of your master by mail, your package should include a cover letter, lyric sheet, a brief biography, a photo of the artist or band, and a self-addressed stamped envelope if you wish the material to be returned to you.

When you're presenting your master in person, you can forgo the cover letter, but you should take along the lyric sheet, biography, and photo of the artist or band. You should have a cassette on hand, and in place of a reel-to-reel you should have a DAT copy of your master, if possible, since so many A & R executives now have DAT machines at their disposal.

Whether you're mailing or presenting a cassette of your master, it should be copied onto a high-bias chrome cassette, and you should review the section "Tip-Top Tapes" in Chapter 4, "Shopping Your Demo," so that your tapes will be in proper order.

The biography should be typed neatly on one page and include a paragraph or two on the artist or band telling who they are and what they've done; a paragraph on the producer stating who he is and what he's produced; and a paragraph on any coproducer or arranger who contributed to the project. I've always made it a point to tell the A & R director what market I feel the song and artist could compete in, and what the goal for the project is, or something as simple as stating my purpose: "to secure an album deal with a major record label." Additionally, across the bottom of the page, the name of a contact should be given, along with a phone number where he or she can be reached "for further discussion."

Remember, the biography serves as a résumé for the production team, and if none of you have done much of anything in the past, make it sound as if you have. I'm not sanctioning the printing of lies, but it's a good idea to find some way you can make things sound a little more appealing than they actually are.

I have out-and-out fibbed on a biography and I got caught at it. What happened is that I had produced an artist who I thought would be more salable as part of a group, so I made up a group name and listed the two main band members. The first member I listed was the artist I was working with, but the second member didn't exist, and the name I used was purely fictional. When the label's president was anxious to meet both of the band members, all I could do at that point was break down and tell the truth that there was only one artist involved. The web I had woven did cause me some embarrassment, but fortunately, the head of the record company liked the master so much that he dropped the band idea altogether, signed the artist, and put out an album under the artist's surname. The moral of the story is: Eventually you'll have to tell the truth, so don't stretch it too far.

## When You Have a Buyer

You've made phone call upon phone call, and trudged all over town with your master until your ego is bruised and your shoes need resoling. And just when you thought it was time to give up and throw your tape on the closet shelf, it finally happened . . . you have a taker.

So what happens next?

Well, when a record company wishes to purchase your master, they'll make you an offer in the form of a master purchase agreement. This agreement provides for the advance and points you'll receive on the record, plus makes mention of future projects which may arise if the first single does well.

The master purchase agreement should always be reviewed by a music attorney. Even so, it benefits you to have some basic knowledge to help you weigh one offer against another and make an intelligent decision.

## The Advance

It's common for a record label to give you an advance for your master, the amount of which is negotiable.

From your side, you want to negotiate for an advance that will allow you to recoup the money you spent on your master, plus provide a few extra dollars for yourself in payment for the time and effort you put into the project. So if you spent $4,000 overall in making your master, a fair request for an advance would be $6,000, the $2,000 being compensation for your headaches, aggravation, and speculation.

During your negotiations, though, keep in mind that you also want to receive enough money to make good on your promises to people involved with the record. So, if you've made a spec deal with a studio and said you'd pay their book rate plus $25 an hour in return for their favor, make sure the advance covers that amount. Or perhaps you promised the singer an extra $250 once you sold the master. Or what about the musician you hired for a minimal fee with the promise that you'd mail him something extra when the master was purchased? And how about your lawyer? How much is he going to charge to look over this agreement? Have all of these figures calculated and at the top of your mind when the negotiations ensue.

If it gets to the point where you've shopped the tape to everyone you possibly can and have found only one buyer and that buyer isn't willing to pay you the amount of advance you need to cover your debts and promises, it's better to take that offer and divvy up the advance you do get as best you can. Believe me, you won't be the first person this has happened to and as long as you're honest about it, most people won't be too upset at getting something as opposed to nothing. If you get the opportunity, you can always try to make it up to them on your next project.

When you review the contract, you should also study the amount of money allotted for budgets on future album projects that may result from this master. For instance, the label may give you a $10,000 advance to purchase your master, and the contract might state that if that single is successful and warrants a follow-up album, the album budget will be $100,000.

Beyond that, both the advanced budgets and the points should escalate over time on any subsequent albums. Because if things are going well enough that the label calls for a second and third album, they can certainly increase your budget. Besides that, all the people involved on the album—the producer, artist, and musicians—are going to grow in stature according to the album's success, so any follow-up albums are going to cost more. At the beginning, the producer might be an unknown lightweight receiving approximately $5,000 to $7,500 to produce an album. Upon reaching middleweight status, he could request $10,000 to $20,000. And a world-class heavyweight producer can get $25,000 to—how high can you count?

So if the first album has a budget of $100,000 and is a success, and you're asked to do a second one, it wouldn't be out of line to expect that you would get an increase of approximately 20 percent. The third album budget should equal the second one plus 25 percent, and the fourth should increase approximately 30 percent. However, remember that this is only going to be true of dealings with major labels; in most circumstances an independent label won't be able to afford those numbers.

## The Points

A point is equal to 1 percent of the suggested retail list price of the record. However, it's based on 90 percent of all records sold instead of 100 percent, to allow for the number of records returned and the number of promotional copies which are distributed for free.

It's standard for record companies to allow between ten and eleven points on a single, and between eleven and thirteen points on an album. We should make a note here that traditionally points have been based on the suggested retail list price, yet today a lot of record companies are going to wholesale selling prices. This is something you need to be aware of. For example, our producer team got one point on the New Kids on the Block remix album, and we just assumed that, as in the past, this was based on the suggested retail. Not! So make sure you know what you're truly dealing with here. The formula for negotiating wholesale points is to take the retail points times two. In other words, if you've got a ten-point album deal on the suggested retail price, it'd be customary that you'd have twenty points on the wholesale price, because remember, wholesale is usually half of retail. Say a record is $10 suggested retail and they sell it to the record store for $5. You'd need to have twice the points on the wholesale deal to make what you would on points based on retail.

When you set out to decide on how your points should be divided, you need to understand a few things about production deals. Production deals are usually made between labels and producers or between producers and artists. The type of production deal we are concerned with here is the one made between the artist and the producer.

When a label offers points in a master purchasing agreement, those points are to be split up between the members of the production team. The production team normally consists of the producer and the artist; sometimes a third party is involved, either a coproducer, a financier, or an agent or lawyer who has been active in putting the deal together. Usually, before the master is sold, the production team will have already established their own production agreement stating how the points will be split up.

In looking at some standard production deals, for the sake of simplicity, let's say the production team consists only of the producer and the artist.

In this instance, if the producer's service is solicited, he'll usually receive two to four points on the deal. However, if he is also expected to shop the master and is functioning as its sales agent, it's common practice for him to receive an extra 10 percent. So, based on a production deal of ten points, let's assume that the producer is receiving three points for producing the master. Later on, though, he's also asked to peddle the tape. He would then get another full point, since 10 percent of ten points is one point, meaning he'll now receive four points, and the artist, six.

If the producer is fronting the money for a project and intends to shop the master, on a ten-point deal he'd normally take five or six points, leaving the artist with five or four points respectively. In actuality, this is an equitable arrangement since the producer has everything to lose (mostly his money), and the artist (especially an unknown artist) has everything to gain.

You can then see that if you hired a producer to do your master, he would expect anywhere from two to four points. On a ten-point deal, that would leave eight to six points to be split between the artist and yourself, you being the person who has financed the project and the one who intends to shop the master.

No royalties are paid until all advance monies are recouped from the earnings of the record. For example, say a record company puts up $100,000 for an album project and gives the production team (the producer and the artist) ten points. The album is given a suggested retail list price of $10, so for each album sold, the production team makes $1.00 ($10 × 10 percent [ten points] = $1.00). That means the advance of $100,000 will be fully recouped once 100,000 records have been sold and not returned ($1.00 × 100,000 = $100,000). Since they have been advanced $100,000 to make the album, the production team will not be paid any additional money until the record sales rise above that 100,000 figure.

To give you an idea of what type of money can be made from production royalties, let's use the same example and assume that the producer has four of the ten points and the artist has six, and overall the record sold 300,000 copies. As noted, the first 100,000 copies went to recoup the $100,000 album advance, and so that leaves 200,000 copies. Of the 200,000, both the producer and the artist are paid on 90 percent, or 180,000 copies. Based on four points, the producer's royalties would come to $72,000 ($10 × 4 percent = 40 cents; 40 cents × 180,000 = $72,000), and the artist would receive $108,000 based on six points ($10 × 6 percent = 60 cents; 60 cents × 180,000 = $108,000).

## What Really Happens When Your Record Sells

The above example is great to show what kind of money you might earn with a particular point deal. However, it seems the more advanced the industry gets, the more costs there are to be recouped before the production team starts seeing some cash. For example, packaging charges on CDs are relatively high, and with the advent of videos another cost has been thrown in. Videos can easily cost $30,000 or so, and what if there's more than one per album? Today, you're just not talking about recouping an album budget, but many other costs as well before any money goes into your pocket.

In somewhat the same vein, ever wonder why an artist will sell millions of records and then you don't hear from him or her for years? Well, sometimes it's that they're touring, or writing, or relaxing—or sometimes, well . . . let me put it this way. If you should ever be fortunate enough to have a huge album that sells tremendously and accordingly the record company owes you—let's say for fun $1,000,000—don't ever agree to do a second album until you've been paid for that first money-maker. There are times when record companies will give you the first $800,000 and hold up the other $200,000, saying that you should get moving on your second album and that money will be used as the budget since ultimately they'll be recouping the budget later anyway. NOT! Most big artists get the money that's due before embarking on their next project.

## When You Don't Have a Buyer

If you can't locate a buyer for your master, you have two choices. Either you chalk it up to experience and go back to the drawing board to do a master of another song, or you can start your own record company and put the record out yourself.

However, starting a record company is not a simple or inexpensive task, and if you thought making a master was a gamble at $4,000, now the stakes are really going to climb.

Establishing a record company and all that goes with it—mastering charges, pressing, promotion, distribution, and so on—is a complicated process that deserves immense consideration, and I advise that you seek the expertise of an entertainment attorney or someone who has taken on this risky venture successfully before plunging into it head-on.

# 12

# Alternative Routes for Your Songwriting Ability

Besides aiming for the Top 40, there are other paths you might consider for showcasing your songwriting skills. Any of these can be just as self-fulfilling and financially rewarding as the recording industry, and may head you toward or even beyond Top 40 status as well.

## Jingles

How does every red-blooded American learn the alphabet? With the aid of a sing-along melody. And how do some advertisers get Americans to remember and use their products? In the same way.

The jingle has long served as an effective advertising tool and bears a close resemblance to pop songs with its catchy, easy-to-sing, easy-to-remember words and melody. It's no wonder that over the years, names like Barry Manilow ("Like a Good Neighbor"—for an insurance company), Randy Newman ("Most Original Soft Drink Ever"—for soda), and Paul Williams ("We've Only Just Begun"—for a bank) either made the transition from jingles to pop status or contributed their talents as songwriters to the jingle field.

But even with their basic similarities, there's still a difference between the pop song and the jingle. That is, jingles aren't really supposed to be songs, they're supposed to be a form of advertising that employs music.

Pick up an advertising book, and you'll find out quickly that advertising is selling. It's the art of persuasion. In the words of Larry Gottlieb, a cowriter on Chrysler's "The Pride Is Back" jingle who later turned successful country songwriter, "All of music is about human emotion. What jingles do is give human emotion to inanimate objects."

Advertising also displays products as answers to people's needs. It's doubtful you'll ever complete an advertising course without the mention of psychologist Abraham Maslow's hierarchy of needs. In listing those needs from lower to higher order, I've also included examples of some "jingle classics" which typify them. They are:

**Physiological Needs.** Basic biological needs like hunger, thirst, sleep, and sex. ("Take Sominex tonight and sleep, safe and restful, sleep . . . sleep . . . sleep.")

**Safety Needs.** Need for security, protection, comfort, and avoidance of pain. (Alka Seltzer's "Plop, plop, fizz, fizz. Oh, what a relief it is!"; "Like a good neighbor, State Farm is there.")

**Affiliation Needs.** Need to be accepted, loved, to fit in and have satisfying relationships with others. (AT&T's "Reach out, reach out and touch someone.")

**Esteem Needs.** Need for recognition, attention, prestige, achievement. (McDonald's "You deserve a break today.")

**Self-Actualization Needs.** Need for self-fulfillment, the need to become what one is capable of becoming. (The U.S. Army's "Be all that you can be . . .")

Along with these needs, you'll also want to keep the following points in mind while crafting your jingle:

1. Emphasize the brand name.
2. Be unique. Don't write something you could apply any brand name to. (Example: the Doublemint Gum jingle uses the phrases "Double your pleasure . . . double your fun.")
3. Use everyday language and write in the present tense. Use personal pronouns to establish a one-on-one relationship with the listener.
4. Remember, there are only thirty to sixty seconds for the product story to unravel, and during that time the jingle is rarely featured for more than twenty seconds or so. For the remainder of the spot, the jingle will be used as a music bed with the announcer's sell message voice-over. So stick to one major idea in your jingle and, if necessary, provide a secondary point to reinforce the product. Let the announcer tell the rest of the story.
5. Compose a hooky melody that expresses the mood, the excitement, and the thoughts about the product in general.
6. Consider the age and social status of the consumers you're trying to reach. Use the type of music and words that they're accustomed to hearing and that will appeal to them.

Also, never forget that you're not only competing with other jingle writers, but in this day and age, you're competing with all of pop music as well. Since music has reached such a sophisticated level and there are so many huge corporations that can afford to pay for the use of songs, today's jingle writer is going head to head with some of the best available music, so he or she is forced to present top-quality, finished productions. Mark Blatt, a friend of mine who has a music house in New York and is the writer of such jingles as "The Pride Is Back," "I'm Going to Disneyland," and also "Hands Across America," tells the following story to prove that point. When he pitched Oldsmobile with his "This Is Not Your Father's Oldsmobile" jingle, 249 other pieces of music were submitted at the same time. Among them were a number of pop songs, including a tune by Paul McCartney and the Billy Ocean hit "Get Outta My Dreams, Get Into My Car." And all of the pieces of music being reviewed, Mark will tell you, were full-blown productions.

### Getting Started

There are a number of ways you can get going in the competitive world of jingle writing, but before you do anything, you first have to make a demo tape of your work. This tape could either:

1. Include several jingles which best display your versatility as well as your creativity. You can achieve that by selecting several well-known products that might range from personal items to food products (beer), to service and retail outlets (record store), to a major consumer item (automobile).
2. If you're a disillusioned songwriter turned jingle writer, you could always put together a demo tape of your five best songs (just a verse and chorus from each one). This should give a fair indication of your songwriting ability.

No matter which type of demo tape displays your talent best, just remember, once again, you need to present a top-notch, quality production that leaves nothing to the imagination. That's because if you're submitting your tape to a jingle house or the creative director at a local ad agency, he or she will know everything there is to know about jingles and will be weighing yours against the competition's. On the other hand, if you're presenting the demo to a client—some small local business you're trying to encourage to adopt a jingle—he or she knows hardly anything about jingles (just everything about the product), so you can't leave anyone guessing on this end either.

So, now that you have your demo, what do you do?

The first thing you can do is submit your demo tape to jingle or music houses. The best way to find these companies is in *The Creative Black Book*. This book lists all of the suppliers to ad agencies and among them are jingle houses. Too, you'll find a listing of commercial music houses in the *Songwriter's Market*, which is a book you're likely to find at the library or in a bookstore, and there's also a publication called *Backstage* which lists names of producers who might be involved with jingle productions.

In your immediate area, there's no reason not to try to sell your talents to local advertising agencies. You'll find the names of the agencies in your community listed in the Business-to-Business Yellow Pages, which you can either order from your phone company or locate at the public library. You should, however, approach the agency with an initial phone call to see if they'd be willing to listen to your demoed jingles. The person you should speak with is the agency's creative director, who at smaller agencies may also be the president of the firm. If you'd like to get information about national agencies, look in the *Standard Directory of Advertising Agencies*, also known as "The Red Book," which you can also find at your public library.

After you present your demo, if the creative director likes it he'll keep it on file until an opportunity arises when one of the agency's clients is in need of a jingle. At that time, if it's felt your particular style is suitable for the job at hand, the agency will solicit your services. The agency will also provide you with some direction for the jingle in the form of a creative worksheet, and you can proceed to create from the facts and objectives outlined there.

And, last, it's a long shot . . . but if there's a little business down the street that you think might benefit from some airtime on the radio, create a jingle for them and ask if you could present your demo to them. Who knows? It might be the start of something big for both of you.

### Getting Paid

Believe it, there are some much-sought-after jingle writers who can make as much as $50,000 for their half-minute tribute to a product. So, now that you have something to shoot for . . .

In the most general application and most usual situation, let's say you're a writer for a jingle house and you've written a jingle that will be used on radio and TV, and twenty or so renditions of that jingle are needed for the client's campaign. It would be typical for the jingle house to receive approximately $10,000 for the TV version of the jingle and $5,000 for the radio version. Of that, 40 percent generally goes to the writer. Now for that amount of money, it wouldn't seem worth it to be a jingle writer— or even a jingle house, for that matter. But what happens is this: When it comes to doing those "twenty or so" renditions, the jingle house is given a production budget. And since the jingle writer is almost always a musician, singer, arranger, or producer on those productions, he's paid a portion of that budget also, and this is really where the bulk of the money is made. Just think how many versions of a jingle would be required by a client like McDonald's!$!$!

For the initial flat fee that the jingle writer receives, he or she is usually expected to relinquish all rights to the jingle. The jingle becomes the property of the client at that point. However, one right the writer will want to try to retain, if at all possible, is the popular song right to the work, which will allow the writer to publish the jingle melody as a song. Many times, the advertiser will permit this, figuring that since his product is already linked to a melody that may receive more radio airplay in the form of a song, it can be construed as free advertising.

Additionally, there does exist the reverse situation, as you know, where a song is adapted for use as a jingle and new lyrics are written to promote a product. When this occurs, the advertiser must pay a license fee to the copyright owner of the popular song. This fee may range from hundreds of dollars to tens of thousands of dollars, based on the extent of the song's use in the commercial and whether the commercial is being run locally, regionally, or nationally.

## Audiovisual Soundtracks

When you sat in a darkened classroom with your attention supposedly turned to the educational film being projected onto a screen in the front of the room, did you ever stop to think about who did the soundtrack for the production? Well, somebody did. And the next time, that somebody could be you.

Today, more than ever, countless schools, organizations, and companies are using audiovisual productions in the form of either slide shows, filmstrips, or videos to inform, train, and educate viewers. As a result, composers now have another means of exhibiting their abilities.

The best part about AV productions is that in any city there are a multitude of viable prospects. Think about it. There are banks, schools, colleges, libraries, industrial firms, zoos, and department stores. For all of these entities and many others, audiovisual productions are utilized for the purpose of either instructing about a particular subject matter, for training personnel, for demonstrating products, or for informing the viewer about the organization's annual budget and costs, benefits, or whatever. With all of these prospects at your disposal, the AV field is one place where your talents can be recognized and handsomely rewarded on a local level.

### Getting Started

Again, before you make your move, you'll have to do a film or slide show on your own which will highlight your expertise in creating the production's musical background. Overall, this production should showcase your ability to create a music bed which is compatible with the particular subject matter, as well as display your good taste in not overpowering the announcer with your music. Quite often in an AV production, silence, more than the music itself, can serve to emphasize the points being made by the pictures or the speaker.

Once you have completed your AV production, you can choose to present it to:

**Advertising Agencies.** Many times an agency's clients will require this type of presentation vehicle for training personnel, relaying consumer benefits, or use at a trade show.

As mentioned previously, you can find the names of ad agencies in the Business-to-Business Yellow Pages, and should speak to the creative director about setting up an appointment to view your production.

**Schools, Organizations, Companies.** Contact any school, organization, or company in your area that you presume would be a likely candidate for AV productions. Find out who's in charge of their AV department or who does the hiring when an AV production is needed for the firm. Once you get to that particular person, ask if you might meet with him or her to introduce yourself and display your work.

**AV Production Firms.** Look in the Yellow Pages under "Audiovisual Companies" for the AV production houses in your area. Any of these firms may be able to use you on a free-lance basis for the films they're contracted to do, and eventually this could lead to a full-time position, if that's what you're looking for. If you're interested in approaching a firm outside your area, you can find the names of AV firms listed in the *Songwriter's Market*.

## Getting Paid

On a local scale, AV soundtracks can typically pay from $250 to $2,500 or more and are generally scaled according to the AV songwriter's experience as well as the length of the film and the intention for the film's use. Once you've established yourself as a free-lance audiovisual songwriter locally, the writing credits earned there can lead you to secure a position with a national AV company and the possibility of bigger dollars.

# Stage Musicals

As with all the other avenues for songwriting, creating the stage musical requires special preparation and much skill.

As a prerequisite to your writing, you should immerse yourself in musicals. See every musical production you possibly can, from the simplest to the most lavish productions. That means you should take in performances by church groups, high school and college drama groups, community theater groups, dinner theaters, and especially those on Broadway if at all possible. While playing the role of spectator, notice how songs are stacked throughout the production and how they embellish the plot and become an integral part of the story line. Digest the audience's reactions to songs. Take note of the types of songs that are being performed. Quite often, dynamic upbeat tunes will hold the viewer's attention, while only one or two ballads are included in a performance and are placed strategically so as not to lose the energy and momentum of the production.

Read everything about every classic musical that you can, and analyze what components (besides the cast) have made these productions all-time favorites. You'll find that many of these classics have been derived from biographies of composers or entertainers, previous works, or have topics that speak of social trends, historical victories and struggles, fantasies, and even the conversion or blossoming of a person, such as the flower girl who became a lady in *My Fair Lady* and the king who came to accept cultural change in *The King and I*.

After you've viewed, critiqued, read, and analyzed, then you can put your own skills to work. Presumably, you're not going to take on the task of writing a script yourself, so you'll have to find an existing play from a book or locate an original work through a playwright in your hometown. And choosing which of these is suitable for adaptation as a musical is a skill in itself. After all, you want something with meat, and don't want to be grasping at straws throughout the course of your composing. So, consider carefully.

After you decide on a script, you're faced with writing not one, but possibly as many as a dozen or more songs. Remember, too, that you'll be writing for not one, but multiple characters. Additionally, keep in mind that every song you write should keep the story moving, provide character development, and generally add to the unfolding of the story's plot.

### Getting Started

Once you have a script and songs in hand, you must find a means of showcasing your work. The best way to get your musical on the road is to start on the local level.

Here, you have several choices. First, you can stage the production yourself in your own garage or in an auditorium you've rented. Maybe you'll require a minimal admission fee or maybe your performance will be viewed for free. But remember, the idea here isn't really to make money (as much as you'd like to); the idea is to present your work so that you can gauge the audience's response, which will ultimately help you improve on your script and songs.

You can also attempt to have your musical performed by local theatrical groups such as college and high school drama groups, church and civic groups, theater guilds, YMCA drama clubs, children's theaters, and dinner theaters. By having any of these local groups perform your material, you may be able to become more involved with the production, and can also witness the reaction of a larger audience. What's more, you may also be able to accumulate newspaper critiques of the production. These newspaper reviews can serve as a résumé when trying to secure national exposure for your work or when attempting to attract financial backers outside your local vicinity.

Additionally, you can and should invite play producers, directors, and actors to your local showing to have a look-see for themselves. However, if they can't or aren't willing to come to you, take the show to them. If possible, get a few members of the cast together and travel to other cities to audition the musical for producers, publishers, and directors in an effort to get national staging for your musical.

Another course of action is to submit your work through the mail to producers and publishers. In your package, you should include the script, typed lyric sheets, and a cassette of your songs, along with any newspaper reviews which you've saved up from local performances. You could also provide video clips from the performance. The names of producers and publishers can be found in *Playbill* and programs, on the label copy of albums, cassettes, and CDs of popular shows, and you can also check out the section devoted to this group in the *Songwriter's Market*. For even more information, you can always contact the following organizations: The Theater Communications Group (TCG), 355 Lexington Avenue, New York, NY 10017; and The Dramatists Guild, 234 West 44th Street, New York, NY 10036.

## Getting Paid

It's doubtful that you'll get rich on local performances of your musical. In fact, if you receive any payment whatsoever, it will probably be in the form of a small percentage of the ticket sales or a very modest fee for each performance. However, the experience these performances afford can be very enriching, and that along with word-of-mouth excitement generated by your work can help launch your career on a national level.

Once you do get national attention for your work, the income can be extremely lucrative indeed. For example, on a Broadway production, the writers (composer, lyricist, and book author) collectively receive a minimum royalty of 6 percent of the theater's gross weekly box-office receipts, which is split equally. Additionally, if the play is licensed for motion pictures or TV, or used for touring company and amateur productions, the writers will receive a share of the license fees and royalties earned from these productions. There's always the possibility that an original-cast album will be produced, and this, too, provides another source of revenues for composers and lyricists. And remember, a song that's a hit on radio earns even more income for its creators. Commercial tunes have sprung from many a Broadway production, like "And I Am Telling You I'm Not Going" from *Dreamgirls* and "Memory" from *Cats*.

## Scoring for Television and Film

Your songwriting ability in itself may not be enough to give you much of an edge in this competitive arena, because scoring for television and motion pictures is a somewhat more specialized field than Top 40 songwriting. "It's not groove or beat-oriented," notes Wes Boatman, part of the Boatman-Kreitler-O'Donnell team that won an Emmy for their music direction and composition for "The Guiding Light," "rather, the music in most circumstances is created as a part of the whole for a cinematic result."

These particular creative partners divide their music tasks into three categories, which gives a clearer understanding of what's expected from them—or from anyone who is supplying music to network TV or even films:

1. *Source Music.* This is music that emanates from the scene itself. For example, if the characters are in a nightclub, music would be playing, but it would have to be something that enhanced the characters and the action and didn't detract from either.
2. *Underscores.* These are emotional cues and backgrounds that will embellish a certain feeling or sentiment as it is dictated by the script.
3. *Character Themes.* These are specially written compositions identified with a particular character or characters.

In this field, too, it's to your advantage to acquire training in complementary areas such as orchestration, composition, and electronic music, and of course you need to become skilled in using all of the gadgets involved with the scoring process. In sound recording, as you know, the two-inch tape doesn't have to sync up with anything. However, in scoring, you're syncing audio with video frame by frame, and that requires knowledge of all the SMPTE equipment that allows the composer to determine where and how much music will be plotted throughout a film.

## Getting Started

Once you feel you have the aforementioned education and skills under your belt, you may begin your quest on a local level. Check into local television stations, public broadcasters, and any audio companies or individuals involved in producing television commercials or films.

Once you have gathered experience here, it may be easier to move on to bigger and better things.

However, if you choose to bypass hometown prospects altogether, you can submit your material on tape to heads of studio music departments, studio publishers, and film music agents. There are also some publications like *Hollywood Reporter* and *Backstage Shoot* which report industry happenings, although these aren't always so helpful for the person just starting out.

If you're really serious about making film scoring your life's work, proximity always helps, so setting your sights on an L.A. or New York residency isn't such a bad idea either. There, you can make firsthand contacts with producers, actors, directors, and screenwriters which may improve your chances of getting your material to the right people. Even more, you may light upon a film composer who's up to his eyeballs in work and needs an assistant. Beyond that possibility, you may have the opportunity to meet a young filmmaker who proposes to do a movie on a shoestring budget, and here each of you may be the springboard for the other's needs.

## Getting Paid

When a film producer arranges to use music for either a film or a TV show, he has two choices. He can either use a previously existing musical composition or he can commission a writer to compose original music for the soundtrack.

In cases where the producer decides to use previously composed music for his film, he must obtain both a synchronization and a performance license from the copyright owner. The synchronization license will give the producer the right to use the work in timed relation with his film. If the producer will be publicly performing the work by exhibiting his film in movie theaters, he must also obtain a performance license. However, if this previously existing composition will only appear in a film being produced for television, only the synchronization license is necessary, the reason being that the performing rights organizations grant blanket licenses to television broadcasters and, therefore, the copyright owner will receive payment for the public performance of his or her work in this medium through the organization he or she is affiliated with.

However, if an original composition is desired, the producer will engage the services of a writer. This can be arranged in two ways:

1. The work is created on a work-for-hire basis. This is the most typical scenario, where the producer or motion picture company acts as the employer and the songwriter as the employee. The producer or company pays the writer a fee and becomes the owner of the composition's copyright. In the matter of the music's publishing, you can see that scoring is very much like popular songwriting, because whoever owns the show or is pulling the strings is going to want your publishing. If you aren't willing to give it up, you may be out of the picture—no pun intended.

2. The writer is commissioned to create the work as a contribution to the film. Here, in addition to receiving a fee, the writer retains copyright ownership of the work and may, therefore, license the use of the copyrighted work.

It should be noted that in some situations, the writer and the producer or film company will come to an agreement whereby the writer accepts a lower fee for his or her work in exchange for an agreed-upon portion of the copyright ownership.

# Glossary of Industry Terms

**AABA.** A popular song structure consisting of two verses, a chorus, and a verse, with the verses repeating the same musical idea.

**A/C.** Adult contemporary music.

**Acetate dub.** An individually cut record (as opposed to multiple pressings), commonly used to reference the effectiveness of the mastering process on a 12" record.

**Administration.** The handling of all copyright, monetary, and contractual aspects of a particular song or catalog of songs.

**Advance.** Money paid prior to the recording of a song or the release of a record, which is then deducted from future royalties.

**AFM.** American Federation of Musicians. Union established for musicians, copyists, arrangers, and contractors (contractors being individuals who hire musicians and/or singers for a recording date).

**AFTRA.** American Federation of Television and Radio Artists. Union established for singers, announcers, actors, narrators, and sound effects artists.

**Analog recording.**   The recording medium in which magnetic particles make up the sound.

**A & R (artist and repertoire) director.**   Record company executive responsible for finding and signing material, talent, and masters.

**AOR.**   Album-oriented rock music.

**Arrangement.**   Adaptation of a musical composition for performance by instruments and voices other than those it was originally written for.

**Arranger.**   Person who creates an arrangement and who may also act as a contractor by finding and hiring musicians to play the parts which have been created.

**Artist.**   Individual or band under a recording contract.

**ASCAP.**   American Society of Composers, Authors and Publishers. A performing rights organization.

**Assignment.**   Transfer of rights to a particular song or songs from one copyright owner to another.

**Biography.**   Concise account of an artist's, group's, producer's, arranger's, and/or songwriter's industry-related experience.

**BMI.**   Broadcast Music, Inc. A performing rights organization.

**Bootlegging.**   Unauthorized recording and selling of a performance of a song.

**Bridge.**   Also known as a release or C section, this section of a song usually introduces a totally different musical idea altogether.

**Bullet.**   Chart notation designating the significant upward movement of a record as indicated by record sales and/or radio add-ons.

**Buyback.**   Contractual option allowing the writer to purchase his or her songs back in an agreed-upon number of years for an agreed-upon sum of money.

**Cassingle.**   A cassette of a single song, has basically

taken the place of a 45 rpm (revolutions per minute) record.

**Casting.** Analyzing what type of material is needed for a particular artist or market, and then slanting or directing material accordingly.

**Catalog.** All of the songs owned by a music publisher or a songwriter.

**CD.** Compact disk (digital recording).

**Charts.** Listings published by industry trades of the best-selling records in the pop, rhythm and blues, country, rock, dance, and rap markets.

**Chord.** Combination of three or more musical notes sounded simultaneously to produce a harmony.

**Chorus.** The section of a song that repeats itself; the hook of a song.

**CHR.** Contemporary Hit Radio.

**Clearance agency.** Another name for a performing rights organization.

**Click track.** A perforated soundtrack which produces click sounds, enabling an individual to hear a predetermined beat in synchronization with a television or movie film or sound recording.

**CMA.** Country Music Association. An organization active in promoting country music.

**Collaborator.** One of two or more persons involved in the writing of a song.

**Commercial record.** A record which has mass appeal and sales potential.

**Commissioned work.** Work used as a contribution to a movie, TV film, etc., whose copyright ownership is retained by the work's creator unless there's a signed agreement stating otherwise.

**Composer.** One who creates music.

**Composition.** A musical work.

**Compulsory license.** After a song has been recorded

once, individuals wishing to manufacture and distribute phonocords of that song must obtain permission to do so from the work's copyright owner in the form of this type of license.

**Co-publishing.**   The joint publishing of one copyrighted work by two or more publishers.

**Copyright.**   Under the U.S. Copyright Act, the exclusive rights granted to composers and lyricists for the protection of their works. *To copyright* is to obtain protection for a musical work or sound recording by filing the appropriate registration forms with the U.S. Copyright Office in Washington, D.C.

**Copyright infringement.**   The violation of any of the copyright owner's exclusive rights.

**Copyright notice.**   A notice placed on a work which informs the world as to the work's creator or whoever owns the copyright. The *copyright symbol* may be expressed with the word "Copyright," the symbol © or the abbreviation "Copr." For published works, the *copyright year* is the year of the work's first publication; for unpublished works, it's the year the work was created; for demos, it's the year the demo is being shopped. The name of the present *copyright owner* follows the year in a copyright notice.

**Copyright owner.**   The individual or company that is the owner of the exclusive rights granted by a copyright.

**Cover record.**   A record that displays another version of a song that has already been recorded; frequently called a remake or cover version.

**Cross-collateralization.**   A means of recouping the money spent on one song or record from the earnings of another song or record.

**Crossover.**   A song receiving airplay in more than one music market.

**Cut.**   A recorded work. *To cut* is to record.

**DAT.**   Digital audiotape.

**Demo.**  A demonstration recording of a song produced for the purpose of displaying the song's potential to music industry personnel.

**Demo firms.**  Companies which specialize in making demos.

**Digital recording.**  A recording medium in which the sound source is turned into a numerical value.

**Distributor.**  Company that handles the sale of a record label's product to jobbers and retail outlets in specific territories.

**DOR.**  Dance-oriented rock music.

**Engineer.**  Individual who operates the studio equipment during a recording session.

**EP.**  Extended-play album, played at 33 ⅓ rpm (revolutions per minute) and generally containing four or five songs instead of the standard eight to twelve songs found on an LP.

**Exclusive songwriter contract.**  A contract that binds the songwriter exclusively to one publisher.

**Folio.**  A printed collection of songs, either created by one writer or taken from a group of writers, which is offered for sale to the public.

**Form PA.**  Copyright registration form filed for the protection of both published and unpublished musical works.

**Form SR.**  Copyright registration form filed to protect sound recordings.

**Gold album.**  An album certified by the RIAA (Recording Industry Association of America) as having sold over 500,000 units.

**Gold single.**  A single certified by RIAA as having sold over 500,000 units.

**Harmony.**  Chords played against a melody in a way or combination that complements the melody and enhances it.

**Harry Fox Agency.**  This organization represents

music publishers in connection with the mechanical reproduction of their copyrights by handling mechanical
licensing and collecting mechanical revenues. The agency
will also handle synchronization licensing upon the request of their music publisher affiliates.

**Head arrangement.**   An arrangement devised on the
spot through trial and error during the course of a song's
production.

**Heads out.**   A term used to describe the way in
which a reel-to-reel tape has been stored. A tape stored in
this way has its loose end at the beginning of the tape and
is ready to be played.

**Hit.**   Description of a record that sells widely and has
usually achieved Top 40 success.

**Hook.**   The melodic, rhythmic, or lyrical section of
a song that repeats itself and pulls the listener in.

**Indie.**   Independent record label.

**Jingle.**   An advertising device that employs short,
catchy musical phrases and words to convey and make
memorable a product's sell message.

**Label.**   A record company.

**Lead sheet.**   Musical notation of a song's melody,
along with the chord symbols and words, which is usually
handwritten (as opposed to printed sheet music).

**Leader.**   White tape or an unrecorded portion of
tape which separates one song selection from another.

**License.**   A legal permit. *To license* is to authorize use
by a legal permit.

**Lick.**   An improvised musical figure.

**Loop.**   A snippet of a previously recorded record
that normally consists of one or two measures which are
continuously cycled to create a drum track for a recording.

**LP.**   A long-playing record played at 33 ⅓ rpm (revolutions per minute).

**Lyric sheet.**  A copy of a song's lyrics, preferably typewritten.

**Lyricist.**  The author of a song's words.

**Lyrics.**  The words to a song.

**Manager.**  Individual who guides an artist and oversees the development of his or her career.

**Market.**  Selling place. Each genre of music (pop, rock, R & B, country, etc.) is considered a market unto itself because each appeals to a specific audience that may purchase that particular type of song.

**Master.**  The final recorded version of a song that's ready to be pressed into records.

**Mechanical right.**  Under the U.S. Copyright Act, a right granted to the copyright owner whereby he or she may profit from the mechanical reproduction (use of a song in records, tapes, electrical transcriptions, and audiotapes for broadcast and background music purposes) of his or her musical work.

**Mechanical rights organization.**  Agency which handles mechanical licensing and collects the money earned from the mechanical reproduction of a copyrighted work for their affiliated publishers (copyright owners).

**Midi.**  Musical instrument digital interface. The language in which synthesizers or sound modules are able to communicate with one another.

**Minimum earnings clause.**  A contractual clause which gives the songwriter added protection by providing that the publisher must not only get the writer's song recorded and released within a specified time frame, but that the writer must also earn a certain sum of money from the tune within that period of time, otherwise the song will revert back to the writer.

**Mix.**  The blending together of different tracks on a multitrack recording in such a way as to achieve an overall desired result.

**Modulation.** The passing from one key to another.

**MOR.** Middle-of-the-road music.

**Music publisher.** An individual or company that works to get songs commercially recorded, handles the administration of copyrights, generates revenue by exploiting the copyright, and collects income earned from mechanical licensing, synchronization licensing, and printed editions, and distributes this income to the songwriter.

**New Age.** Usually thought of as an adult music format which is often instrumental and very mood-oriented.

**One-stop.** Wholesale operation from which record store owners and jukebox operators may purchase record products from various manufacturers.

**Overdub.** The addition of instruments or vocals to preexisting tracks.

**Payola.** Money illegally paid to a broadcaster to sway him into playing a certain record.

**Performance royalty.** Money earned when a copyrighted work is either performed live or broadcast in some manner.

**Performing right.** Under the U.S. Copyright Act, a right granted to copyright owners of musical works which allows them to license their works for public performance.

**Performing rights organization.** Organization that monitors the public performance of songs by various music users, and collects and distributes monies earned from those performances to their writer and publisher affiliates.

**Phonocord.** The physical audiotape, phonograph record, or any analog or digital format that embodies the fixed sounds of a sound recording.

**Pick hit.** A song reviewed by the trades that's predicted to do well in its designated market.

**Pirating.**  Unauthorized reproduction and selling of records and/or tapes.

**Platinum album.**  An album certified by the RIAA as having sold one million units.

**Platinum single.**  A single certified by the RIAA as having sold one million units.

**Point.**  A percentage of money earned on a record which is equal to 1 percent of the suggested retail list price of the record and is usually paid on 90 percent of all records sold.

**Printed editions.**  The printing of a song in the form of sheet music or for inclusion in songbooks, folios, or stage and marching band arrangements, made available for sale to the public.

**Producer.**  Individual responsible for all aspects of a recording, from the selection of the song to the final mix.

**Professional manager.**  Music publisher employee responsible for screening new material and placing material with artists and producers.

**Program director.**  Radio station executive who determines which songs will be added to the station's playlist.

**Prosody.**  The marriage of words and music.

**Public domain.**  Status of a musical work which is no longer protected by copyright due to either an expired copyright or an invalid copyright notice.

**Publication.**  The issuing of copies of a work to the public for sale.

**Rackjobber.**  Dealer that supplies records from a variety of manufacturers to specific retail outlets such as drugstores and variety stores.

**R & B.**  Rhythm and blues.

**Release.**  The bridge of a song; or the issuing of a record by a record label.

**Rhythm.**  The repetitious sounds or pulses that give a song its feel, movement, groove, or beat, generally established by instruments comprising the rhythm section, that is, keyboard, guitar, bass, and drums.

**RIAA.**   Recording Industry Association of America.

**Royalty.**   Money earned from the use of a song or the sale of a record.

**Sampling.**   When sounds are electronically taken from a master recording and through technological imitation placed within the context of another composition.

**Self-contained artist.**   An artist who writes and performs his or her own material.

**SESAC.**   Society of European Stage Authors and Composers. This performing rights organization also handles mechanical and synchronization licensing.

**SGA.**   Songwriters Guild of America. A protective association for the songwriter.

**Sheet music.**   A printed edition of a song made available for sale to the public.

**Showcase.**   A presentation by means of a live performance of new material and/or new talent.

**Single.**   An individual song or a song from an album that is used as a promotional tool, promoted to radio stations to gain recognition, airplay, and ultimately sales for that particular song or album.

**SMPTE.**   The most commonly used time code which allows you to sync up external devices with an alternate sound source.

**Song shark.**   Individual or company that profits from dealing unethically with songwriters.

**Sound recording.**   A work that is a series of recorded sounds.

**Spec recording.**   A recording done on the basis that payment will be made to the studio from the advance money received once a deal has been secured.

**Split publishing.**   Same as Co-publishing.

**Staff writer.**   Songwriter who writes exclusively for one publisher and receives a salary from same.

**Standard.**   A song that retains its popularity over the years and is usually covered by a number of artists.

**Studio.**   Facility where songs are recorded.

**Subpublishing.**   Publishing situation wherein the original publisher (or U.S. publisher) enters into an agreement with a foreign publisher so that the foreign publisher will represent and promote the original publisher's song in the foreign territory.

**Synchronization.**   Using music in timed relation (in sync) to film.

**Synchronization right.**   The right to use a musical composition in sync with a film or videotape.

**Synthesizer.**   Most commonly, a keyboard instrument on which sounds can be manipulated by separate controls for oscillators and filters, enabling the player/programmer to create and custom-tailor sounds.

**Tails out.**   A term used to describe a way in which a reel-to-reel has been stored. A tape stored in this way has its loose end at the end of the tape, and it must be rewound before it can be played.

**Take.**   An accepted recording of an instrumental or vocal part. To take is to put down a track or vocal and listen to the result.

**Time reversion clause.**   A contractual clause stating that a publisher must get a writer's song recorded and released within a specified period of time. If he fails to do so, the song reverts back to the writer.

**Top 40.**   Radio station format with a playlist that primarily includes only the top-selling records, as indicated from the trade pop charts. Top 40 is also called CHR.

**Track.**   One of the individually controlled specific components that make up a multitrack; for example, one of the tracks in a 24-track recording. "Track" could also be used as song or title when referring to a specific cut on an album.

**Trades.**   Music industry publications.

**Union scale.**   Minimum wage scale earned during the course of employment by members of AFM and AFTRA.

**Urban.**   Radio station format with a playlist that primarily includes R & B, dance, and rap music.

**Verse.**   In any song pattern, the A section which precedes and generally sets up the chorus.

**Virtual recording.**   When SMPTE or some other time code has been generated to operate a sequencer so as to enable that sequencer to communicate with sound modules in a particular section of a live performance or recording.

**Work-for-hire.**   Situation wherein the songwriter is hired by a film producer, motion picture company, or music publisher to create a musical composition for a fee, while the copyright ownership of that composition is retained by the film producer, motion picture company, or music publisher.

**Writer's signature.**   The unique style or characteristics that identify a songwriter's material.

# APPENDIX A

# MUSIC PUBLISHERS

## Pop Publishers

Almo Music
360 N. La Cienega
Boulevard
Los Angeles, CA 90048

Alpha Music, Inc.
1619 Broadway
New York, NY 10019

Amokshasong
c/o Cosh Management
P.O. Box 102
London E15 2HH, England

Apache Red
c/o Irving Music
360 N. La Cienega
Boulevard
Los Angeles, CA 90048

Aquarian Fire
c/o Guardian Angel
Productions
P.O. Box 38683
Hollywood, CA 90028

Arista Music, Inc.
c/o BMG Music Publishing
1133 Avenue of the
Americas
New York, NY 10036

AVI Music Publishing
Group, Inc.
7060 Hollywood Boulevard
Hollywood, CA 90028

Badams
c/o Bruce Allen Talent
406–68 Water Street
Vancouver, BC, V6B 1A4
Canada

Hal Bernard
P.O. Box 8385
Cincinnati, OH 45208

Big Pig Publishing
ADM: Warner/Chappell
1290 Avenue of the
Americas
New York, NY 10019

Biv Ten
c/o Katz & Cherry
3423 Piedmont Road, NE
Atlanta, GA 30305

Black Doors
c/o Eric Johnson
189–22 Tioga Drive
St. Albans, NY 11414

BMG Music Publishing
1133 Avenue of the
Americas
New York, NY 10036

Bust-It-Music
c/o Louis Burrell
80 Swan Way
Oakland, CA 94612

Cashola
c/o Grajonca Music
P.O. Box 1994
San Francisco, CA 94101

Chappell Music
1290 Avenue of the
Americas
New York, NY 10019

Chrysalis Music
9255 Sunset Boulevard
Los Angeles, CA 90069

Colgems-EMI
c/o Screen Gems-EMI
810 Seventh Avenue
New York, NY 10019

The Company of the Two
P(i)eters, Inc.
2055 Richmond Street
Philadelphia, PA 19125

Controversy Music
ADM: Warner/Chappell
9000 Sunset Boulevard
Los Angeles, CA 90069

Country Road Music
c/o Gelfand, Rennert
1880 Century Park E.
Los Angeles, CA 90067

Creeping Death
c/o Manatt Phelps
11355 W. Olympic
Boulevard
Los Angeles, CA 90064

Walt Disney Music
500 S. Buena Vista Street
Burbank, CA 91521

Dog Turner Music
c/o EMI Music
810 Seventh Avenue
New York, NY 10019

E/A Music
ADM: Warner/Chappell
9000 Sunset Boulevard
Los Angeles, CA 90069

EMI April
810 Seventh Avenue
New York, NY 10019

EMI Blackwood
810 Seventh Avenue
New York, NY 10019

EMI Music
c/o Screen Gems-EMI
810 Seventh Avenue
New York, NY 10019

EMI Unart
c/o EMI Music
810 Seventh Avenue
New York, NY 10019

End of Music
c/o Virgin Songs
827 N. Hilldale Avenue
West Hollywood, CA
90069

Fantasy, Inc.
2600 Tenth Street
Berkeley, CA 94710

Full Keel Music
c/o Windswept Pacific
9320 Wilshire Boulevard
Beverly Hills, CA 90212

Al Gallico
9301 Wilshire Boulevard
Beverly Hills, CA 90210

Gamble-Hugg Music
c/o Mighty Three Music
309 South Broad Street
Philadelphia, PA 19107

Global Music, Inc.
1345 Avenue of the
Americas
New York, NY 10105

The Goodman Group
488 Madison Avenue
New York, NY 10022

Gratitude Sky
c/o Virgin Music
1790 Broadway
New York, NY 10019

Green Skirt Music
c/o Carter Turner & Co.
1 Capitol City Plaza
3350 Peachtree Road
Atlanta, GA 30326

Rick Hall Music, Inc.
P.O. Box 2527
Muscle Shoals, AL 35660

Harrindur Music
c/o Ensign Music Corp.
1 Gulf & Western Plaza
New York, NY 10023

Henry Suemay Music
c/o EMI Music
810 Seventh Avenue
New York, NY 10019

Hidden Pun Music
c/o Hit & Run Music
Publishing, Inc.
1841 Broadway
New York, NY 10023

Hit & Run Music
Publishing, Inc.
1841 Broadway
New York, NY 10023

Island Music, Inc.
6525 Sunset Boulevard
Los Angeles, CA 90028

Jobete Music Co., Inc.
6255 Sunset Boulevard
Los Angeles, CA 90028

Joe Public
c/o Ensign Music Corp.
15 Columbus Circle
New York, NY 10023

Joel Music
ADM: EMI Music
810 Seventh Avenue
New York, NY 10019

Kear Music
c/o Carter Turner & Co.
1 Capitol City Plaza

3350 Peachtree Road
Atlanta, GA 30326

Keith Sweat Publishing
ADM: Warner Brothers
Music Corp.
9000 Sunset Boulevard
Los Angeles, CA
90069-0305

Kip Teez Music
6350 Reseda Boulevard
Reseda, CA 91335

Last Song
c/o I.D. Productions
9520 W. 47th Street
Brookfield, IL 60513

Leiber-Stoller Songs, Inc.
9000 Sunset Boulevard
Los Angeles, CA 90069

Hal Leonard Publishing
Corp.
7777 W. Blue Mound Road
Milwaukee, WI 53213

Level 42
c/o Paul Crockford
Management
59 Islington Park Street
London N1, England

Lipservices
1841 Broadway
New York, NY 10023

Loc'd Out
c/o Decent Management
7932 Hillside Avenue
Los Angeles, CA 90046

Macola Music
8831 Sunset Boulevard
West Hollywood, CA
90069

Mark King & Mike Lindup
c/o Warner Brothers Music
Corp.
9000 Sunset Boulevard
Los Angeles, CA
90069-0305

Eric Martin Songs
2062 Union Street
San Francisco, CA 94123

MCA Music
1755 Broadway
New York, NY 10019

Mike Ten
c/o Katz & Cherry
3423 Piedmont Road, NE
Atlanta, GA 30305

Moebetoblame
c/o Lindy Goetz
Management
11116 Aqua Vista
Studio City, CA 91602

Charlie Monk Music
3991 Hobbs Road
Nashville, TN 37215

Mood Music
c/o Warner Brothers Music
Corp.
9000 Sunset Boulevard
Los Angeles, CA
90069-0305

MPL Communications
c/o Eastman & Eastman
39 W. 54th Street
New York, NY 10019

Neville Music
c/o Irving Music
360 N. La Cienega
Boulevard
Los Angeles, CA 90048

New Jersey Underground
c/o Gelfand, Rennert, &
Feldman
6 East 43rd Street
New York, NY 10017

Northern Pikes Songs
c/o Ed Smeall
4442 Saw Mill Valley Drive
Mississauga, Ontario
L5L 3N2, Canada

One Word
c/o Scott Daine Ent.
P.O. Box 9026
New Haven, CT 06532

Orion
c/o Next Decade
Entertainment, Inc.

730 5th Avenue
New York, NY 10019

Painted Desert Music Corp.
10 E. 53rd Street
New York, NY 10022

Peasant Mart
c/o Richard Green, Esq.
11 Music Circle South
Nashville, TN 37203

Pecot
827 N. Hilldale Avenue
Hollywood, CA 90069

Peer-Southern Organization
810 Seventh Avenue
New York, NY 10019

Pillarview
c/o Chrysalis Songs
9255 Sunset Boulevard
Los Angeles, CA 90069

Play the Music
c/o Metropolitan Records
900 Passaic Avenue E.
Newark, NJ 07029

Elvis Presley Music
9000 Sunset Boulevard
Los Angeles, CA 90069

Realsongs
c/o Manatt Phelps

11355 W. Olympic
Boulevard
Los Angeles, CA 90064

Rendezvous Entertainment
1133 Avenue of the
Americas
New York, NY 10036

Rightsong
c/o Warner Tamerlane
9000 Sunset Boulevard
Los Angeles, CA 90069

SBK Entertainment World,
Inc.
1290 Avenue of the
Americas
New York, NY 10104

Shakeji
ADM: MCA Music
70 Universal City Plaza
Universal City, CA 91608

Shanice 4 U
c/o Bill Dern Management
8455 Fountain Avenue
Los Angeles, CA 90069

Shapiro, Bernstein & Co.,
Inc.
10 E. 53rd Street
New York, NY 10022

Silver Blue Music
220 Central Park South
New York, NY 10019

So What
48 Princess Street
Manchester M16 HR,
England

Solar
1635 N. Cahuenga
Boulevard
Los Angeles, CA 90028

Somethin' Stoopid
c/o Almo Music
360 N. La Cienega
Boulevard
Los Angeles, CA 90048

Sony Songs
666 Fifth Avenue
New York, NY 10103

Tajai Music
c/o Mighty Three Music
209 South Broad Street
Philadelphia, PA 19107

Tarpell Music
1080 N. Delaware Avenue
Philadelphia, PA 19125

TCF Music
c/o Warner Brothers Music
Corp.
9000 Sunset Boulevard
Los Angeles, CA
90069-0305

Testatyme
c/o Almo Music

360 N. La Cienega
Boulevard
Los Angeles, CA 90048

Third Coast
c/o I.D. Productions
9520 W. 47th Street
Brookfield, IL 60513

Tom Sturges
c/o Chrysalis Music
9255 Sunset Boulevard
Los Angeles, CA 90069

Tree Publishing Co., Inc.
c/o Sony-Tree Publishing
8 Music Square West
Nashville, TN 37203

Tuareg
c/o Richard Green, Esq.
11 Music Circle South
Nashville, TN 37203

Ultrawave
c/o Boulevard Management
16130 Ventura Boulevard
Encino, CA 91431

Virgin Music
1790 Broadway
New York, NY 10019

Virgin Songs
827 N. Hilldale Avenue
W. Hollywood, CA 90069

Warner/Chappell Music, Inc.
9000 Sunset Boulevard
Los Angeles, CA 90069

Warner Elektra Asylum Music, Inc.
9000 Sunset Boulevard
Los Angeles, CA 90069

Wordiks
c/o Siegel & Feldstein
1990 S. Bundy Drive
Los Angeles, CA 90025

Zomba
137–139 W. 25th Street
New York, NY 10001

## R & B Publishers

Across 110th St. Music
c/o EMI Publishing
810 Seventh Avenue
New York, NY 10019

ADRA
c/o Select Records
16 W. 22nd Street
New York, NY 10010

April Joy Music
ADM: Island Music
8920 Sunset Boulevard
Los Angeles, CA 90069

ATV Music
c/o EMI Music
810 Seventh Avenue
New York, NY 10019

AZ Music
c/o Warner Brothers Music Corp.
9000 Sunset Boulevard
Los Angeles, CA
90069-0305

Barjosha
c/o Zomba
137–139 W. 25th Street
New York, NY 10001

Biv Ten
c/o Katz & Cherry
3423 Piedmont Road NE
Atlanta, GA 30305

Black Doors
c/o Eric Johnson
189–22 Tioga Drive
St. Albans, NY 11414

Chumpy Music
c/o Kevin Glickman
372 5th Avenue
New York, NY 10018

Cold Chillin'
c/o Warner/Chappell Music, Inc.
9000 Sunset Boulevard
Los Angeles, CA 90069

Deswing Mob
c/o Uptown Enterprises
1755 Broadway
New York, NY 10019

Divineland
c/o Protoons
740 Broadway
New York, NY 10003

Donril Music
ADM: Zomba
137–139 W. 25th Street
New York, NY 10001

Dyad Music
c/o Mason & Co.
400 Park Avenue
New York, NY 10022

E. Sharp
c/o Tommy Boy Records
1747 First Avenue
New York, NY 10128

EMI April
810 Seventh Avenue
New York, NY 10019

Forceful Music
c/o Mrs. C. George
702 Lenox Road
P.O. Box 284
Brooklyn, NY 11203

Franne Gee
8685 Lookout Mountain
Avenue
Los Angeles, CA 90046

Jon Gass
c/o Sandy Fox
1900 Avenue of the Stars
Los Angeles, CA 90067

Genric
c/o Stanton Scott
Productions
3519 Via Del Prado
Woodland Hills, CA 91364

Getaloadofatso
c/o Uptown Enterprises
1755 Broadway
New York, NY 10019

Rick Hall Music, Inc.
P.O. Box 2527
Muscle Shoals, AL 35660

Harlem Music, Inc.
1800 Main Street
Buffalo, NY 14208

Heritage Hill
c/o Warner/Chappell
Music, Inc.
9000 Sunset Boulevard
Los Angeles, CA 90069

Howie Tee Music
976 Schenectady Avenue
Brooklyn, NY 11203

Island Music
3500 West Olive Avenue
Burbank, CA 91505

Jobete Music Co., Inc.
6255 Sunset Boulevard
Los Angeles, CA 90028

R. Kelly
c/o Barry Hankerson
23460 Hatteras Street
Woodland Hills, CA 91367

King's Kid
c/o Warner Tamerlane
9000 Sunset Boulevard
Los Angeles, CA 90069

Leftover Soupped
c/o EMI April
810 Seventh Avenue
New York, NY 10019

Loc'd Out
c/o Decent Management
7932 Hillside Avenue
Los Angeles, CA 90046

London
c/o Bill Dern Management
8455 Fountain Avenue
Los Angeles, CA 90069

MCA Music
1755 Broadway
New York, NY 10019

Mike Ten
c/o Katz & Cherry
3423 Piedmont Road, NE
Atlanta, GA 30305

Milteer
c/o EMI Music
810 Seventh Avenue
New York, NY 10019

Money in the Bank
c/o Joel Katz, Esq.
3423 Piedmont Road, NE
Atlanta, GA 30305

Mudslide
c/o Bill Dern Management
8455 Fountain Avenue
Los Angeles, CA 90069

Next Plateau Music
1650 Broadway
New York, NY 10019

Peer-Southern Organization
810 Seventh Avenue
New York, NY 10019

Protoons
c/o Profile
740 Broadway
New York, NY 10003

Purple Heart Music
c/o Richardson Consultants
1000 Corporate Pointe
Culver City, CA 90230

Rightsong
c/o Warner Tamerlane
9000 Sunset Boulevard
Los Angeles, CA 90069

SBK Entertainment World,
Inc.
1290 Avenue of the
Americas
New York, NY 10104

Shaman Drum
c/o Artists Only, Inc.
152–18 Union Turnpike
Flushing, NY 11367

Shapiro, Bernstein & Co.,
Inc.
10 E. 53rd Street
New York, NY 10022

Stanton's Gold Music
3519 Via Del Prado
Woodland Hills, CA 91364

Steveland Morris Music
4616 Magnolia Boulevard
Burbank, CA 91505

Stone Jam
c/o Untouchables
Entertainment
1560 Broadway
New York, NY 10036

Sula
c/o Warner Brothers Music
Corp.

9000 Sunset Boulevard
Los Angeles, CA
90069-0305

Sun Face
c/o Artists Only, Inc.
152–18 Union Turnpike
Flushing, NY 11367

Tarpell Music
1080 N. Delaware Avenue
Philadelphia, PA 19125

Varry White Music
6607 Sunset Boulevard
Los Angeles, CA 90028

Virgin Songs
827 N. Hilldale Avenue
W. Hollywood, CA 90069

Warner/Chappell Music,
Inc.
9000 Sunset Boulevard
Los Angeles, CA 90069

Warner Tamerlane
9000 Sunset Boulevard
Los Angeles, CA 90069

Welbeck Music
c/o EMI April
810 Seventh Avenue
New York, NY 10019

Whole Nine Yards
ADM: John Davimos, Esq.

6380 Wilshire Boulevard
Los Angeles, CA 90048

Willesden Music
c/o Zomba
137–139 W. 25th Street
New York, NY 10001

Wokie Music
19713 Saticoy Street
Canoga Park, CA 91306

Writing Staff
c/o EMI April
810 Seventh Avenue
New York, NY 10019

Yah Mo Music
867 S. Muirfield Road
Los Angeles, CA 90005

Zomba
137–139 W. 25th Street
New York, NY 10001

## Country & Western Publishers

Acuff-Rose Music
c/o Opryland Music Group
65 Music Square West
Nashville, TN 37203

Atlantic Music
c/o Criterion Music
6124 Selma Avenue
Hollywood, CA 90028

Bellamy Bros. Music
1102 17th Avenue South
Nashville, TN 37212

Belwin Mills Publishing
Corp.
15800 NW 48th Avenue
Miami, FL 33014

BMG Music Publishing
1 Music Circle North
Nashville, TN 37203

Bobby & Billy Music
c/o Bill Deaton
1300 Division Street
Nashville, TN 37203

Cabin Fever
ADM: SBK Songs
35 Music Square East
Nashville, TN 37203

Cadillac Pink
c/o Criterion Music
6124 Selma Avenue
Hollywood, CA 90028

Glen Campbell Music, Inc.
P.O. Box 158717
Nashville, TN 37215

Buddy Cannon
ADM: PolyGram Music
54 Music Square East
Nashville, TN 37203

Chante Clair
c/o Bug Music
1026 16th Avenue South
Nashville, TN 37202

Tom Collins Music
P.O. Box 121407
Nashville, TN 37212

Criterion Music
6124 Selma Avenue
Hollywood, CA 90028

Cross Keys Music
c/o Sony-Tree Publishing
8 Music Square West
Nashville, TN 37203

Danny Boy
c/o Affiliated Publishers
11 Music Square East
Nashville, TN 37203

Edge O' Woods
10 Music Circle South
Nashville, TN 37203

EMI April
35 Music Square East
Nashville, TN 37203

Ensign
c/o Famous Music
65 Music Square East
Nashville, TN 37203

Famous Music
65 Music Square East
Nashville, TN 37203

First Release
c/o Criterion Music
6124 Selma Avenue
Hollywood, CA 90028

Forrest Hills Music
65 Music Square West
Nashville, TN 37203

Funky But Music, Inc.
P.O. Box 1770
153–155 Sanders Ferry
Road
Hendersonville, TN 37077

Al Gallico
9301 Wilshire Boulevard
Beverly Hills, CA 90210

Grand Haven Music
2020 21st Avenue South
Nashville, TN 37212

Rick Hall Music, Inc.
P.O. Box 2527
Muscle Shoals, AL 35660

Heartland Express
14300 Terra Bella Street
Panorama City, CA 09107

Heartscratch
c/o Irving Music

1904 Adelicia Street
Nashville, TN 37212

Hit & Run Music
Publishing, Inc.
1841 Broadway
New York, NY 10023

Hookem Music
c/o Terrace Music
217 E. 86th Street
New York, NY 10028

Irving Music
1904 Adelicia Street
Nashville, TN 37212

Kentucky Thunder
122 Maureen Drive
Hendersonville, TN 37075

Kinetic Diamond
c/o Hamstein Music
P.O. Box 163870
Austin, TX 78716

Long Run Music
c/o Raposa Productions
P.O. Box 120551
Nashville, TN 37212

Macola Music
8831 Sunset Boulevard
West Hollywood, CA
90069

Maypop Music
P.O. Box 121192
Nashville, TN 37212

Miss Hazel Music
P.O. Box 882
Mt. Juliet, TN 37122

Moline Valley
c/o Hamstein Music
P.O. Box 163870
Austin, TX 78716

Charlie Monk Music
3991 Hobbs Road
Nashville, TN 37215

Myrt & Chuck's Boy
1915 Wildwood Avenue
Nashville, TN 37212

Nocturnal Eclipse
8730 Sunset Boulevard
Los Angeles, CA 90069

Opryland Music Group,
Inc.
65 Music Square West
Nashville, TN 37203

Paul & Jonathan Songs
Route 2, Box 129
Kingston Springs, TN
37082

Peer-Southern Organization
810 Seventh Avenue
New York, NY 10019

Pier Five
1106 18th Avenue South
Nashville, TN 37212

Polly Girl
6251 Tuttle Place
Anchorage, AK 99507

Post Oak
c/o Sony-Tree Publishing
8 Music Square West
Nashville, TN 37203

Elvis Presley Music
9000 Sunset Boulevard
Los Angeles, CA 90069

PRI Music
c/o PolyGram
54 Music Square East
Nashville, TN 37203

Tex Ritter Music
Publishing
6124 Selma Avenue
Hollywood, CA 90028

SBK Entertainment World,
Inc.
1290 Avenue of the
Americas
New York, NY 10104

Scarlet Moon Music
c/o Copyright Management,
Inc.
1102 17th Avenue South
Nashville, TN 37212

Screen Gems-EMI
35 Music Square East
Nashville, TN 37203

Shapiro, Bernstein & Co.,
Inc.
10 E. 53rd Street
New York, NY 10022

Songs of PolyGram
International
54 Music Square East
Nashville, TN 37203

Songwriters Ink
c/o Affiliated Publishers
11 Music Square East
Nashville, TN 37203

Sony-Tree Publishing
8 Music Square West
Nashville, TN 37203

Texas Wedge
c/o Affiliated Publishers
11 Music Square East
Nashville, TN 37203

Thankxamillion Music
c/o Tree Publishing
8 Music Square West
Nashville, TN 37203

Tree Publishing
c/o Sony-Tree Publishing
8 Music Square West
Nashville, TN 37203

Warner/Chappell Music,
Inc.
9000 Sunset Boulevard
Los Angeles, CA 90069

Word, Inc.
5221 N. O'Connor
Boulevard
Irving, TX 75039

Warner Tamerlane
21 Music Square East
Nashville, TN 37203

Zoo II
c/o Frank Miller
4205 Hillsboro Road
Nashville, TN 37215

# APPENDIX B
## RECORD LABELS

*Note:* Throughout the following listing, the names in parentheses indicate which labels these record companies are divisions of or which companies distribute their product. This information is for your benefit only—just to give you a better perspective on how interlocking this label network can be—and it's actually even more involved than it appears here. However, this information needn't be included in the company's mailing address when you're submitting songs.

## Pop Labels

A & M Records
(PolyGram)
595 Madison Avenue
New York, NY 10022

American Gramophone
9120 Mormon Bridge
Road
Omaha, NE 68152

Arista Records (BMG)
6 W. 57th Street
New York, NY 10019

ATCO (Atlantic)
75 Rockefeller Plaza
New York, NY 10019

Atlantic Records (WEA)
75 Rockefeller Plaza
New York, NY 10019

Bearsville Records
P.O. Box 135
Bearsville, NY 12409

Beggar's Banquet (BMG)
274 Madison Avenue
New York, NY 10016

BMG Records
1133 Avenue of the
Americas
New York, NY 10036

Capitol (Thorn/EMI)
1750 N. Vine Street
Hollywood, CA 90028

Capricorn Records
534 Broadway
Macon, GA 31201

CBS/Sony Records, Inc.
51 W. 52nd Street
New York, NY 10019

Charisma Records
(Atlantic)
1790 Broadway
New York, NY 10019

Cheetah Records
605 E. Robinson Street
Orlando, FL 32801

Chrysalis Records
(Thorn/EMI)
810 Seventh Avenue
New York, NY 10019

Columbia/Sony Records
(Sony)
P.O. Box 4450
New York, NY 10101-4450

Criterion Music Corp.
6124 Selma Avenue
Hollywood, CA 90028

Critique Records, Inc.
800 W. Cummings Park
Woburn, MA 01801

Curb Records (Thorn/EMI)
3907 W. Alameda Avenue
Burbank, CA 91505

Cypress Records
1525 Crossroads of the
World
Los Angeles, CA 90028

Def American (Reprise)
c/o Rick Rubin
3500 W. Olive Avenue
Burbank, CA 91505

Delicious Vinyl
6607 Sunset Boulevard
Los Angeles, CA 90028

DGC Records
9130 Sunset Boulevard
Los Angeles, CA 90069

East West (ATCO)
75 Rockefeller Plaza
New York, NY 10019

Elektra Entertainment
(WEA)
75 Rockefeller Plaza
New York, NY 10019

EMI Records (Thorn/EMI)
810 Seventh Avenue
New York, NY 10019

Enigma Entertainment
11264 Playa Court
Culver City, CA 90231

Epic Records (Sony)
P.O. Box 4450
New York, NY 10101-4450

Fantasy, Inc.
2600 Tenth Street
Berkeley, CA 94710

Frontline Records
2955 E. Main Street
Irvine, CA 92714

Geffen Records (MCA)
9126 Sunset Boulevard
Los Angeles, CA 90069

Giant Records (Warner
Bros.)
345 N. Maple Drive
Beverly Hills, CA 90210

ICON Records
57 Greene Street
New York, NY 10012

Impact Records (MCA)
6255 Sunset Boulevard
Hollywood, CA 90046

Interscope
10900 Wilshire Boulevard
Los Angeles, CA 90024

IRS Records (Cema Dist.)
3939 Lankershim Boulevard
Universal City, CA 91604

Island Records (PolyGram)
14 E. 4th Street
New York, NY 10012

Jive Records (BMG)
137–139 W. 25th Street
New York, NY 10001

Laface Records (Arista)
3500 Parkway Lane
Atlanta, GA 30092

London Records
(PolyGram)
825 Eighth Avenue
New York, NY 10019

MCA Records
70 Universal City Plaza
Universal City, CA 91608

Mercury Records
(PolyGram)
825 Eighth Avenue
New York, NY 10019

Metropolitan Records
900 Passaic Avenue
E. Newark, NJ 07029

Motown Records (MCA)
6255 Sunset Boulevard
Los Angeles, CA 90028

Paisley Park (Warner Bros.)
7801 Audubon Road
Chanhassen, MN 55317

Philadelphia International
Records
309 S. Broad Street
Philadelphia, PA 19107

Polydor Records
(PolyGram)
825 Eighth Avenue
New York, NY 10019

PolyGram Records, Inc.
825 Eighth Avenue
New York, NY 10019

Priority Records, Inc.
6430 Sunset Boulevard
Hollywood, CA 90028

Private Music
9014 Melrose Avenue
Los Angeles, CA 90069

Profile Records
740 Broadway
New York, NY 10019

Qwest Records (Warner
Bros.)
3800 Barham Boulevard
Los Angeles, CA 90068

RCA Records (BMG)
1133 Avenue of the
Americas
New York, NY 10036

Rendezvous Entertainment
1133 Avenue of the
Americas
New York, NY 10036

Reprise Records (Warner
Bros.)
3300 Warner Boulevard
Burbank, CA 91505

Rhino Records, Inc.
2225 Colorado Avenue
Santa Monica, CA 90404

Ruthless Records
61430 Strathern
Canoga Park, CA 91304

Rykodisc, Inc.
Pickering Wharf
Salem, MA 01970

SBK Records (ERG/EMI
Records Group)
1290 Avenue of the
Americas
New York, NY 10104

Scotti Bros. Records
2114 Pico Boulevard
Santa Monica, CA 90405

Sire Records (Warner
Bros.)
75 Rockefeller Plaza
New York, NY 10019

Slash
c/o Warner Brothers
3300 Warner Boulevard
Burbank, CA 91505

Starway Records
7600-B Leesburg Pike
Falls Church, VA 22043

The Strugglebaby
Recording Co.
P.O. Box 8385
Cincinnati, OH 45208

Ultra Records
5250 Santa Monica
Boulevard
Hollywood, CA 90029

Virgin Records (Atlantic)
338 North Foothill Road
Beverly Hills, CA 90210

Warner Bros. Records
(WEA)
3300 Warner Boulevard
Burbank, CA 91505

WEA,
Warner/Elektra/Atlantic
Corp.
111 N. Hollywood Way
Burbank, CA 91505

Wing Records (Mercury)
3800 Alameda Avenue
Burbank, CA 91505

Zomba Recording Corp.
(BMG)
137–139 W. 25th Street
New York, NY 10001

## R & B/Dance/Rap Labels

A & M Records
(PolyGram)
1416 N. La Brea Avenue
Hollywood, CA 90028

Arista Records (BMG)
6 W. 57th Street
New York, NY 10019

Atlantic Records (WEA)
75 Rockefeller Plaza
New York, NY 10019

Bassment Records
234 Christopher Columbus
Drive
Jersey City, NJ 07302

Beat Street Records
850 Seventh Avenue
New York, NY 10019

BMG Record Labels
1133 Avenue of the
Americas
New York, NY 10036

Bust It Records
80 Swan Way
Oakland, CA 94612

Capitol (Thorn/EMI)
1750 N. Vine Street
Hollywood, CA 90028

Cardiac Records
1790 Broadway
New York, NY 10019

CBS/Sony Records, Inc.
51 W. 52nd Street
New York, NY 10019

Charisma Records
(Atlantic)
1790 Broadway
New York, NY 10019

Chrysalis Records
(Thorn/EMI)
810 Seventh Avenue
New York, NY 10019

Cold Chillin' (Warner
Bros.)
c/o Warner Bros.
1995 Broadway
New York, NY 10023

Columbia/Sony Records
(Sony)
P.O. Box 4450
New York, NY 10101-4450

Criterion Music Corp.
6124 Selma Avenue
Hollywood, CA 90028

Critique Records, Inc.
800 W. Cummings Park
Woburn, MA 01801

Curb Records (Thorn/EMI)
3907 W. Alameda Avenue
Burbank, CA 91505

Cutting Records
104 Vermilyea Avenue
New York, NY 10034

Cypress Records
1525 Crossroads of the
World
Los Angeles, CA 90028

Def American (Reprise)
c/o Rick Rubin
3500 W. Olive Avenue
Burbank, CA 91505

Delicious Vinyl
6607 Sunset Boulevard
Los Angeles, CA 90028

Discos CBS International
2190 NW 89th Place
Miami, FL 33172

East West (ATCO)
75 Rockefeller Plaza
New York, NY 10019

Elektra Entertainment
(WEA)
75 Rockefeller Plaza
New York, NY 10019

EMI Records
(Thorn/EMI)
810 Seventh Avenue
New York, NY 10019

Enigma Entertainment
11264 Playa Court
Culver City, CA 90231

Epic Records (Sony)
P.O. Box 4450
New York, NY 10101-4450

Fantasy, Inc.
2600 Tenth Street
Berkeley, CA 94710

Frontline Records
2955 E. Main Street
Irvine, CA 92714

Full Effect Records
2894 E. Grand Boulevard
Detroit, MI 48202

Geffen Records (MCA)
9130 Sunset Boulevard
Los Angeles, CA 90069

Giant Records (Warner
Bros.)
345 N. Maple Drive
Beverly Hills, CA 90210

GRP Records (MCA)
555 W. 57th Street
New York, NY 10019

Ichiban Records, Inc.
P.O. Box 724677
Atlanta, GA 30339

Jive Records (BMG)
137–139 W. 25th Street
New York, NY 10001

Jump Street Records, Inc.
200 W. 72nd Street
New York, NY 10024

JVK Records
c/o Quality Records
8484 Wilshire Boulevard
Beverly Hills, CA 90211

Laface Records (Arista)
3500 Parkway Lane
Atlanta, GA 30092

Lefrak-Moelis Records
(BMG)
40 W. 57th Street
New York, NY 10019

Luke Records (Atlantic)
8400 N.E. 2nd Avenue
Miami, FL 33138

Macola Record Group
8831 Sunset Boulevard
West Hollywood, CA
90069

Malaco Records
P.O. Box 9287
Jackson, MS 39286

MCA Records
70 Universal City Plaza
Universal City, CA 91608

Mercury Records
(PolyGram)
825 Eighth Avenue
New York, NY 10019

Motown Records (MCA)
6255 Sunset Boulevard
Los Angeles, CA 90028

Next Plateau Records
1650 Broadway
New York, NY 10019

Paisley Park (Warner Bros.)
7801 Audubon Road
Chanhassen, MN 55317

Pendulum Records (Elektra)
75 Rockefeller Plaza
New York, NY 10019

Perspective Records
(A & M)
1416 N. La Brea Avenue
Hollywood, CA 90028

Philadelphia International
Records
309 S. Broad Street
Philadelphia, PA 19107

PolyGram Records, Inc.
825 Eighth Avenue
New York, NY 10019

Profile Records
740 Broadway
New York, NY 10003

RAL/Columbia
c/o Columbia/Sony
P.O. Box 4450
New York, NY 10101-4450

RCA Records (BMG)
1133 Avenue of the
Americas
New York, NY 10036

Rendezvous Entertainment
1133 Avenue of the
Americas
New York, NY 10036

Reprise Records (Warner
Bros.)
3300 Warner Boulevard
Burbank, CA 91505

Sam Records
76-05 51st Street
Elmhurst, NY 11373

SBK Records (ERG/EMI
Records Group)
1290 Avenue of the
Americas
New York, NY 10104

Select Records
16 W. 22nd Street
New York, NY 10010

Sire Records (Warner
Bros.)
75 Rockefeller Plaza
New York, NY 10019

Solar Records (Epic)
1635 N. Cahuenga
Los Angeles, CA 90028

Soul Records (MCA)
594 Broadway
New York, NY 10012

Tabu Records
9229 Sunset Boulevard
Los Angeles, CA 90069

Tommy Boy Records
(Warner Bros.)
1747 First Avenue
New York, NY 10128

Uptown Enterprises (MCA)
1755 Broadway
New York, NY 10019

Virgin Records (Atlantic)
30 W. 21st Street
New York, NY 10010

Warner Bros. Records
3300 Warner Boulevard
Burbank, CA 91505

WEA,
Warner/Elektra/Atlantic
Corp.
111 N. Hollywood Way
Burbank, CA 91505

Zomba Recording Corp.
(BMG)
137–139 W. 25th Street
New York, NY 10001

Zoo Entertainment (BMG)
6363 Sunset Boulevard
Hollywood, CA 90028

## Country & Western Labels

Arista Records (BMG)
1 Music Circle North
Nashville, TN 37203

Atlantic Records (WEA)
c/o Warner Bros.
P.O. Box 120897
Nashville, TN 37212

BMG Records
1 Music Circle North
Nashville, TN 37203

Capitol Records
(Thorn/EMI)
1111 16th Avenue
Nashville, TN 37212

CBS/Sony Records, Inc.
34 Music Square East
Nashville, TN 37203

Charisma Records
(Atlantic)
1790 Broadway
New York, NY 10019

Chrysalis Records
(Thorn/EMI)
645 Madison Avenue
New York, NY 10022

Country International
Records
23 Music Circle East
Nashville, TN 37203

Criterion Music Corp.
1925 17th Avenue
Nashville, TN 37212

Curb Records (Thorn/EMI)
47 Music Square East
Nashville, TN 37203

Cypress Records
1525 Crossroads of the
World
Los Angeles, CA 90028

EMI Records (Thorn/EMI)
810 Seventh Avenue
New York, NY 10019

Enigma Entertainment
11264 Playa Court
Culver City, CA 90231

Epic Records (Sony)
34 Music Square East
Nashville, TN 37203

Fantasy, Inc.
2600 Tenth Street
Berkeley, CA 94710

Frontline Records
2955 E. Main Street
Irvine, CA 92714

Geffen Records (MCA)
9130 Sunset Boulevard
Los Angeles, CA 90069

Giant Records (Warner
Bros.)
45 Music Square West
Nashville, TN 37203

Jewel Records
1594 Kinney Avenue
Cincinnati, OH 45231

Liberty Records
3322 West End Avenue
Nashville, TN 37203

MCA Records
1514 South Street
Nashville, TN 37212

Mercury Records
(PolyGram)
901 18th Avenue
Nashville, TN 37212

PolyGram Records
901 18th Avenue
Nashville, TN 37212

Pyramid Records
P.O. Box 140316
Nashville, TN 37214

RCA Records (BMG)
1 Music Circle North
Nashville, TN 37203

Reprise Records (Warner
Bros.)
1815 Division Street
Nashville, TN 37203

SBK Records (ERG/EMI
Records Group)
3322 West End Avenue
Nashville, TN 37203

Scotti Bros. Records
2114 Pico Boulevard
Santa Monica, CA 90405

Sire Records (Warner
Bros.)
75 Rockefeller Plaza
New York, NY 10019

Soundwaves
c/o Joe Gibson
1012 18th Avenue South
Nashville, TN 37212

Staircase Records
P.O. Box 161630
Austin, TX 78716

Starway Records
7600-B Leesburg Pike
Falls Church, VA 22043

Step One Records
1300 Division Street
Nashville, TN 37203

Stop Hunger
c/o Capitol Management
1300 Division Street
Nashville, TN 37203

Tug Boat Records
c/o Doc Holiday
Productions
5405 W. Echo Pines Circle
Ft. Pierce, FL 34951

Warner Bros. Records, Inc.
1815 Division Street
Nashville, TN 37203

WEA,
Warner/Elektra/Atlantic
Corp.
111 N. Hollywood Way
Burbank, CA 91505

Word, Inc.
5221 N. O'Connor
Boulevard
Irving, TX 75039

# APPENDIX C
# INDUSTRY PUBLICATIONS

## Industry Trades

*Billboard*
One Astor Plaza
1515 Broadway
New York, NY 10036

*Gavin Report*
140 Second Street
San Francisco, CA 94105

## Industry-Related Publications

*Dance Music Report*
636 Broadway
New York, NY 10012

(Dance, urban music)

*Down Beat*
180 West Park Avenue
Elmhurst, IL 60126

(Jazz news)

*Mix Magazine*
6400 Hollis Street
Emeryville, CA 94608

(Contains articles about professional recording, sound and music production)

*Music City News*
50 Music Square West
Nashville, TN 37203

(Nashville news)

*R-E-P*
Intertec Publishing Corporation
9800 Metcalf
Overland Park, KS 66212-2215

(Recording, engineering, and production updates and overviews)

*Rolling Stone*
745 Fifth Avenue
New York, NY 10151

(Rock-related articles and insights)

## Periodicals and Tip Sheets

*AWC News/Forum*
American Women Composers
1690 36th Street NW
Washington, DC 20007

(For women composers; articles of interest, competition information)

*Close Up Magazine*
1 Music Circle South
Nashville, TN 37203

(Tips for songwriters regarding country music)

*The Magic of Songwriting*
5832 S. 2000 West
Roy, UT 84067

(For beginning songwriters; published bimonthly)

*Song Placement Guide*
4376 Steward Avenue
Los Angeles, CA 90066-6134

(Tip sheet for songwriters and music publishers)

## Reference Guide

*Songwriter's Market*
F & W Publications
1507 Dana Avenue
Cincinnati, OH 45207

(Gives listings of contacts for all facets of songwriting)

## Film Industry Publications

*Back Stage*
330 W. 42nd Street
New York, NY 10036

(For the songwriter interested in scoring for television or film)

*Variety*
475 Park Avenue South
New York, NY 10016

(Helpful to songwriters interested in creating film scores. Gives latest show business scoop, plus lists of future films to be produced and the companies connected with these productions.)

# APPENDIX D

# ASSOCIATIONS AND PROFESSIONAL ORGANIZATIONS

American Composers Alliance
170 West 74th Street
New York, NY 10023

For serious music composers. Prints catalogs of members' compositions, subsidizes recordings, and promotes radio broadcasts.

American Federation of Musicians (AFM)
1501 Broadway
New York, NY 10036

Entertainment union which enhances musician members' employment opportunities by enforcing employers' observance of wage scales and working conditions. Aids in contract negotiations and protects musicians on federal, state, and local levels.

American Federation of Television and Radio Artists
(AFTRA)
260 Madison Avenue
New York, NY 10016

Labor organization designed to protect and enhance employment opportunities for vocalists, announcers, narrators, and sound effects artists.

American Guild of Music
5354 Washington Street
Downers Grove, IL 60515

For musicians, teachers, and students. Was formed to improve educational methods through lectures, newsletters, and workshops, and also to provide performance opportunities.

American Mechanical Rights Agency, Inc. (AMRA)
200 West 20th Street, Ste. 714
New York, NY 10011

For songwriters and publishers. Collects mechanical, synchronization, and background royalties.

ASCAP (American Society of Composers, Authors and Publishers)
1 Lincoln Plaza
New York, NY 10023

7920 Sunset Boulevard
Hollywood, CA 90046

2 Music Square West
Nashville, TN 37203

Kingsbury Center
350 West Hubbard Street
Chicago, IL 60610

52 Haymarket
London SW1 Y4RP, England

First National Bank Building
1519 Ponce de Leon Avenue
Santurce, Puerto Rico 00910

For songwriters and publishers. The oldest performing
rights organization in the U.S.; owned and operated by its
members. (See Chapter 9 for additional information.)

BMI (Broadcast Music, Inc.)
320 West 57th Street
New York, NY 10019

8730 Sunset Boulevard
Third Floor West
Hollywood, CA 90069

10 Music Square East
Nashville, TN 37203

79 Harley House
Marylebone Road
London NW1 5HN, England

For songwriters and publishers. Performing rights organization with the largest number of affiliates. (See Chapter 9
for additional information.)

Copyright Management, Inc.
1102 17th Avenue South, Ste. 400
Nashville, TN 37212

Handles administration, licensing, and royalties for
music publishers.

Country Music Association, Inc. (CMA)
7 Music Circle North
Nashville, TN 37203

Members include writers who earn a portion of their
income from country music. Promotes the use and sale of
country music.

The Dramatists Guild, Inc.
234 West 44th Street
New York, NY 10036

Professional association for playwrights and composers
and lyricists of musicals. Protects rights of members in conjunction with their work and provides legal counseling. Also
encourages the work of its members through lectures, seminars, field trips, and workshops.

Gospel Music Association (GMA)
38 Music Square West
Nashville, TN 37203

Full membership open to those who make a portion of
their income from either writing, publishing, recording, or
performing gospel music. Associate membership open to
individuals interested in or supportive of gospel music. Promotes gospel music, publishes an annual directory of people
involved in gospel music, and offers awards programs.

The Harry Fox Agency, Inc.
205 East 42nd Street
New York, NY 10017

For publishers only. The oldest and largest mechanical
rights organization in the world. Collects mechanical royalties, audits record companies at regular intervals, and will
take legal action on behalf of their affiliates if necessary. Also
handles synchronization licensing. (See Chapter 9 for additional information.)

Nashville Songwriters Association, International
(NSAI)
1025 16th Avenue South
Nashville, TN 37212

Active and associate membership for songwriters. Association's purpose is to advance recognition of songwriters on
a worldwide basis.

National Academy of Recording Arts and Sciences
(NARAS)
303 North Glenoaks Boulevard
Burbank, CA 91502

Members include vocalists, musicians, songwriters, producers, recording engineers, album-cover art directors, liner-
note writers, i.e., anyone who's involved in making records.
This nonprofit organization presents the annual Grammy
Awards, issues scholarships, and conducts seminars.

National Academy of Songwriters (NAS)
6381 Hollywood Boulevard
Hollywood, CA 90028

Nonprofit organization offering education and protection for songwriters at any level, from novices to superstars.
Provides song evaluations, toll-free hotline, collaborators
network, tip sheet, newspaper, workshops, and group legal
discounts.

National Association of Composers/USA
P.O. Box 49652
Los Angeles, CA 90049

Active in the promotion, publication, performance, and
broadcasting of new material by its songwriter members.

National Music Publishers Association, Inc.
205 East 42nd Street
New York, NY 10017

Trade association for publishers of popular music. Offers
newsletters, special reports, and workshops to its members.

Radio and TV Registry
1317 Third Avenue
New York, NY 10021

Works directly with music contractors. Tracks down
and directs musicians to session dates.

Recording Industry Association of America, Inc.
(RIAA)
1020 19th Street
Washington, DC 20036

Nonprofit trade association for recording companies, organized to promote their interests and better the industry.

SESAC, Inc. (Society of European Stage Authors and Composers)
156 West 56th Street
New York, NY 10019

55 Music Square East
Nashville, TN 37203

For songwriters and publishers. Performing rights organization which additionally handles mechanical and synchronization licensing. (See Chapter 9 for more information.)

Songwriters Association of Washington
1377 K Street NW
Washington, DC 20005

A nonprofit organization which sponsors workshops, seminars, showcases, and contests in order to help writers improve their craft, learn about the business, and gain more exposure in the industry.

Songwriters Guild of America (SGA)
276 Fifth Avenue
New York, NY 10001

Founded as the Songwriter's Protective Association in 1931 and formerly known as AGAC, the American Guild of Authors and Composers. Represents songwriters in their dealings with publishers and will conduct audits on behalf of the writer. Sponsors the SGA Contract (also referred to as the AGAC contract); the Royalty Collection Plan (to ensure that prompt and accurate payments are made to writers); the Catalog Administration Plan (to relieve writers who wish to act as their own publishers of the paperwork involved in the financial administration of their works); the Copyright Renewal Service (to inform writers ahead of time of a song's copyright renewal date); plus a collaboration service, workshops, "ASK-A-PRO" question and answer sessions, and newsletters. (See Chapter 7 for additional information.)

Theatre Communications Group, Inc.
355 Lexington Avenue
New York, NY 10017

National arts organization supported by nonprofit professional theaters which serves composers, lyricists, and librettists for the theater. Provides casting, personnel, and management services to organizations and individuals. Publishes numerous journals, newsletters, books, and directories. Membership not open to individuals, but individuals may receive publications and directories.

# Index